BELOVED OF GOD AND MEN

+BELOVED+ OF GOD AND MEN

Essays in Honour of
BLESSED·COLVMBA·MARMION

EDITED BY
THE CENACLE PRESS
AT SILVERSTREAM PRIORY

THE CENACLE PRESS
AT SILVERSTREAM PRIORY

© 2023 Silverstream Priory

All reservable rights reserved.

The Cenacle Press at Silverstream Priory
Silverstream Priory
Stamullen, County Meath, K32 T189, Ireland
www.cenaclepress.com

ppr 978-1-915544-79-7

Book design by Michael Schrauzer

CONTENTS

Introduction ix

PART I: THAT YOU MAY BE CHILDREN OF YOUR FATHER
(*Ut sitis filii Patris vestri*). 1

1 Blessed Columba Marmion—*An Fior Uisce*:
  'The Authentic Water' by Fr Kilian Byrne 3

2 'I use the *Summa* as Text-book': The Thomism of
  Blessed Columba Marmion by Fr John Saward . . . 28

3 St Thérèse's Influence on Marmion
  by Fr Cassian Koenemann, OSB. 43

4 Christ's Mysteries and Imitating What They Contain
  by Fr Peter Martyr Yungwirth, OP 56

5 Meditations for the Rosary from the
  Writings of Blessed Columba Marmion
  by Sr Claire Waddelove, OSB 84

PART II: BE YE THEREFORE PERFECT
(*Estote ergo vos perfecti*) 93

6 Blessed Columba Marmion: Guide for
  the Monastic Life by The Cenacle Press. 95

7 Blessed Columba Marmion, OSB:
  Spiritual Father to the Spouses of the Word
  by Mother Maria Regina van den Burg, FLM . . . 139

8 A Spiritual Friendship: Dom Columba Marmion
  and Mother Marie-Joseph van Aerden
  by Monsignor Joseph Murphy. 162

9 Blessed Columba Marmion and
  the Spiritual Direction of Priests
  by Raymond Leo Cardinal Burke 192

Appendix. 225

Further Reading .249

INTRODVCTION

IN THE HUNDRED YEARS THAT HAVE passed since Blessed Columba Marmion's death in 1923, his contributions to the Church as handed down in his books, letters, and example have only become increasingly relevant and necessary. It would seem a sufficient contribution even if we only were to mention that Marmion opened the door to two of the greatest saints in the last hundred and fifty years, St Thérèse of Lisieux and St Teresa of Calcutta. For St Thérèse, it was to Marmion that Pius XI went to ask whether she should be beatified; for St Teresa of Calcutta, Marmion's writings were those dearest to her and those which most helped her through her decades of darkness. Yet the treasury that Marmion left to us goes far beyond these two saints, and his is a light waiting to be rediscovered that it might illuminate the Church once again.

Born in Dublin in 1858, Joseph Marmion was the seventh of nine children. His birth followed the deaths of two of his older brothers, both of whom died in their infancy. Begging the intercession of St Joseph, Marmion's parents were blessed with their third boy whom they consecrated to God's service and named Joseph in thanksgiving for the great saint's intercession. His consecration to God took its first step towards being fully realized in 1881 when he was ordained a priest of the Archdiocese of Dublin. After an intellectually active seminarian formation and several years spent studying in Rome, Marmion's early priestly life was spent not only in the academic halls for which his lively intellect so well suited him, but also in ministering to prisoners, both male and female.

The experiences that he underwent in serving these prisoners shaped him for the rest of his life, for, as Marmion's biographer, Dom Raymond Thibaut, writes: his service 'aroused in him the sense of merciful compassion.... He loved these protégées of his and felt a strange consolation in pouring balm from his priestly hands on their wounds'.[1] Indeed, in this ministry to the outcasts of society, he became particularly attuned to the infinite mercy of God.

After some years serving as priest in the Archdiocese of Dublin, in 1886 Marmion took the next step in realizing his consecration to God when he answered the call to leave 'his country, his kindred, and his father's house' (Gen. 12:1) in order to give himself irrevocably to God in monastic life. On November 21st, 1886, Marmion entered the Abbey of Maredsous in Belgium and received the name Columba, that of the great missionary-monk of Ireland. For the next two decades, Marmion grew and developed into the 'chosen arrow' of God: first through the many trials and humiliations of a difficult novitiate and early monastic life, then through his move to Maredsous' foundation of Mont-César in Louvain where Marmion was named Prior, theology professor, and spiritual director to the monks. Having been formed through these decades of experience, Marmion eventually was elected as abbot of his parent monastery of Maredsous in 1909, an office he would retain until his death in 1923.

In the last decade of his life and for several more after his death, the great abbot of Maredsous was renowned throughout all of Europe and the Americas for his uniquely powerful spiritual teaching, his undaunted governance of the great Beuronese Abbey of Maredsous, and his incomparable Irish wit and wisdom. It is thus a great tragedy that this preeminent figure of the Church in the first half of the century fell away from memory in the second half. Yet despite the

---

[1] Thibaut, Raymond, OSB, *Abbot Columba Marmion: A Master of the Spiritual Life 1858–1923*, trans. Mother Mary St Thomas (London: Sands & Co. 1932), 33.

layers of ash burying any knowledge of this saint, his wisdom remains as glowing embers, ready to ignite with the flame of Divine Charity anyone who approaches his writings, which, as Pope Benedict XV declared, contain 'the pure doctrine of the Church'.

Just as Marmion's writings were *dilectus Deo et hominibus*, 'beloved of God and men', so too was the man himself. Like the great patriarchs and saints of all times, he knew God face to Face, knew Him as his greatest friend. Only from this Fountain of Life could Marmion hope to supply nourishment for the souls entrusted to his care; only if he beheld God's Light could his monks benefit from his lights. So, following in the path of St Benedict, Marmion devoted himself 'more to profit than to preside' over the people he governed.

Although all of Marmion's published works come from his time as abbot of Maredsous in the 1910s, the teaching that is presented in these works—*Christ, The Life of the Soul, Christ in His Mysteries, Christ, The Ideal of the Monk, Sponsa Verbi*, and *Christ, The Ideal of the Priest* (published posthumously)—had been carried with him from the earliest days of his priestly and monastic life. From the very beginning, Marmion's interior and exterior life focused on God's merciful Fatherhood; the place of the soul as beloved child of God; abandonment to His providential care; the ineffable indwelling of the Trinity in the soul; and the centrality of the liturgy in the spiritual life of the Church as well as that of each individual. Through these movements of grace, God was guiding Marmion's heart towards a teaching not unlike that of St Thérèse of Lisieux. Yet not only was his comprehensive view of the spiritual life to be developed parallel to that of St Thérèse, but it also found echoes in other saints of that period, such as St Elizabeth of the Trinity, St Charles de Foucauld, and St Pius X. Rarely does God raise up saints who stand alone, and in His providential timing, Marmion would share in the great currents of spiritual thought that were running through the turn of the twentieth century. Yet in a masterful way, Marmion's writings contain their entire scope, embracing them all and helping to undergird them. With incomparable clarity and simplicity, Marmion lays out the great vista of sanctity, the 'unsearchable riches of Christ' (Eph. 3:8), and traces its sublime path to God.

It was a great blessing to the Church, then, when Pope St John Paul II beatified Columba Marmion on September 3rd, 2000. As the pope said: 'Marmion left us an authentic treasure of spiritual teaching for the Church of our time. In his writings he teaches a simple yet demanding way of holiness for all the faithful, whom God has destined in love to be His adopted children through Jesus Christ.'[2] Twenty-three years later, this statement still rings true.

The essays contained in the present volume are a testament to this fact for they demonstrate the great breadth of souls that Blessed Marmion speaks to even down to our own day and age. From Marmion's doctrine based upon our spiritual adoption by the Father to the centrality of Christ's mysteries lived and participated in through the Church's liturgy; from his firm foundation in Scripture, particularly the writings of St Paul, to his absolute adherence to the teachings of the Church, particularly as transmitted by St Thomas Aquinas; from his exposition of the beauty and goodness of the religious life to his care for the universal call to holiness; and from his soaring insights into the great heights of Truth to his dwelling in the particularities of each individual and each circumstance, all with an eminently human touch, Marmion has something to say to 'all the faithful'. To each Marmion offers Christ: 'Christ today, yesterday, and forever' (Heb. 13:8). With a heart attuned to and beating with the heart of the Church, Christ's beloved Bride, Marmion presents to us Christ contemplated, loved, and lived, not with a theoretical knowledge, but with a real and lively faith. The Church is gifted but rarely with souls so comprehensive as to reach all of Her children, but

---

2 "Homily of His Holiness John Paul II for the Beatification of Pius IX, John XXIII, Tommaso Reggio, William Chaminade and Columba Marmion", September 3, 2000.

Introduction

there is no doubt that Blessed Columba Marmion was one such soul: a soul beloved of both God and men.

It is our prayer that the present volume will share more widely the teaching and writings of Blessed Columba Marmion, the 'pure doctrine of the Church', so as to enrich all God's children with the unsearchable riches of Christ, and to rekindle the hearts of the faithful through one who is undoubtedly a saint for our times.

The Cenacle Press
Feast of Blessed Columba Marmion
3 October 2023

+ PART · I +
VT · SITIS · FILII · PATRIS · VESTRI

I

BLESSED COLVMBA MARMION

AN FÍOR UISCE[1]

FR KILIAN BYRNE

INTRODUCTION: TODAY'S CONTEXT

I WOULD LIKE TO BEGIN WITH TWO PERsonal anecdotes. In 2000, the year in which Pope John Paul II beatified Dom Columba Marmion, I called into a Catholic religious bookshop, here in Ireland. I asked whether they had anything written by Marmion. They did not. The best they could do for me was to sell me a short biography on Marmion, written by Mark Tierney OSB. I purchased it, but left dissatisfied.

On Thursday, 25 January 2023, the centenary year of Blessed Columba Marmion's death, I returned to the same religious bookshop. Once again, I inquired whether they had anything written by Marmion. This time, however, not only did they not have anything by Marmion, but it seemed to me that the young shop assistant had never even heard of Columba Marmion. The best the shop could do this time was to offer me yet another biography about Marmion. This time I declined and left somewhat disgruntled. Qoheleth informs us that: 'What has been is what will be, And what has been done is what will be done; and there is nothing new under the sun' (Eccles. 1:9).

It seems that this shop must pride itself in the application of what the Preacher teaches here. Strangely enough this same Catholic bookshop was not without a number of books,

---

[1] English translation from the Irish: 'the genuine/authentic water'.

indeed shelves of them, dealing with 'mindfulness' and other dubious works, posing as Catholic spirituality.

The Prophet Jeremiah was born in Anathoth, a small town situated in the Kingdom of Judah, to the north of Jerusalem.[2] He was of the tribe of Benjamin, descended from a priestly family. His prophetic ministry lasted for over forty years, beginning during the reign of Josiah, 627 B.C. He ministered at a time when the Children of Israel, God's chosen people, had, once more, turned their backs on the Covenant and the Law of God and chose instead the idols and morality of the surrounding pagan nations. The Navarre Commentary points out that: 'Like the other Prophets, Jeremiah teaches that the God of Israel, [Adonai] is the only true God. The other gods are idols, the product of human hands, lifeless bits of wood, stone or metal; there is nothing they can do for man'.[3]

Out of His jealous love for man, God complains about the infidelity of His people in words which may very well resonate throughout our churches and many retreat centres today (that is, those retreat centres not yet closed down!). For thus saith the Lord: '... My people have committed two evils: they have forsaken me, the fountain of living water, and hewed out cisterns for themselves, broken cisterns, that hold no water' (Jer. 2:13).

In his excellent Apostolic Exhortation on 'Evangelization in the Modern World', *Evangelii Nuntiandi*, Paul VI warned against the idolization of techniques over trust in the living God:

> Techniques of evangelization are good, but even the most advanced ones could not replace the gentle action of the Spirit. The most perfect preparation of the evangelizer has no effect without the Holy Spirit. Without the Holy Spirit the most convincing dialectic has no power over the heart of man. Without him the most highly developed schemas resting on

---

2 *The Navarre Bible: Major Prophets: Text and Commentaries* (Dublin: Four Courts Press, 2003), p. 293.
3 Ibid., p. 295.

a sociological or psychological basis are quickly seen to be quite valueless.[4]

Or, in the immortal words of the Bard, such activity, without the supernatural perspective, becomes a clear case of *'Much Ado About Nothing'*.[5]

THE CALL TO AUTHENTIC HOLINESS

Like the late Holy Father it is quite clear that Marmion was well able to distinguish between what we might call authentic and fake spirituality. In fact, it is true to say that like the darnel fake spirituality often tries to ape what is real, what is true, what is good, and what is beautiful.[6] It does this in order to seduce the foolish, the unspiritual. It is the real, alone, which constitutes 'the springs of salvation' and from which comes forth true evangelization. As distinct from the murky waters of the 'broken cisterns'.

In his introduction to Marmion's great masterpiece, *Christ, The Life of The Soul*, Dom Mark Tierney, OSB, recounts the story often told by Marmion about his own spiritual director when he was a seminarian for Dublin Diocese at Clonliffe College. According to Marmion, this spiritual director 'maintained that there was only one road to holiness: *practise the virtues, and keep on practising them,* until in the end—after many long years—you come to love God. Marmion had no sympathy with such an approach, which, he said, was in fact *difficult and impossible'*.[7]

In fact, from the very start, Marmion underlines the absolute futility and sterility of what might very well be called 'fake holiness' or 'fake spirituality'. Here are his own words:

> Some have no precise idea of what holiness is. Unaware of, or setting aside the plan of Eternal Wisdom, they

---

4   Paul VI, *Evangelii Nuntiandi*, 8 Dec. 1975, §75.
5   Title of play by William Shakespeare, first published in 1623.
6   cf. Parable of the weeds and wheat in Mt. 13:24–30.
7   Marmion, Columba, *Christ, The Life of the Soul* (Bethesda, MD: Zaccheus Press, 2005), p. xiv.

> make holiness consist of this or that conception stemming from their own mind; they wish to find their way entirely on their own. Attached to purely human ideas which they have worked out for themselves, they wander from the path. If they take great strides, it is outside the way traced by God; they are victims of those illusions against which St Paul was already putting the first Christians on their guard (Col. 2:8).
>
> Others have clear notions on points of detail but lack a view of the whole. Losing themselves in minutiae, not having any synthesis of the view, often they merely lift one foot after the other on the place where they were before. Their life becomes real toil, subject to incessant difficulties; a toil without élan, without an opening-out to flower; and, often, without much results—because these souls accord their acts a greater importance, or give them a lesser value, than those acts ought to have in the full picture.[8]

Here one is reminded of the decades of innumerable ecclesiastical programmes to renew religious life, the priesthood, the parish, very often to no great avail. On the contrary, with a few honourable exceptions, what are left today are abandoned seminaries, closed religious houses, and empty pews. So often is the Holy Spirit invoked by those who set out to renew the Church by mere human means: human and not Divine Wisdom. Any success, if indeed there be any, is usually short lived and fairly sparse. The fruit simply does not endure! Such diligent 'reformers' need to pay close attention to the afore-mentioned Apostolic Exhortation of Paul VI on 'Evangelization in the Modern World'. For not only does the Pontiff warn against mere human toil without the Divine input, but he also makes crystal clear what in fact constitutes fruitful and lasting evangelization under the action of the Holy Spirit. Having said that 'evangelization will never be possible without the action of the Holy Spirit' (nor indeed, the much desired renewal of the Church), he then goes on to explain what this means for the individual and for the entire Church.

---

8 *Ibid.*, p. 4.

Here he writes: 'It is the Holy Spirit who, today, just as at the beginning of the Church, acts in every evangelizer, *who allows himself to be possessed and led by Him.*'[9]

Here, the Holy Father is pointing not so much to mere human wisdom but rather to Divine Wisdom. In other words, to evangelize effectively (as well as to renew the Church), we have to become 'holy' and therefore fruitful, according to God's Wisdom and Truth. Here Marmion is totally clear about this:

> ...if we are holy pursuant to our own will, we shall never be truly so; we have to be holy according to God's will. Divine Wisdom is infinitely above human wisdom; God's thought contains fertile riches that no created thought possesses. This is why the plan established by God is one of such wisdom that it can never fail to reach its goal because of intrinsic insufficiency; only through our own fault. If we let the Divine Idea have complete power to operate in us, if we adapt ourselves to it with love and fidelity, it becomes extremely fruitful and can bring us to the most sublime holiness.[10]

Where then can we find the Divine Plan, traced out as it were, for our lives? For Marmion, the answer lies in the rich teachings of St Paul. More precisely, it is traced out for us in the opening chapter of Paul's Letter to the Ephesians, described by the Scripture scholar Fr Francis Martin as the jewel in the Pauline corpus. As a 'prisoner of the Lord' St Paul begins his letter with a type of Hebrew blessing, a *berakah:* 'Blessed be the God and Father of Our Lord Jesus Christ, who has blessed us in Christ with every spiritual blessing in the heavens, as he *chose* us in him, before the foundation of the world, to be *holy and without blemish* before him' (Eph. 1:3–4).

Sometime during his twenties, that great apostolic and prophetic layman, Venerable Frank Duff penned his first ever pamphlet under the title *Can We Be Saints?* His provocative opening line continues to astound and challenge, perhaps even

---

9   *Evangelii Nuntiandi,* §75; emphasis added.
10 Marmion, *Christ, The Life of the Soul,* p. 5.

more so today than when it was first written: 'In the heart of every right-thinking Catholic, God has implanted the desire to become a Saint'.[11]

It's almost as if the author were saying that if you do not have this desire, or have not allowed this good seed planted in baptism go to seed, then your thinking has become crooked, false, perverse, and ultimately bad for yourself and for all humanity.[12] We see this spelled out, as it were, in the teachings of Venerable Fulton Sheen. In his series *Life Is Worth Living*, Sheen explains how

> life is monotonous if it has no goal or purpose. When we do not know why we are here or where we are going, then life is full of frustrations and unhappiness. When there is no goal or overall purpose, people generally concentrate on motion.... They do not know where they are going, but they are certainly "on their way".[13]

The alternative to real holiness is what Pope John Paul II calls 'a life of mediocrity [the dreaded Laodicean lukewarmness[14]], marked by a minimalistic ethic and a shallow religiosity'.[15] He continues:

> To ask catechumens: 'Do you wish to receive baptism?' means at the same time to ask them: 'Do you wish to become holy?' It means to set before them the radical nature of the Sermon on the Mount: 'Be perfect as your heavenly Father is perfect'.[16]

This same question carries equal force for all of us who have received baptism as infants. Nothing could be clearer than the simple assertion of St Louis M. de Montfort—a member of

---

[11] Duff, Frank, *Can We Be Saints?* (Dublin: Praedicanda Publications, 1958), p. 1.
[12] Cf. Parable of the Sower in Lk. 8:4–15
[13] Sheen, Fulton., *Life Is Worth Living* (San Francisco: Ignatius Press, 1999), p.15.
[14] Cf. Rev. 3:15–16.
[15] John Paul II, *Novo Millennio Ineunte*, 6 Jan, 2001, §31.
[16] *Ibid.*; cf. Mt. 5:48.

the French (Bérullian) School of spirituality, of which Marmion was reckoned to be the last—'Chosen soul... your sure vocation is the acquisition of the Holiness of God'.[17] That is, we are called to the summit, and beyond! Do you truly believe this? So much so as to be willing to swim against the prevailing and toxic culture of atheistic secularism? To follow the Lamb where He goes, as Pope John Paul pointed out at World Youth Day, outside Rome, at the start of this millennium?[18]

If we want to become holy then, we should ask, what constitutes 'true holiness'? Authentic Christianity? The kind which yields the fruit that endures? For Marmion the answer lies in the next verse of Paul's Letter to the Ephesians: 'Blessed be the God and Father of Our Lord Jesus Christ, who has blessed us in Christ with every spiritual blessing in the heavens, as he chose us in him... to be holy and without blemish. In love he destined us for *adoption* to himself through Jesus Christ...' (Eph. 1:5).

But how does God the Father adopt us? Very simply, by communicating His Divine Life to us. What does this Divine Life do in us? It raises us up—just as sin drags us down—and we become in a way like unto God Himself. This is the clear teaching of the *Catechism of the Catholic Church*, quoting from Sts Athanasius and Thomas Aquinas: 'For the Son of God became man so that we might become God'; 'The Only-Begotten Son of God, wanting to make us sharers in his divinity, assumed our nature, so that he, made man, might make men gods'.[19]

---

17 De Montfort, St Louis M., *The Secret of Mary: With Preparation for Consecration* (Marian Apostolate Publishing, 2013), §3.
18 'Dear friends, to believe in Jesus today, to follow Jesus as Peter, Thomas, and the first Apostles and witnesses, demands of us, just as it did in the past, that we take a stand for Him, almost to the point at times a new martyrdom: the martyrdom of those who, today as yesterday, are called to go against the tide in order to follow the divine Master, to follow "the Lamb where He goes" (Rev. 14:4).' World Youth Day, Tor Vergata, 19 August 2000.
19 Catholic Church, *Catechism of the Catholic Church: Revised in Accordance with the Official Latin Text Promulgated by Pope John Paul II* (Washington, DC: United States Catholic Conference, 2000), §440.

The implications of this truth for how we live our life of faith are spelled out powerfully by Venerable Fulton Sheen. In his great book *The Mystical Body of Christ*, first published in 1935, Sheen spells out the supreme importance of this Divine Life for the human race:

> The great tragedy of history is not that men should fall, but that they should fail to rise to the full realisation of their vocation as children of God, in other words, that they should miss so much. All about us we see vast multitudes of men and women of refinement and culture, endowed with intelligence and possessed of every natural virtue and every now and then swept by noble emotions and ideals, but who are living second-rate, superficial, unimportant, and morally insignificant lives, because they have never had their nature inflamed by the Spirit of Christ. They may do so much for the world in the material order, they may build bridges, harness waterfalls, accomplish great pieces of research, but they never sound the depths of their souls which can only be filled by God. The world of the supernatural has no more appeal to them than heroism has appeal to a coward. They have become so used to the dense atmosphere of the material, that they stifle the more rarified atmosphere of the supernatural.
>
> And in this lies the danger of our civilisation, which is gradually turning away from God. Nothing great, nothing really good was ever done in the world by any human life that had not a baptism of God's Holy Spirit.[20]

What then constitutes true holiness? Here Marmion gives the clearest and most succinct answer of all. For Marmion, holiness is nothing other than the 'mystery of divine life, communicated and received'.[21] When these words are read in the context of what has already been written we begin to see something of the depth and breadth of Marmion's description

---

20 Sheen, Fulton, *The Mystical Body of Christ* (Christian Classics, 2015), pp. 184–185.
21 Marmion, *Christ, The Life of the Soul*, p. 8.

of holiness. In fact, it might be true to say that it is this basic insight, this fundamental principle, which underpins and shapes all his writings on the Church, the sacraments, the liturgy, the priesthood, the religious life, and his letters of spiritual direction, which were written for the layperson as well as for the religious. In the words of the great Belgian Cardinal Mercier when asked the secret of the success of Marmion's books, he replied: 'He makes you *touch God*'.[22] And, surely, this experience should be, as indeed it is, available to *all* the baptized.

From Marmion's description of true holiness, three practical questions arise:

    I. Where is this Divine Life communicated?
    II. How is it communicated?
    III. How do we 'receive' or draw down this Divine Life into our souls?

I. WHERE IS THIS DIVINE LIFE COMMUNICATED?

From the outset it is important to note the Church's own teaching on the necessity of baptism as set out in the *Catechism of the Catholic Church*. Here the Church is crystal clear:

> The Lord affirms that baptism is necessary for salvation (cf. Jn 3:5). He also commanded his disciples to proclaim the Gospel to all nations and to baptize them... The Church does not know of any means other than baptism that assures entry into eternal beatitude; this is why she takes care not to neglect the mission she has received from the Lord to see that all who can be baptized are 'reborn of water and the Spirit'. *God has bound salvation to the sacrament of Baptism, but He, Himself, is not bound by His sacraments*'.[23]

In a similar way, Marmion, while insisting on the necessity of the Church for receiving the gift of Divine Life, is not in any way limiting the provenance of God's grace. As Jesus

---

22 *Ibid.*, p. xiii.
23 CCC § 1257.

taught Nicodemus: 'The wind blows where it wills' (Jn 3:8). Nonetheless, it is the Church, as the Mystical Body of Christ, animated by His Spirit, wherein we find what Marmion calls 'the All' in order to draw with immense confidence from 'the authentic and official wellsprings'.[24]

It is here that we find both the divine element and the human element: the holiness of the Church because of Christ's fidelity to her (and His invisible, but real, presence within her) and the harlotry of the Church because of our infidelity to Him, who is our Head. For that reason, in an era in which the sins of the Church are becoming more and more exposed to public scrutiny, and indeed disgust, the wise person will take note of what Marmion counsels regarding the Mystery of the Church. His words are so apt for today:

> The faithful soul sees through the human element to the Divine element: the indefectibility of the doctrine, kept safe throughout all the ages and despite all the assaults of heresies and schisms the unity of this same doctrine preserved by the infallible magisterium; the heroic and uninterrupted holiness manifested in so many ways, in this Church; the unbroken succession by which, link by link, the Church of our day can be traced back to the foundations established by the Apostles; the force of universal expansion that characterises it—so many certain signs by which we recognise that Our Lord is with His Church "to the end of time" Mt. 28:20).
>
> Let us then have trust in the Church that Jesus left us: it is another "Himself".[25]

And for these very reasons, Marmion insists on us belonging *totally* to the Church. Hear him:

> It is in the Church that we shall find Christ. No one goes to the Father—and going to the Father [as His adopted child!] is what salvation and holiness is all about; no one goes to the Father except through

---

24 Marmion, *Christ, The Life of the Soul*, p. 120.
25 *Ibid.*, p. 119.

Christ: "No one comes to the Father but through me" (Jn 14:6). But remember well the following truth which is of no less capital importance. No one goes to Christ except through the Church; we only belong to Christ if we belong in fact or in desire to the Church; we only life the live of Christ in the unity of the Church.[26]

Adding, a little earlier that 'Christ, indeed, cannot be conceived without the Church'.[27]

A similar point, and so necessary for today, was made by St John Paul II, in his book *Memory and Identity*. Here, the Pontiff is addressing those people who claim that they are into spirituality, while at the same time they reject the Church. The Pontiff writes:

"Christ yes. The Church no!" is the protest from some of our contemporaries. Despite the negative element, this stance appears to show a certain openness to Christ, which the Enlightenment excluded. Yet it is only an appearance of openness. Christ, if He is truly accepted, is inseparable from the Church, which is His Mystical Body. There is no Christ without the Incarnation, there is no Christ without the Church. The Incarnation of the Son of God in a human body is prolonged, in accordance with His will, in the community of human beings that He constituted, guaranteeing His constant presence among them: "And remember, that I am with you always, to the end of the age" (Mt. 28:20).[28]

II. HOW DOES GOD COMMUNICATE HIS DIVINE LIFE?

Prayer: Private

But how does God communicate His Divine Life to us? Preeminently, God communicates His Divine Life to us through the personal prayer of the individual and most especially through the public prayer of the Church, *Sponsa Christi*.

---

26 *Ibid.*, pp. 114–115
27 *Ibid.*, p. 107.
28 John Paul II, *Memory and Identity* (Weidenfeld & Nicholson, 2005), p. 132.

For Marmion, personal prayer is nothing other than a conversation 'in which one listens and one speaks: the soul delivers itself up to God and God communicates Himself to the soul'.[29] This calls to mind the teaching one St John Chrysostom set out in his sixth homily on prayer: 'There is nothing more worthwhile than to pray to God and to converse with Him, for prayer unites us to God as His companions...(For true) prayer is the light of the soul, giving us true knowledge of God'.[30] Or, perhaps, what Marmion might call 'a flavoursome knowledge of spiritual things'.[31]

Clearly this is the type of prayer to which St John Paul II sees the Church being called in the New Millennium. In fact, he insists that our parishes become schools of prayer and places where 'genuine training in holiness is given'.[32] The Holy Father writes about this deep, personal prayer to which the baptized are called:

> Is not one of the signs of the times that in today's world, despite widespread secularisation, there is *widespread demand for spirituality*, a demand which expresses itself in large part as *a renewed need for prayer?*... Yes, dear brothers and sisters, our Christian communities must become *genuine schools of prayer*, where the meeting with Christ is expressed not just in imploring help but also in thanksgiving, praise, adoration, contemplation, listening and ardent devotion, until the heart truly 'falls in love'. Intense prayer, yes, but it does not distract us from our commitment to history: by opening our heart to the love of God it also opens it to the love of our brothers and sisters and makes us capable of shaping history according to God's plan.[33]

---

29 Marmion, *Christ, The Life of the Soul*, p. 423.
30 St John Chrysostom in *The Divine Office: The Liturgy of the Hours according to the Roman Rite*, vol. 2 (London: Wm Collins Sons & Co. Ltd., 1976), p. 21.
31 Marmion, *Christ, The Life of the Soul*, p. 153.
32 John Paul II, *Novo Millennio Ineunte*, 7 May 2000, §31.
33 *Ibid.* §33; emphasis added.

Prayer: Public

However, it is the public prayer of the Church to which Marmion points us as one of the supreme sources of Divine Life for each baptized individual. In particular, three areas of such prayer present themselves:

> 1. The Liturgy of the Hours
> 2. The Liturgical Year
> 3. The Sacramental Life of the Church—Penance and the Eucharist

1. The Liturgy of the Hours. It would be a supreme injustice to think that Marmion's great classic, *Christ, The Life of the Soul*, was written primarily for priests and religious. No. This is for all the baptized who want to grow in true holiness. Therefore, Marmion's chapter dealing with the *Vox Sponsae*, or what he calls 'the homage of public prayer', is undoubtedly for all the faithful.[34]

In this, Marmion, like Frank Duff, may have been somewhat ahead of his time. Addressing his legionaries, the great Frank Duff poses the question: 'Why should people say an Office?' From there he sets out to reveal something of the extraordinary spiritual power of this great prayer in clear and precise terms:

> The special value of the liturgy is that it is the official prayer of the Church, the voice of the Mystical Body in which all our poor voices intermingle with the voice of Our Lord and take on the quality of His prayer. This places liturgical prayer on an eminence above our own individual prayers.
>
> Some of the verses are set in the mouth of God and some in the mouth of the person addressing God. Therefore, it is a case of dialogue between God and that person. There we have the ideal form of prayer: a conversation with God.[35]

---

34   Marmion, *Christ, The Life of the Soul*, p. 389
35   Legion of Mary, *A Shorter Breviary* (Collins Liturgical Publications, 1989), p. ix.

Straight away this brings us right into another of Marmion's descriptions of prayer as 'a conversation of child of God with its heavenly Father' under the action of the Holy Spirit.[36]

But Duff has yet another reason for why we 'should...say an Office'. He writes: 'Every line of the Psalms affords food for thought and love. There is literary beauty in them...All the emotions and the trials of life are covered'.[37]

Like his predecessors, Pope Benedict XVI not only called all the baptized to holiness, but he also invited the Church, lay and clerical, to enrol in a kind of school of prayer as set out in the Scriptures. Thus began his great journey through the Bible in which he invited the Church, together with the first disciples, to turn with humble trust to the Teacher and to ask Him: 'Lord, teach us to pray' (Lk. 11:1).

Furthermore, it is the Psalms (which we encounter in the Liturgy of the Hours) that draws us into 'the book of prayer' par excellence. In words not unlike Frank Duff, but in a vastly expanded way, the Holy Father sees these great prayers of the Psalms as our way of relating to God. He writes:

> This Book expresses the entire human experience with its multiple facets and the whole range of emotions that accompany human experience. In the Psalms are expressed and interwoven joy and suffering, the longing for God and the perception of our own unworthiness, happiness and the feeling of abandonment, trust in God and sorrowful loneliness, fullness of life and fear of death. The whole reality of the believer converges in these prayers...Since the Psalms are prayers, they are expressions of the heart and of the faith with which everyone can identify and in which that experience of special closeness to God ['a child of God with its heavenly Father'!]—to which every human being is called—is communicated. Moreover, the whole complexity of human life is distilled in the complexity of the different literary forms of the Psalms: hymns, laments, individual entreaties and

---

36 Marmion, *Christ, The Life of the Soul*, p. 417.
37 Duff, *The Spirit of the Legion of Mary*, p. ix.

collective supplications, hymns of thanksgiving, penitential Psalms, sapiential Psalms, and the other genres that are to be found in these poetic compositions.[38]

But, also, in and through the Psalms God communicates to us His Divine Life, His Wisdom, His Light, His Courage, His Strength, His Beauty, His Love, and His Mercy so that He is continually building us up in Faith, Hope, and Charity—those supernatural virtues by which, in the words of Dom Marmion, 'we are able to act as children of God and to produce acts that are worthy of our supernatural end'.[39]

For Marmion, however, the two greatest sources of Divine Life are to be found in the Liturgical Year and the Sacramental Life of the Church to which we now turn.

2. *The Liturgical Year.* According to Marmion, it is the Liturgical Year which puts us into direct contact with the Mysteries of Jesus. Each year, we are told, the Church celebrates the Mysteries of Christ's birth, life, death, resurrection, and outpouring of His Spirit. These are the Seasons of Advent, Christmas, Lent, Holy Week, Easter, and Pentecost. All of these illustrious seasons flow from and are, as it were, completed in the supreme mystery which is the Heart of Christ. Here we find 'the very love that inspired them all'.[40] Furthermore, each of these Mysteries is the source of a particular grace, each has its own spiritual gift for us.

From the outset Marmion insisted that these divinely life-giving Mysteries are also our Mysteries. This is so in three ways. Firstly, because Jesus Christ lived these Mysteries for us. And so, writes Marmion, they are as much ours as they are His. Secondly, because in each and all of these Mysteries Jesus reveals Himself as our Exemplar, our Model. To become, as it were, 'the ideal of our souls'.[41]

---

38   Benedict XVI, *A School of Prayer: The Saints Show Us How to Pray* (San Francisco: Ignatius Press, 2013), p. 48.
39   Marmion, *Christ, The Life of the Soul*, p. 299.
40   Marmion, *Christ in His Mysteries* (Bethesda, MD: Zaccheus Press, 2008), p. 419.
41   *Ibid.*, p. 13.

Christ Jesus was God living in our midst; God who had appeared to us, God made visible, tangible, brought within our reach, and showing us the way of holiness, by His life as much as by His words. We have no need to search beyond Him for the model of our perfection. Each one of His Mysteries is a revelation of His virtues. The humility of the manger, the toil and self-effacement of the hidden life, the zeal of the public life, the abasement of His immolation on the cross, the glory of His triumph—these are virtues we ought to imitate, feelings we ought to share, or states in which we ought to participate. At the Last Supper, after having washed the feet of the apostles and having thus—He, their Master and Lord—giving them an example of humility, Our Lord said to them: "I have given you an example, *that as I have done to you, so you should do*"(Jn 13:15). He could have said that about everything He did.[42]

Thirdly—and here we see the more intimate and deeper reason which makes the Mysteries of Jesus ours—not only did Jesus live them for us, not only are they models for us, but '*in His Mysteries Christ is but one with us*... Christ and we are but one, *in the mind of God*'.[43] 'There is no truth' writes Marmion, 'that St Paul could have insisted on more than that, and my liveliest desire is that you [the reader!] understand the full depth of it'.[44]

Even though these Mysteries in their historical and material sense are now past, since Christ's life on earth is past, *'their power'*, Marmion insists, *'remains, and the grace that allows us to share in them operates always'*.[45] Consequently Marmion speaks about, what the Fathers of the Church used to call the *'vis mysterii'*—'the power, the strength, of the mystery celebrated, the significance proper to it'.[46] He adds in a quote

---

42 *Ibid.*, p. 15
43 *Ibid.*, p. 16–17.
44 *Ibid.*
45 *Ibid.*, p. 20.
46 *Ibid.*, p. 27.

from St Gregory Nazianzen that 'it is impossible to present to God a more acceptable gift than that of offering ourselves with a right understanding of the mystery'.[47]

For these reasons, then, Marmion insists that 'by following Christ Jesus in all His Mysteries in that kind of way, by uniting ourselves with Christ, we share little by little, but surely, in His divinity, in His divine life; and each time in greater measure and with a deeper intensity'.[48] This is what we might call the divine fecundity of these mysteries.

Here it is very noteworthy how Marmion links his teaching with that of St Pius X who wrote that 'active participation of the faithful in the sacred mysteries and in the public and solemn prayer of the Church *is the first and indispensable source of the Christian spirit*'.[49]

How far removed is this rich and deep understanding of 'active participation' from what passes as such in so many of our liturgies today! Rightly did Cardinal Ratzinger see how these words 'active participation' have been 'very quickly misunderstood to mean something external, entailing a need for general activity, as if as many people as possible, as often as possible, should be engaged in [liturgical] action'.[50] The good Cardinal continues:

> The word "part-icipation" refers to a principal action in which everyone has a "part". And so, if we want to discover the kind of doing that active participation involves, we need, first of all, to determine what this central *action* is in which all members of the community are supposed to participate.

'The real "action" in the liturgy in which we are all supposed to participate is the action of God Himself (*actio Dei*)'. So that, for example, in the Eucharist, 'God himself has become man,

---

47 *Ibid.*
48 *Ibid.*, p. 30.
49 *Ibid.*, pp. 30–31; cf. St Pius X, *Motu Proprio*, Nov. 23, 1903.
50 Ratzinger, *The Spirit of the Liturgy* (San Francisco: Ignatius Press, 2000), p. 171.

become body.... He comes to us, through His Body...[and] draws man into co-operation with Himself'.[51]

Like Marmion the good Cardinal invites us to go beneath the visible to the invisible, to rise above 'the exterior elements of the celebration of the mysteries' so that through the visible we may 'be seized with a love of things invisible'.[52] Otherwise we will continue to miss the power and beauty of these Mysteries which are truly capable of transforming us into children of the Father at the service of the Church and the world.

Take, for example, the Season of Lent. Here we can ask: what is the grace proper to this season as set out most particularly on Ash Wednesday? In answering this we come now to Marmion's teaching on the Sacramental Life of the Church and, in this particular case, to the Sacrament of Penance.

3. The Sacramental Life of the Church: Penance. This great Penitential and Holy Season is entered into through the portal of Ash Wednesday. On this day, through the Prophet Joel, the Lord urgently calls His people to true repentance, authentic contrition: 'Now, now'—it is the Lord who speaks—'come back to me with all your heart, fasting, weeping and mourning. Let your hearts be broken, not your garments torn' (Joel 2:12–13).

This '*contritio*', through which alone the Church can be properly renewed, is impossible without God's grace. For that reason, the Church presents in her Liturgy of the Hours for Ash Wednesday the Letter of Pope St Clement to the Corinthians that we might consider its sentiments. The Pontiff invites us to 'fix our thoughts on the Blood of Christ, and reflect how precious that Blood is in God's eyes, inasmuch as its outpouring for our salvation has opened *the grace of repentance* for all mankind'.[53] Admittedly, the tried and tested ways of opening our lives to this grace are prayer, fasting, and almsgiving. However, it is grace which changes hearts and re-focuses minds.

---

51 *Ibid.*, pp. 171, 173.
52 Marmion, *Christ in His Mysteries*, p. 28.
53 *The Divine Office*, vol. 2, p. 6.

What is meant here is what Marmion, drawing from a rich liturgical tradition, calls 'compunction of heart'. He asks: 'What do we mean by compunction of heart? It is an habitual feeling of regret for having offended the divine goodness... a feeling of sorrow inspired by love and maintained in full vigour in the soul [which] will produce in it a state of irreconcilable opposition to all consent to sin'.[54]

It is 'the constant sorrow for our past faults: "My sin is always before me" (Ps. 50:3)... [which] must be based, not on the circumstances of each sin, but on the fact of having offended God'.[55] He continues:

> We must not call to mind the specific details, the recollection of which may sometimes be dangerous, but rather repent of having opposed our human will to God's will, of having outraged His sovereignty, repudiated His love, of having neglected, wasted, or even lost, the great treasure of grace.[56]

Interestingly, and no doubt drawing from his experience of religious community life, Marmion goes on to point out: 'As I advance in life, I see ever more clearly that our lack of stability and of progress in virtue is most often the consequence of a lack of compunction'.[57]

Perhaps we see this spirit of compunction most clearly expressed in the short, sharp, and succinct prayer of the Publican, who hardly dared to raise his eyes to heaven, but beat his breast and cried out: 'O Lord, be merciful to me a sinner' (Lk. 18:13).

However, this spirit of compunction, as we have said, must always be first and foremost a work of divine grace in our lives. A divine work to which we must open ourselves daily by allowing God to reveal to us the hidden depths of our

---

54 Marmion, *Christ, The Ideal of the Priest* (Gracewing Publishing, 2005), p. 117.
55 *Ibid.*, p. 118.
56 *Ibid.*
57 *Ibid.*, p. 117.

human misery. How God does this is often through life's little events! This is, in a certain sense, also part of the matter of true prayers. Does not the *Catechism of the Catholic Church* describe prayer as 'a covenant drama', 'in which God gradually reveals Himself and reveals man to himself'?[58] Without this undeniably painful process, there is the great danger that, like the unfortunate Pharisee, we too could end up doing no more in our prayer than conversing with ourselves (Lk. 18:11).

In his letters of spiritual direction, Marmion is at pains to insist on the necessity of coming to know ourselves, or more accurately, to recognize the misery within. To a person living in the world, he offered the following advice:

> In the measure we approach God through Jesus Christ we approach the light for "God is Light, and in Him there is no darkness" (cf. 1 Jn 1:5). Now this light produces two effects:
>
> 1. It reveals to us the greatness of our God. His love, His perfections.
> 2. It also reveals to us the abyss of misery, of pettiness, the possibilities of sin and betrayal, hidden in the depth of our heart.
>
> This is the great prayer of St Augustine: "May I know Thee, O my God, may I know myself". The knowledge of one does not go without the knowledge of the other.
>
> When God discovers to us the abyss of our misery, it needs all the strength of the Holy Spirit, all our confidence in the love of our Heavenly Father, all our faith in the Blood of Jesus Christ in order not to be crushed by the weight of our weakness, and yet what glorifies God is when, in the full knowledge of our misery, we persist in hoping in His love.[59]

Here Marmion is being true to his Irish heritage. For had not that great Apostle of Ireland, *Aspal Mór na h-Éireann*, begun

---

58 Cf. CCC §2567
59 Marmion, *Union with God: Letters of Spiritual Direction* (Bethesda, MD: Zaccheus Press, 2005), p. 94.

his *Confessio* with these immortal words: '*Ego Patricius, peccator ...*', 'I, Patrick, a sinner, the most awkward *(rusticissimus)*, the least of all the faithful and very contemptible in the estimation of most people...'[60] How well does the Church in Ireland (and the Irish nation) measure up to these words today? A question worth exploring someday!

But there is something more here. Where does one go or how does one deal with one's misery (original and actual sin)? That great Secretary of Divine Mercy tells us. In her Diary, Sr Faustina describes the Lord's own description of the moment of sacramental absolution. It is here, in the Sacrament of Confession, the Tribunal of Divine Mercy, that 'the misery of the human soul meets the mercy of God'.[61]

And it this statement by the Lord which draws us right back into Dom Marmion's teaching on the Sacrament of Penance, wherein God reveals His Mercy. 'What', Marmion asked, 'indeed *is* being merciful? It is taking the misery of others into one's own heart, in some way—the Latin word is *misericordia*'.[62] And that Heart is the Sacred Heart of Jesus!

The Sacramental Life of the Church: The Eucharist. Now, we come to the greatest source of Divine Life, the Sacrament of the Eucharist. It is clear here that Marmion is not only addressing the Mystery of Holy Communion but also the Sacrifice of the Mass by which the immolation of Calvary is reproduced and renewed and in which the 'Communion brings the Sacrifice to an end'.[63]

Unfortunately, it is not possible to develop Marmion's rich teaching on this matter in so short an article. Nonetheless, I would like to return to the notion of active participation in

---

60 *Confessio Patricii, Patrick the Pilgrim Apostle of Ireland*, ed. Máire B. de Paor PBVM (Veritas Publications, 1998), pp. 220–21. 'Ego, Patricius, Peccator, rusticissimus, et minimus omnium fidelium, et contemptibilissimus apud plurimos...'
61 Kowalska, St Faustina, *Divine Mercy in My Soul*, ed. Congregation of Marians of the Immaculate Conception, 3rd ed. (2009), §1602.
62 Marmion, *Christ, The Life of the Soul*, p. 243.
63 *Ibid.*, p. 341.

the Mystery of the Eucharist. While it is true to say 'that only priests, who participate, through the sacrament of holy orders, in the Priesthood of Christ—only they have the power to offer officially the body and blood of Jesus Christ', it is also true that the faithful, through their baptism, 'participate in some way in the Priesthood of Christ... as a chosen race, a royal priesthood, a holy nation'—and as such, 'the faithful, then, can offer the Sacred Host in union with the priest'.[64]

How then can the faithful actively do so? How do they actively participate in the Eucharistic Sacrifice? From what Cardinal Ratzinger has already said, it should be clear to us that activities such as reading, serving, singing, chanting, distributing Holy Communion, etc., are, at most, external and secondary. They do not constitute the essence of active participation at the Eucharist. Returning to the words of Cardinal Ratzinger we might say that when the priest, acting *in persona Christi Capitis*, pronounces the words of consecration, God Himself becomes present, through His Body and through His Blood, in order to draw us into co-operation with Himself so that in surrendering ourselves to this *Actio Dei* we become a source of blessing and renewal not just for the Church but for the whole world. This surely is not just active but also fruitful participation in the Holy Sacrifice.

Furthermore it is the 'more intimate participation we ought to seek to achieve': that is, 'to identify ourselves as fully as possible with Jesus Christ in His twofold capacity of High Priest and Victim in order to be transformed into Him'.[65] Stefano Manelli tells the story that someone once said to Padre Pio, 'Father, how much you must suffer by standing on the bleeding wounds of your feet for the entire time of Mass!' Padre Pio replied: 'During Mass I am not standing, I am hanging.'[66]

---

64 Cf. *Ibid.*, p. 351.
65 Cf. *Ibid.*, p. 349.
66 Manelli, Stefano, *Jesus, Our Eucharistic Love* (Academy of The Immaculate, 1996), p. 26.

An Fíor Uisce

This would have been undoubtedly understood and practiced by Marmion's Irish ancestors, who risked all in order to attend Mass during the Penal Laws. They demonstrate what constitutes 'active participation'. We see this in a description given by a traveller through eighteenth century Ireland, when the Penal Laws were in full force. This is what he came across:

> I had taken only a few steps on my way when my attention was attracted by the appearance of a man who knelt at the foot of one of the firs. Several others became visible in succession in the same attitude; and the higher I ascended the larger became the numbers of these kneeling peasants. At length, on reaching the top of the hill, I saw a cruciform building badly built of stone, without cement, and covered by thatch. Around it knelt a crowd of robust and vigorous men, all uncovered, though the rain fell in torrents and mud quivered beneath them. Profound silence reigned everywhere. It was the Catholic chapel at Blarney (at Waterloo) and the priest was saying Mass.
>
> I reached the door at the moment of the Elevation, and all this pious assembly had prostrated themselves with their faces on the earth. I made an effort to penetrate under the roof of the chapel thus overflowed by worshippers. There were no seats, no decorations, not even a pavement; the floor was of earth, damp and stony, the roof dilapidated, and tallow candles burned on the altar in place of tapers...
>
> When the Holy Sacrifice was ended, the priest mounted his horse and rode away. Then each worshipper rose from his knees and went slowly homeward; some of them, wandering harvestmen carrying their reaping hooks, turned their steps towards the nearest cottage to ask hospitality to which they considered to have a right, others... went off to their distant homes. Many remained for a much longer time in prayer, kneeling in the mud in that silent enclosure chosen by the poor and faithful in the time of ancient persecutions.[67]

---

[67] Hayden, Fr Augustine, *Ireland's Loyalty to the Mass* (The Neumann Press, 2007), pp. 195–197.

It is small wonder that Pope Benedict XVI in his Pastoral Letter to the Catholics of Ireland called on us 'to remember the rock from which you were hewn' (cf. Is. 51:1) and to which scholars like Marmion call us back.[68]

III. FAITH AS THE GENERAL MEANS FOR DRAWING THE DIVINE LIFE INTO OUR SOULS

Finally, how do we draw down this Divine Life into our souls? Through what Marmion calls the exercise of the virtue of faith. For, according to Marmion, 'it is [this] faith that introduces every soul into the region of the super-natural', and 'the more pure and living it is, the more it will envelop our whole existence: the more, also, will our spiritual life be solid, true, luminous, sure and fruitful'.[69]

In short, not unlike the Letter to the Hebrews, Marmion calls on us in the Ireland of today, to live as 'just men', that is, to live by faith and faith alone. Mary Healy tells us that the Letter to the Hebrews was written 'to a community of Christians who were struggling. They had had times of fervour in the past but had become discouraged in the midst of a hostile culture with the threat of further persecution. Some had stopped regularly attending the liturgy and some were even tempted to abandon the faith'.[70]

Here the author of Hebrews is very clear. His words could well be aimed at the Church in Ireland today. He exhorts us 'not to take our eyes off Jesus, the leader and perfecter of our faith' (Heb. 12:2), to abandon ourselves to His service, to make what Marmion, borrowing from St Thomas, describes as 'the adhesion of our intellect, not to man's word, but to God's; God [who] can neither deceive us nor be deceived: [a] faith [which] is a homage tendered to God considered

---

68 Benedict XVI, "Pastoral Letter to the Catholics of Ireland", 19 March 2010.
69 Marmion, *Christ, The Life of the Soul*, pp. 187, 183.
70 Healy, Mary, *Catholic Commentary on Sacred Scripture: Hebrews* (Baker Publishing Group, 2016), p. 29.

as supreme truth and supreme authority'.[71] To live and walk by faith. 'The just man' Marmion reminds us, *'lives* by faith. To live is to have within one an inner mainspring which is the source of one's movements and operations' whereby more and more one acts as a true child of the Father.[72] There is no better way today. And this is so even though 'that faith will be tried by this age of unbelief, of blasphemy, of scepticism, of naturalism, of human respect, that surrounds us with its unhealthy atmosphere'.[73] We can, if you will, learn to make our own the words of St Patrick: 'Whether I received good or ill, I return thanks equally to God, who taught me always to trust Him *unreservedly*'.[74]

Such then is the faith to which Marmion is calling us today. For such, indeed, is the faith which not only can the darkness not overpower, but which in the words of St John, constitutes 'our victory over the world' (cf. 1 Jn 5:4). Moladh go deo le Dia![75]

---

71 Marmion, *Christ, The Life of the Soul*, p. 176.
72 *Ibid.*, p. 187.
73 *Ibid.*, p. 194.
74 *The Divine Office*, vol. 2, p. 50*.
75 Praise God forever!

2

'I VSE THE SVMMA AS TEXT-BOOK'

THE THOMISM OF BLESSED COLUMBA MARMION

FR JOHN SAWARD

WHEN THE OXFORD CONVERT JOHN Henry Newman arrived at the College of Propaganda in the autumn of 1846, there was next to no Thomism in the Roman schools. His friend James Robert Hope, who had spent eight months in Rome in the early 40s, told him he would find 'very little theology' of any kind. A Jesuit professor confessed that in philosophy neither Aristotle nor St Thomas were in favour: 'St Thomas is a great saint—people don't care to speak against him; they profess to reverence him, but put him aside.'[1] Thirty years later, when the Dublin seminarian Joseph Marmion started his studies at Propaganda, the Angelic Doctor's philosophy and theology were enjoying, to redeploy a famous phrase of Newman's, a Roman 'second Spring'. In 1879, two years before Marmion's ordination, the encyclical *Aeterni Patris* of Pope Leo XIII propagated the seeds of the Spring for the benefit of the whole Church. The teacher at Propaganda destined to shape Marmion's theological thinking more than any other was Francesco Satolli, a Thomist long admired by Pope Leo and sent by him 'to teach the *Summa theologica* of the Angel of the Schools at the Propaganda'.[2] To

---

1 Letter of John Henry Newman to J. D. Dalgairns (November 22, 1846); *The Letters and Diaries of John Henry Newman*, vol. 11 (London: Thomas Nelson, 1961), p. 279.
2 Dom Raymond Thibaut, *Abbot Columba Marmion: A Master of the Spiritual Life, 1858–1923* (London, Edinburgh, & St Louis: Sands & Herder,

the end of his life, Abbot Marmion recalled with gratitude Satolli's lectures and his demonstration of 'the luminous plan, powerful structure, vigorous logic, and marvellous unity' of the *Summa*.3 In a letter of November 1902, when the by then Benedictine Columba Marmion was teaching dogmatic theology at Mont César, he told his friend Bishop Vincent Dwyer: 'I use the *Summa* as text-book'.4 His advice to a doctoral student was 'above all to go deeply into the thought of St Thomas'.5 The purpose of this essay is to show how deeply Columba Marmion himself went into the thought of the Angelic Doctor, especially in his understanding of Christian holiness as a participation in the holiness of Christ.

MARMION'S THOMISM: QUOTING FROM ST THOMAS

Blessed Columba's Thomism can be considered in two ways: materially, as exemplified by quotations from the works of St Thomas; and formally, as demonstrated by his use, with or without quotation, of the Angelic Doctor's 'method, doctrine, and principles'.6 Some authors quote the words of St Thomas abundantly, while feeling free to depart from his thought. Others, such as Blessed Columba, are sparing in their citations, but prove by their arguments and conclusions that they think according to the mind of the *Doctor communis*. He quotes St Thomas less frequently than he does Sacred Scripture and the Sacred Liturgy, but on almost every page of his writings, with or without accompanying footnotes, he proves that, like the Egyptians who went to Joseph to save them from famine, he was one who had gone to Thomas to find the 'the nourishment of sound doctrine'.7

1932)[= Thibaut], p. 22–23.
3 *Ibid.*, p. 23.
4 *The English Letters of Abbot Marmion, 1858–1923* (Dublin: Helicon, 1962) [= English Letters], p. 37.
5 Thibaut, p. 123.
6 Cf. *Codex iuris canonici* (1917), can. 1367/2.
7 The analogy with Joseph and the Egyptians and the phrase quoted can be found in Pope Pius XI's Encyclical Letter *Studiorum ducem* (*Acta*

Dom Marmion draws for his nourishment from the sound doctrine to be found not only in the three parts of the *Summa* but in other works such as the commentary on the *Sentences* and the *De veritate*. From the treatise on the One God in the *Prima pars* he takes up the Thomistic and Boethian definition of eternity, 'the simultaneous and perfect possession of endless life', and tells us it means that 'God, in a *nunc stans*, that is, in a *now* that surpasses all limit and all succession, "possesses, in a perfect way, the fulness of a life without beginning or end".'[8] Like the Angelic Doctor, he is confident that human reason can demonstrate the existence of 'a supreme Being, first cause of every creature, the Providence of the world, the one who sovereignly rewards, the final end of all things', and that from this natural knowledge of God derive 'duties toward God and neighbour, duties that together form the basis of what is called the natural law, and the observance of which constitutes natural religion'.[9] But, though natural reason can attain these great truths, it has no access to God's innermost life. And so 'Divine Revelation comes, inundating us with its light',[10] and teaching us that 'in God there are the Father, the Son, and the Holy Spirit: three distinct Persons, yet all Three with but one and the same divine nature or essence'.[11] For

---

apostolicae sedis [=AAS] 15 (1923), 323). The detailed references in footnotes to the works of St Thomas in *Christ, vie de l'âme* were doubtless often supplied by Dom Raymund Thibaut, Abbot Marmion's disciple and editor.
8   Marmion, Columba, *Le Christ, idéal du prêtre* (Maredsous: Éditions de Maredsous, 1952) [= *Prêtre*], p. 197. All translations of Marmion's works from the original French are my own unless otherwise noted; cf. *Summa theologiae* [= ST]1a q. 10, a. 1.
9   Marmion, Columba, *Le Christ, vie de l'âme: Conférences spirituelles* (Paris: Desclée de Brouwer, 1935)[= *Vie*], p. 5–6. Marmion does not cite St Thomas in this passage, but what he says is manifestly faithful to St Thomas's thought (cf. ST 1a q. 2, aa. 1 & 2 (on the possibility of demonstrating God's existence and the Five Ways of actually demonstrating His existence); q. 22 (on the Providence of God); 1a2ae q. 91, a. 2 (on the existence of the natural law); and 2a2ae q. 81 (on the virtue of religion)).
10   Marmion, Columba, *Le Christ dans ses mystères: Conférences spirituelles* (Cadillac: Saint-Remi,2019) [= *Mystères*], p. 366; cf. 1a q. 32, a. 1 (on the impossibility of knowing the three Divine Persons by natural reason).
11   *Vie*, p. 13.

Blessed Columba as for St Thomas, the Son proceeds from the Father by way of intellect, as Word: 'As infinite intellect, the Father knows His perfections perfectly and expresses this knowledge in a unique Word (*Verbe*), the living, substantial Utterance (*Parole*), the adequate expression of what the Father is.'[12] The Holy Spirit proceeds from the Father and the Son by way of will, as Love: He 'seals the union of the Father and the Son by being Their substantial and living Love'.[13] It is precisely because He is the Love of the Father and the Son that the Spirit is the *Holy* Spirit.[14]

It is from St Thomas that Marmion derives his understanding of the theological virtues and Gifts in general, as presented in the *Prima secundae*, and of each virtue and Gift in particular, which is the subject-matter of the *Secunda secundae*. His understanding of the seven Gifts of the Holy Spirit in relation to the seven virtues, theological and moral, is likewise Thomistic. The Gifts perfect the virtues, says St Thomas, for, while we exercise the virtues under the movement of our own reason, the Gifts prepare us to be moved by *God*.[15] Marmion holds the same opinion: 'By the Gifts, the Holy Spirit keeps hold and reserves to Himself the guiding of all our supernatural conduct.'[16]

---

12   *Ibid.*, p. 14; cf. ST 1a q. 34.
13   *Ibid.*, p. 14; cf. ST 1a q. 37.
14   *Ibid.*, p. 14n; 'Since the good that is loved has the characteristic of being an end, and from the end a movement of the will is rendered good or bad, it is necessary that the love by which the supreme good, which is God, is loved should possess eminent goodness, which is expressed by the name "holiness"... Therefore, the Spirit, whom we think of as the love by which God loves Himself, is named "the Holy Spirit"' (*Compendium* lib. 1, cap. 47).
15   Cf. ST 1a2ae q. 68, a. 1.
16   *Vie*, p. 142. 'The Gifts are not... the inspirations of the Holy Spirit themselves, but dispositions that make us obey the inspirations promptly and easily... True, by the virtues the soul in the state of grace acts supernaturally, but it acts in a way that conforms to his rational and human condition, and with his own movement and initiative. By the Gifts it is disposed to act directly and solely under the divine impulsion, while of course retaining its liberty, which is manifested by acquiescence with the inspiration from above, and this happens in a way that does not always fit in with its rational, natural way of seeing and envisioning things' (*Vie*, p. 142). In his book on the priesthood, Marmion considers the particular case

Quoting from the commentary on the *Sentences*, he says that 'faith is the first attitude we must have in our relations with God, *prima conjunctio ad Deum est per fidem*'.[17] He defines the act of faith in the Angelic Doctor's own words: 'To believe, says St Thomas, is, under the command of the will moved by grace, to give the assent, the adherence, of our intellect to the divine truth: *Ipsum autem credere est actus intellectus assentientis veritati divinae ex imperio voluntatis sub motu gratiae.*'[18] Although we walk in this life by faith, not sight, and have the face-to-face vision of God in Heaven as the object of hope rather than as a present possession, our Lord tells us that 'he who believes in the Son *has* eternal life' (cf. Jn 3:36). St Paul likewise connects faith with what we hope to see in Heaven when he says that 'faith is the substance of things to be hoped for, the evidence of things that appear not' (cf. Heb. 11:1). In fidelity to this teaching of our Lord and His Apostle, Marmion, quoting St Thomas, defines faith as 'a habit of the mind by which eternal life is begun in us.'[19] Charity, for Marmion as for Aquinas, is a kind of friendship: 'man's friendship with God.'[20] We love God and neighbour by one and the same charity: we love our neighbour for God's sake, that he may inherit eternal life in God: 'To love our neighbour supernaturally is to love him in view of God, to gain for him or to preserve for him the grace of God that will lead him to eternal beatitude.'[21] If we exercise the other virtues with charity, they acquire a new beauty and power. 'If each of these acts is carried out with an explicit

---

of the Gift of Counsel in relation to the virtue of prudence: 'God does not give the Gift of Counsel to His children to suppress the virtue of prudence, but "to come to its aid and perfect its exercise". *Ipsam [prudentiam] adjuvans et perficiens*' (*Prêtre*, p. 295; cf. ST 2a2ae q. 52, a. 2).

17 *Ibid.*, p. 161; cf. *Sent.* lib. 4, d. 39, q. 1, a. 6, ad 2.
18 *Ibid.*, p. 166; cf. ST 2a2ae q. 2, a. 9.
19 *Prêtre*, p. 73; cf. ST 2a2ae q. 14, a. 1.
20 *Ibid.*, p. 156; cf. ST 2a2ae q. 23, a. 1.
21 *Vie*, p. 445, quoting in a footnote two texts from the *Summa*: 'God is the reason for loving our neighbour, for this is what we must love in our neighbour: that he be in God' (ST 2a2ae q. 25, a. 1); 'To love is nothing other than willing the good for someone' (ST 1a q. 20, a. 2).

intention to love God, that motive colours, so to speak, the acts of the other virtues, and without depriving them of their particular merit, it adds to it a new one.'[22] In *Le Christ, idéal du moine*, the chapter on the virtue of humility is based upon St Thomas's exposition, in the *Secunda secundae*, of St Benedict's twelve degrees of humility in the Holy Rule. If these pages are proof of the Thomism of Dom Columba Marmion, they show, too, the Benedictine sympathies of Friar Thomas of Aquino.[23]

The *Tertia pars* is the source of Marmion's thinking about the Incarnate Word, His saving work, and the application of His saving work to individual souls through faith, charity, and the grace of the sacraments.[24] Like St Thomas in the opening questions of the *Tertia pars*, he expounds the Hypostatic Union in exact conformity to the great Councils of the Patristic age.[25] With St Thomas, and before him St

---

22 *Ibid.*, p. 288; cf. ST 2a2ae q. 23, a. 8 (on charity as 'the form of the virtues').
23 'It is well known that St Thomas was a Benedictine oblate at Monte Cassino and remained there for nine years...During his stay at Cassino the young Thomas studied the text of the Rule of the Holy Patriarch. "The writings of the future Doctor...[writes P. Mandonnet OP] bear witness to his familiarity with St Benedict's great legislative monument"' (Columba Marmion OSB, *Le Christ, ideal du moine* (Paris: Desclée de Brouwer, 1936) [*Moine*], p. 291n).
24 'Christ's Passion works its effect in those to whom it is applied through faith and charity, and through the Sacraments of faith' (ST 3a q. 49, a. 3, ad 1). 'All these [Sacraments] spring from the Cross, from the love of Christ; all apply to us the fruits of the Saviour's Death by the power of the Blood of Jesus' (Marmion, *Vie*, p. 94)
25 'Christ is the Incarnate Word. Revelation teaches us that the Second Person of the Holy Trinity, the Word, the Son, has taken a human nature upon Himself to unite it to Himself in person. This is the mystery of the Incarnation...Christ is perfect God and perfect man...He is perfect God. In taking our human nature upon Himself, the Word remains what He was, *Quod fuit permansit*: God, the eternal Being, possessing in plenitude all life, all perfection, all sovereignty, all power, and all beatitude...Perfect God, Christ is also perfect man...He has taken upon Himself a human nature that He has made His own by uniting it to Himself physically, substantially, personally, by ineffable bonds, *Quod non erat assumpsit*...The human nature, altogether integral, altogether perfect in its essence, in its constitutive elements, nevertheless only has existence through the Word, in the divine person of the Word. It is the Word who gives the human nature its reality of existence, which, in this case, means its personal "subsistence"' (*Mystères*, p. 70–75).

Athanasius and St John Damascene, he tells us that the sacred humanity is an *instrument*, living and united, of the eternal Word: the divine person saves us by means of His sufferings and actions in human nature.[26] 'It is by one and the same act of Divine Wisdom [says Marmion, paraphrasing St Thomas] that Christ and we have been predestined',[27] thus, in Marmion's own words, 'the Father makes of all the disciples of Christ who believe in Him and live by his grace one and the same object of His good pleasure'.[28] When we are in the state of grace on earth, and finally, when by God's mercy we attain heavenly glory, God the Father sees His Son in us and us in Him, and delights in us, as in Him. Marmion's theology of the priesthood of Christ, and of men's participation in it through the Sacrament of Holy Orders, is the fruit of an attentive reading of the treatise *de sacerdotio Christi* in the *Tertia pars*. To help his readers understand the priestly life of Christ in Heaven, he distinguishes, as St Thomas does, between Christ's offering of His Sacrifice and its consummation: having offered His Sacrifice on Calvary, the Eternal High Priest communicates its fruits from Heaven.[29]

Although Marmion cites no authority for it from the works of St Thomas, his theology of *Christ in His Mysteries* without doubt conforms to the Angelic Doctor's teaching in the *Summa*.

---

26 'It is in His human nature that Jesus suffers, makes expiation, and merits. His humanity becomes the instrument of the Word, and these sufferings of the sacred humanity *work* our salvation, are the *cause* of our redemption, and restore life to us' (Marmion, *Vie*, p. 83). In a footnote Marmion cites 'a beautiful proposition of the Angelic Doctor: "Inasmuch as He was with God in the beginning, the Word vivifies our souls as principal agent, but His flesh and the mysteries enacted in the flesh work instrumentally in giving life to the soul"(ST 3a q. 62, a. 5, ad 1)' (*Vie*, p. 83n).
27 *Vie*, p. 118; cf. ST 3a q. 24, a. 4.
28 *Ibid.*, p. 118.
29 *Prêtre*, p. 26. Having distinguished between the offering and the consummation of the Sacrifice, St Thomas concludes: 'Christ entered into the Holy of Holies—that is, into Heaven—and prepared the way for us, that we might enter by the power of His blood, which He shed for us on earth' (ST 3a q. 22, a. 5).

The Thomism of Blessed Columba Marmion

In the Prologue of the *Tertia pars* St Thomas states his intention to speak, first, of 'the mystery of the Incarnation' and, secondly, of 'the things that our Saviour, that is, God Incarnate, did and suffered'. The mystery of the Incarnation is the subject-matter of twenty-six questions. The things that God Incarnate did and suffered, from the Blessed Virgin's womb to the Father's right hand in Heaven, are then dealt with in thirty-three questions, one for each year of the Saviour's earthly sojourn. Now, the incarnate Word has the use of His human free will, and is able to merit, in and from the first moment of His conception.[30] Therefore, in each of His mysteries, in every state and at every stage of His human life on earth up to His giving up of the ghost on the Cross, He can and does merit graces that from Heaven He will communicate to the souls of His members. These are the special graces for which the Church prays in the successive seasons and feasts of the Liturgical Year, and which Columba Marmion unfolds in *Christ in His Mysteries*: 'In His glorious state, Christ no longer merits. He could merit only during His mortal life, up to the hour in which He breathed His last on the Cross, but the merits He acquired He never ceases to place in our possession.'[31]

Marmion's doctrine of the sacraments in general, and of each sacrament in particular, is thoroughly Thomistic. He uses the Angelic Doctor's analogy between natural life and the supernatural life imparted in the sacraments,[32] and argues, in agreement with St Thomas, that the sacraments are efficacious with an instrumental causality, like the power of a chisel in the hand of the sculptor.[33] It should not surprise us to dis-

---

30 Cf. ST 3a q. 34, aa. 2 & 3.
31 *Mystères*, p. 27.
32 *Vie*, p. 90; cf. ST 3a q. 65. a. 1.
33 '[The Sacraments] produce grace, not as principal cause—sanctifying grace flows from Christ alone, as from its unique source—but as instruments, in virtue of the motion they receive from Christ's humanity united to the Word and filled with divine life' (*Vie*, p. 88–89). In a footnote, he quotes two texts from the treatise on the Sacraments in general in the *Tertia pars*: 'Bodily Sacraments by their own operation, which they exercise on the body they touch, accomplish by divine power an instrumental operation on the

cover that Marmion's thinking about the Bread of Life and the Eucharistic Sacrifice is modelled on that of the Church's supreme *Doctor eucharisticus*.[34] In his book on the priesthood, he speaks of the transforming power of Holy Communion, and quotes St Thomas as his authority: 'In virtue of this Sacrament, through love, a certain transformation of man into Christ takes place.'[35] The Mass, writes Marmion, is 'not just a simple representation of the Sacrifice of the Cross, nor does it have the value of a simple memorial, but is a true Sacrifice, the same as that of Calvary, which it reproduces and continues, and of which it applies the fruits'.[36] This is the doctrine of the Council of Trent,[37] and before it of St Thomas; in St Thomas's words, quoted by Marmion in his book on the priesthood: 'The effect that the Passion of Christ had in the world this Sacrament has in man.'[38]

---

soul. For example, the water of Baptism, by cleansing the body by its own power, cleanses the soul as an instrument of divine power, for from soul and body comes one thing. And so Augustine says that "[the water] touches the body and cleanses the heart" (ST 3a q. 62, a. 1, ad 2).' 'A spiritual power is in the Sacraments inasmuch as they are ordained by God to produce a spiritual effect' (ST 3a q. 62, a. 4, ad 1).

34 'Just as in the natural order food preserves, sustains, increases, and restores the life of the body, and causes it to flourish, so this heavenly Bread is the food of the soul: it sustains and restores the life of grace in the soul, causing it to grow and rejoice, because it gives the soul the Author of grace Himself' (*Vie*, p. 344). In a footnote Marmion cites St Thomas's application of the four effects of natural food to the spiritually nourishing power of the Eucharist in ST 3a q. 79, a. 1.

35 *Prêtre*, p. 232; cf. *Scriptum super Sententiis* [= *Sent.*] lib. 4, d. 12, q. 11, a. 2.

36 *Vie*, p. 326.

37 Marmion quotes the Council's *Doctrina de ss. Missae sacrificio* (Session 22, 17th September 1562) throughout his chapter on the Eucharistic Sacrifice in *Vie* (pp. 314–340). In ch. 1 of the *Doctrina*, the Council Fathers tell us that 'our Lord and God' institutes the Most Holy Sacrifice of the Mass 'in order to leave His beloved Bride, the Church, a visible sacrifice (as the nature of men requires), by which the bloody Sacrifice He was to accomplish on the Cross would be represented, its memory remain to the end of the world, and its saving power be applied for the forgiveness of the sins we daily commit' (*Enchiridion symbolorum, definitionum, et declarationum de rebus fidei et morum*, 33rd edition, ed. H. Denzinger & A. Schönmetzer SJ (Barcelona, Freiburg, Rome, and New York: Herder, 1965) [= DS], n. 1740).

38 *Prêtre*, p. 207; cf. ST 3a q. 79, a. 1.

MARMION'S THOMISM: THINKING WITH ST THOMAS—SHARING THE HOLINESS OF CHRIST

In his understanding of Christian holiness Blessed Columba Marmion shows himself to be a disciple of St Thomas, but first of all, like St Thomas, a disciple of the Apostles St John and St Paul, and of the divine Master whose teaching they transmit. Christian holiness is a participation in the holiness of Christ, the Father's incarnate Only-begotten Son. Christ *is* our holiness, says Marmion, quoting St Paul: 'God has made [Him] our wisdom, our justice and *sanctification* and redemption' (1 Cor. 1:30).[39] Here is the 'fundamental axiom' of Dom Marmion's theology, as Fr Philipon OP calls it: 'All our sanctity consists in becoming by grace what Jesus Christ is by nature, the child of God.'[40]

According to St Thomas and Blessed Columba, it is by the grace of Christ Himself that we are made holy and become what He is by nature, adopted sons incorporated into the true and natural Son. Christ is 'the life of our souls' through our share in His holiness by His grace.[41] To understand this

---

[39] Marmion quotes these words of St Paul repeatedly: for example, *English Letters*, p. 36; *Vie*, p. 80; *Moine*, p. 40. At Christmas 1908, in Louvain, he composed his 'Consecration to the Blessed Trinity', in which he prays: 'O Jesus, unite us to thee, in thy life all holy, entirely consecrated to thy Father and to souls. *Be thou our justice, our holiness, our redemption, our all* (*The Trinity in our Spiritual Life*, ET [Cork: Mercier Press, 1953], p. 9). 'Christ is not only holy in Himself; He is *our* holiness. All the holiness that God has destined for souls has been placed in the humanity of Christ, and it is from that source that we must draw' (*Vie*, p. 24). 'The plan of the Eternal Father, the mystery hidden in God from ages to generations (cf. Col. 1:26) is to "to re-establish all things" (cf. Eph. 1:10), to sanctify the world by His Son. Jesus Christ is the only "way" by which one may go the Father (cf. Jn 14:6)' (Retreat for Priests, Louvain, 1898, quoted by M. M. Philipon OP in *The Spiritual Doctrine of Dom Marmion*, ET (London & Glasgow: Sands, 1956) [= Philipon], p. 92–93).

[40] Retreat at Hayward's Heath, August 1905, quoted by Philipon, p. 98.

[41] 'All holiness... will consist in receiving divine life from Christ and through Christ, who possesses its fulness and who has been established as the one Mediator... Holiness, then, is a mystery of divine life communicated and received: communicated, in God, from the Father to the Son by "an ineffable generation", communicated outside of God by the Son to the humanity that He personally unites to Himself in the Incarnation, then by

mystery, Marmion makes his own St Thomas's doctrine of the 'capital' grace of Christ, the grace proper to Him as Head of the Mystical Body of which we are the members. First, as St Thomas does, he speaks of 'the grace of union', and of the sanctifying grace deriving from it, the grace of Christ as individual man, *singularis homo*:

> The 'grace of union' (the hypostatic union) unites the human nature to the person of the Word, and thus renders everything in Christ divine. Christ is by this grace a divine 'subject'... But it is still fitting that this human nature be adorned with 'sanctifying grace' in order to operate divinely in each of its faculties. This sanctifying grace is 'connatural' to the grace of union, in the sense that it derives from the grace of union in a kind of natural way. It places the soul of Christ at the height of its union with the Word, and enables the human nature, which subsists in the Word in virtue of the grace of union, to be able to act as befits a soul elevated to such an eminent dignity, and to produce divine fruits.[42]

Now the habitual grace of Christ as individual man is not, so to speak, a private possession. 'This grace in Jesus', says Marmion, 'is not confined to Him alone; it is not solely personal in character, but enjoys the privilege of universality. Christ has been predestined to become our Head, our representative.'[43] Christ as man has grace not only as individual man, but as

---

this humanity restored to souls and received by each of them in the measure of their particular predestination, *secundum mensuram donationis* (Eph. 4:7)' (*Vie*, p. 8). 'There are two starting-points (*principia*) for the human race: one, according to the life of nature, viz. Adam; the other according to the life of grace, viz. Christ' (St Thomas, *Super 1 Corinthios* cap. 15, lect. 7).

42 *Vie*, p. 132. Fr Garrigou-Lagrange defines the grace of union as Christ's 'personal being, which is given gratuitously and divinely to the human nature' (Reginald Garrigou-Lagrange OP, *De Verbo incarnato* [Turin: Marietti, 1949], p. 179). St Thomas considers the grace of Christ as individual man in ST 3a q. 7 and the grace of Christ as Head in q. 8. To explain the relation of Christ's grace as individual man to the grace of union, Marmion quotes St Thomas: 'The habitual grace of Christ is a consequence of the hypostatic union, as brightness comes from the sun' (ST 3a q. 7, a. 13).

43 *Ibid.*, p. 65.

Head of the Church, of men and angels: He has the *gratia capitis*.[44] Because of the grace of union, Christ has grace of the greatest eminence, and because of the eminence, He can bestow grace on others as their Head; thus, St Thomas concludes, the grace of Christ as individual man and the grace of Christ as Head of the Church are really identical. 'From His fulness have we all received, grace upon grace' (Jn 1:16). It is because Head and members together are, as St Thomas says, like 'one mystical person' that 'the satisfaction of Christ extends to all the faithful as to His members', and that He can merit not only for Himself but for us.[45] Everything that Christ is, has, and does as man is for sharing with His members.[46]

As members of Christ sanctified by His grace, we participate in His Sonship and in the life that He lives within the Godhead with the Father and the Holy Spirit. Our adoptive sonship, says Blessed Columba echoing St Thomas, is 'a resemblance of the eternal sonship'.[47] Sanctifying grace (habitual grace) is, in the Thomistic definition, 'a participated likeness of the divine nature'.[48] The Holy Spirit makes us partakers of the holiness of Christ through the grace we receive in the sacraments,[49] through faith and charity and His sevenfold Gifts,[50] and

---

44 Cf. ST 3a q. 8, aa. 1, 3, & 4.
45 'Christ Jesus, as Head, has then merited everything for us, just as, by substituting Himself for us, He made satisfaction for us' (*Vie*, p. 66); cf. ST 3a q. 48, a. 2, ad 1 (on Christ's work of satisfaction); and 3a q. 48, a. 1 (on Christ's merits).
46 But, of course, the grace of union is 'unique and found only in Jesus Christ' (*Vie*, p. 45n).
47 ... *filiatio adoptiva est quaedam participata similitudo filiationis naturalis* (ST 3a q. 3, a. 5, ad 2), quoted by Marmion in *Vie*, p. 45; cf. *Le Christ, idéal du prêtre* (Maredsous: Éditions de Maredsous, 1952), p. 34.
48 ... *grata nihil est aliud quam quaedam participata similitudo divinae naturae* (ST 3a q. 62, a. 1, on grace as the principal effect of the Sacraments), quoted by Marmion in *Vie*, p. 18. He goes on to say: 'Participation in this divine life is made a reality for us by grace, in virtue of which our souls become capable of knowing God as God knows Himself, of loving God as God loves Himself, of enjoying God as God is filled with His own beatitude, and thus living the life of God Himself' (*Vie*, p. 18).
49 Cf. *Vie*, pp. 85–87.
50 Cf. *Ibid.*, pp. 144–150.

through the daily renewal of our baptismal renunciation of Satan and death to sin.[51] Thus the Spirit of Christ transforms us into the likeness of Christ (cf. 2 Cor. 3:18), and enables us to live as adopted sons who, in union with the true and natural Son incarnate, in all things give glory to the Father.

> Holiness for us is nothing other than the complete fulfilment, the full development of that first grace which is our divine adoption, the grace given in our Baptism, ... and by which we become children of God and brothers of Jesus Christ.[52]

The saints are those who become most perfectly what they already are by their baptism: children of God, members and brethren of Christ, temples of the Holy Spirit, partakers of the life of the Most Holy Trinity.

CONCLUSION

By 1923, the year of Blessed Columba Marmion's death, the Thomistic revival had passed from the freshness and uncertainty of spring to the brightness and established warmth of high summer. The Leonine Commission, inaugurated a year after *Aeterni Patris*, had already published its critical edition of the *Summa theologiae* and was half-way through its work on the *Summa contra gentiles*. The *Revue thomiste* was founded in 1893. In 1907, in the encyclical *Pascendi dominici gregis*, which condemned the doctrines of the Modernists, St Pius X reminded professors that they could not 'abandon Aquinas, especially in metaphysics, without grave detriment'.[53] Seven years later the Sacred Congregation for Studies published the twenty-four *Approved Theses of Thomistic Philosophy*.[54] In 1922, in his Apostolic Letter, *Officiorum omnium*, Pius XI declared St Thomas to be the principal guide for those studying

---

51 Cf. *Ibid.*, pp. 184–204.
52 *Ibid.*, p. 138.
53 Pope St Pius X, Encyclical Letter *Pascendi dominici gregis*, On the Doctrines of the Modernists, 8th September 1907; AAS 40 (1907), p. 640.
54 DS 3601–3624.

the great disciplines of philosophy and theology,[55] and a few months after Marmion's death in 1923, in *Studiorum ducem*, the same Pope showed how the Angelic Doctor exemplifies the mutual fruitfulness of holiness and devotion to the truth and again urged teachers and pupils to be assiduous in their study of his works.[56]

The Thomistic revival inspired a renewal not only of philosophy and dogmatic and moral theology, but also of the theology of the spiritual life, as is evident in the writings of the Dominican Thomists Ambroise Gardeil (†1931), Juan González Arintero (+1928), and Reginald Garrigou-Lagrange (†1964),[57] each of whom, in his own way, held that the call to mystical union with the Incarnate Word and the whole Trinity is not restricted to those rare souls who receive extraordinary graces (*gratiae gratis datae*), but is in principle for all Christians who participate in the life of the Blessed Trinity through the sanctifying grace of Christ (*gratia gratum faciens*) received in the sacraments.[58] Now, though he does not address the specific questions posed by his Dominican contemporaries, Blessed

---

55 Pope Pius XI, Apostolic Letter *Officiorum omnium*; AAS 14 (1922), 449–458.
56 Pope Pius XI, Encyclical Letter *Studiorum ducem*; AAS 15 (1923), 309–326.
57 Cf. Ambroise Gardeil OP, *La structure de l'âme et l'expérience mystique*, vols. 1 & 2 (Paris: Gabalda, 1927); Juan González Arintero OP, *La evolución mística*, new ed. (Salamanca: Editorial San Esteban, 1989); Reginald Garrigou-Lagrange OP, *Perfection chrétienne et contemplation selon S. Thomas d'Aquin et S. Jean de la Croix* (Paris: Éditions de la Vie spirituelle, 1923).
58 'The basic principle of the mystical life is sanctifying grace or "the grace of the virtues and Gifts"' (Reginald Garrigou-Lagrange OP, *Christian Perfection and Contemplation according to St Thomas Aquinas*, ET (St Louis & London: Herder, 1949), p. 349). This opinion has now been endorsed by the teaching Church herself in the *Catechism of the Catholic Church*: 'Spiritual progress tends toward ever more intimate union with Christ. This union is called "mystical" because it participates in the mystery of Christ through the Sacraments—"the holy mysteries"—and, in Him, in the mystery of the Holy Trinity. *God calls us all to this intimate union with Him, even if the special graces of extraordinary signs of this mystical life are granted only to some for the sake of manifesting the gratuitous gift given to all*' (*The Catechism of the Catholic Church*, n. 2014).

Columba Marmion was likewise confident that the summit of the spiritual life was within the reach of every Christian, for the holiness to which God calls us is but the flowering of the grace of our baptism, that grace which is a participation in the divine nature and confers a likeness to the natural sonship of Christ. As we have seen, these 'master ideas'[59] of the theology of Dom Marmion derive ultimately from the *Summa theologica* of the Angel of the Schools expounded by Francesco Satolli at Propaganda. The holiness that the Church recognizes in Columba Marmion—the doctrine of holiness she has praised through the Popes and the holiness of his life that she has declared makes him worthy of beatification—is characteristically Benedictine, but also unmistakeably Thomistic.

---

59 This phrase comes from the title of Dom Thibaut's book, *L'idée maîtresse de la doctrine de Dom Marmion* (Maredsous: Éditions de Maredsous, 1947).

3
ON ST THÉRÈSE'S INFLVENCE ON MARMION[1]

FR CASSIAN KOENEMANN, OSB

MAHATMA GANDHI WAS CREDITED as having said 'I like your Christ. But not your Christianity.'[2] Abstracting from him in particular, I want to use this point of view to posit a thoughtful external Observer looking into Christianity for its best witness. Approached by such an Observer, I would offer St Thérèse as our best modern witness, and I'd like to think such an Observer, attentive to subtleties lost on the common lot, would find her little way of spiritual childhood intriguing. Put another way, this recent Doctor of the Church may be the least unlike our Christ in a manner that could best speak to a contemporary Observer. Why? It has less to do with her beautiful opening lines about being a little flower, glorious though those lines are, and much more to do with her following the royal road of the cross in her accepting of her nothingness and in her offering of herself as a victim to God's merciful love, trusting in God's mercy for her. She did not see Christ as someone who died so that she could live a high-status life or a high-influence life or a pleasant life or a tranquil life; rather, she saw Christ as someone to imitate, fully, aided by His power, by taking up

---

1 If you would like to read a more researched treatment on this topic, please see my book, *The Grace of Nothingness: Navigating the Spiritual Life with Blessed Columba Marmion*, most especially the section on St Thérèse's influence on Marmion in Chapter 2 and the various practical spiritual lessons common to the both of them shared throughout Chapter 3.
2 Mahatma Ghandi, "Mahatma Ghandi says he believes in Christ but not Christianity" in *The Harvard Crimson*. https://www.thecrimson.com/article/1927/1/11/mahatma-gandhi-says-he-believes-in/

her own cross. She knew her weakness well, so she counted not on it but on the loving Father's transformative mercy.

Won over by the grace of God, St Thérèse trusted Jesus. She simply took Jesus at his word. 'Blessed are the poor in spirit...' Yes, she believed the life of beatitude was outlined right there in the great reversals of the Sermon on the Mount. Period. So, she would go to God by way of a humble confidence in His ways. It was as if, when Jesus said to her, 'Take up your cross and follow me' (cf. Mt. 16:24–26), her only reply was, 'You have the words of eternal life' (Jn 6:68).

Let us pause for a moment to savour the peace that comes from trusting God that deeply. Allow me to set a reflection on this reality from the *Imitation of Christ* next to her own words and follow them both with a comment of my own. The *Imitation of Christ*, so beloved by St Thérèse that she memorized chapters of it early in her life, asks rhetorically, 'Can the man whose heart is truly obedient to God ever be puffed up with empty pride?' Thomas à Kempis goes on to provide the answer, 'Nothing in this world will make him, whom Truth has subjected to Itself, yield to pride, nor will the man who has firmly placed his hope in God be moved by the praises of other men.'[3] Now let us read to St Thérèse's self-disclosure on this topic:

> All creatures can bow toward her, admire her, and shower praises upon her. I don't know why this is, but none of this could add one single drop of false joy to the true joy she experiences in her heart. Here she sees herself as she really is in God's eyes: a poor little thing, nothing at all.[4]

There is on display here a tremendous transformation to unpack:

---

[3] À Kempis, Thomas, *Imitation of Christ*, ed. and trans. Joseph Tylenda (New York: Vintage Spiritual Classics, 1998), Bk III.14, pp. 96–97.
[4] St Thérèse of Lisieux, "Manuscript C, 02r," in Archives du Carmel de Lisieux. http://www.archives-carmel-lisieux.fr/english/carmel/index.php/c01-10/c02/c02r.

> Notice that St Thérèse is not captivated by the praises of others, for she knows deeply the greatest praise from the One who matters most. God constantly loves her, even in her nothingness, and his love for her is always enough. Let us think here of an art exhibition. The artist wins the admiration of the greatest aesthetes and connoisseurs, she receives the acceptance of her gift by her family and friends. She has brought the inspiration within her to masterful conclusion. Yet most importantly, she recognizes the Grand Master Artist has always been at work in her.[5]

In short, she had gone to God 'with empty hands', as her offering makes explicit, and received grace back plentifully, 'good measure, pressed down, shaken together, running over' (Lk. 6:38), albeit in a novel and hidden way.[6] Her graces were in fact so hidden that she heard, through the window by her deathbed, her sisters in the garden commenting that there was nothing to say for her eulogy. That phenomenon occurred because those religious were looking for the wrong indicators of sanctity. Thanks be to God that a few other persons could recognize her novel contributions.

Her actions demonstrated that her trust in God had reached a great maturity. That truth is evident in her taking up her cross daily in the straitjacket limitations of a convent of misguided, even immature and unhealthy, humans. Let us here take off the rose-coloured glasses about religious. Do her accounts not inadvertently reveal persons with whom we would not want to live? If we use motherliness as a measure, well, then, several, if not many, of her sisters fell well short. Now let us speak of her love towards them. We see her love of God in her love of those who offer her so little in return—or worse yet, who offer her only priggish attacks. Yet in that

---

[5] Koenemann, Cassian, OSB, *The Grace of Nothingness: Navigating the Spiritual Life with Blessed Columba Marmion* (Brooklyn, NY: Angelico Press 2021), pp. 153–154.
[6] See Thérèse of Lisieux, "Prayer 6," in *Archives du Carmel de Lisieux*. www.archives-carmel-lisieux.fr/english/carmel/index.php/pri-6.

constrained circumstance, we see her embrace God through her embrace of her sisters.

Her view of perfection was different. 'Perfection seems simple to me, I see it is sufficient to recognize one's nothingness and to abandon oneself as a child into God's arms,' wrote St Thérèse. We see in this short summary of her doctrine that there was no mercenary love for Jesus in her, no give and take for worldly rewards. There wasn't even any spiritual transaction in her, no seeking of mystical states; all was foregone as a transformational gift of self to God, counting only on His mercy to provide whatever her weakness needed along the journey, along the journey towards whatever offering He wanted to effect in her life. If to love God (first) and neighbour (second) is the meaning of life, and if it is thus also the measure of life, then her offering as a victim soul to God's merciful love, her abandonment to Divine Providence, and her practical outpouring of herself, both towards God and her fellow inmates, were great indeed, far greater than her dreamy ambitions.

Let me put it yet more forcefully: she could come closest to saying to the rest of us anew, 'You are thinking not as God does, but as human beings do' (cf. Mt. 16:23). Do you doubt me on that audacious point? See how well you agree with this comment from her: 'Ah! how little known are the goodness, the merciful love of Jesus, Brother! [....] It is true, to enjoy these treasures one must humble oneself, recognize one's nothingness, and that is what many souls do not want to do.'[7] Indeed, the worldly soul will never find her sense of nothingness and her offering; the mercenary soul may miss it at first glance; the spiritual seeker may notice it but fear it; but an Observer, whom we can here endow with great psychological and spiritual maturity, would perhaps note, 'Ah, this Little Flower is a mature human and Christian, and a marvel of grace at such a young age.'

---

7   Thérèse of Lisieux, "Letter 261, to Fr. Bellière, 26 July 1897," in *Archives du Carmel de Lisieux*. http://www.archives-carmel-lisieux.fr/english/ carmel/index.php/lt-261-a-266/1172-lt-261-a-labbe-belliere.

If we can recognize St Thérèse's greatness today, it is only because others have helped us to do so. Early in the process, Marmion aided the reception of St Thérèse's novel influence within the Church. Pope Pius XI was seemingly inclined to beatify this new prodigy, who was already well loved by the people of God, but he nonetheless sought Marmion's opinion on the matter. We have Marmion's reply to him, which is ample grounds to establish her influence on him and his keen observation of her deep contributions:

> It seems that in this age when few feel called to go to God by the career of the sublime austerities of former times, God wills to show us that love can supply for everything, and that this way of love is the easiest and shortest way of perfection.
>
> Sister Thérèse of the Holy Child Jesus, Carmelite of the Carmel of Lisieux, appears to us to be a shining confirmation of this truth. She said of herself that in Christ's Mystical Body she desired to be the heart and to do all through love. And this love, mother of every virtue, was expressed in her by that perfect fidelity to all her duties, by that absolute abandon to God's good pleasure, by that boundless confidence in the goodness and love of her Heavenly Father, which are the perfect expression of the Spirit of Adoption.[8]

Abbot Columba recognized what would eventually become a more common observation in the soon-to-emerge field of Spiritual Theology: St Thérèse's little way marks a transition away from the 'austerities of former times' to a new 'easiest and shortest way of perfection.' Put another way, the little way was the organic development, the flowering so to speak, of a science of the saints that had previously pushed upward from the earth by way of austerities. Early investigators into the ways of holiness like Sts Cassian and Benedict were the roots; greats like Sts Bernard and John of the Cross were the

---

8 Marmion, Columba, *Union with God: Letters of Spiritual Direction by Blessed Columba Marmion*, ed. Raymond Thibaut, trans. Sr Mary St Thomas (Bethesda, MD: Zaccheus Press, 2006), p. 21.

stem and leaves; refinements like Sts Teresa and Francis de Sales were the sepal; but St Thérèse was the pistil and petals. (I suppose we can make Marmion the stamen that spreads this flower's characteristics.)

Blessed Marie Eugene, a great Carmelite commentator who was also gifted with the ability to live out his research into the science of the saints, summarized St Thérèse's impact as:

> In order to combat a generalized pride, Saint Thérèse constructs a spirituality of humility, her 'way of spiritual childhood.' To remain a child, to cultivate carefully in oneself the awareness of one's littleness and trusting weakness, to rejoice in one's poverty, to display it gladly before God as an appeal to His mercy; such, in her opinion, is the most proper attitude to attract God's glance and the plenitude of His transforming and consuming love. Really to acquire this attitude and to keep it, demands a complete immolation.[9]

Now Blessed Marie Eugene wrote those insights at the distance of several decades of his own and others' research into St Thérèse's worldwide impact. They combine well with Marmion's initial assessment, hopefully providing you with enough confidence in that assessment to dig deeper into the subtleties that make this new and 'easiest' way to holiness so much superior. Both commentators speak of 'love supplying for everything,' to use Marmion's phrase. Blessed Marie Eugene was more explicit about it supplying for one's weakness. Yet we can see the same insights coming through in Marmion's writings, such as in these lines of spiritual direction, seemingly derived directly from St Thérèse: 'We ought not to strive to dazzle God by our perfection, but rather to draw down His mercy by the confession of our weakness'[10]; 'It is God's will to be glorified by the union of our weakness with the power

---

9 Fr Marie Eugene, *I Want to See God: A Practical Synthesis of Carmelite Spirituality*, vol. 1, trans. M. Verda Clare (Chicago, IL: FIDES Publishers, 1953), p. 93.
10 Marmion, Columba, *Christ, The Ideal of the Monk*, Translator unknown (Ridgefield, CT: Roger A. McCaffrey, n.d.), p. 216.

of Christ'[11]; and, 'It is our wretchedness and our weakness which win us the strength of God.'[12] In these short phrases we have the complete reversal from the approach of acquiring spiritual importance to one of surrender. In the perfect scenario, I would hope our posited Observer would respond to such phrases, 'Now this is a different way of thinking and of living that seems so uniquely Christian.'

In a superb letter of spiritual direction, Marmion indeed reframes the Christian life as one that becomes an expression of mercy:

> Be a monument of His mercy for all eternity. The greater the wretchedness and the unworthiness, the greater and more adorable His mercy: *Abyssus abyssum invocat* [abyss calls upon abyss]: the abyss of our wretchedness invokes the abyss of his mercy. It is an immense consolation for me to see that you are travelling by this road which is so sure, which leads to such heights, and which glorifies the precious blood of Jesus Christ and the mercy of God. It is the way I have chosen too. Help me by your prayers.[13]

The notion from Alcoholics Anonymous of a Higher Power lifting one out of addiction can help us to unpack this reversal. We have been saved and are being actively restored, actively made better, and even actively perfected by God's transforming power (grace) at work within each person's life. It transforms us from the inside out, but only as we rely on it for that transformation. The way we do so is to realize that it is only when we are weak (that is, when we recognize our dependence on God for this transformation) that we are strong (that is, transformed by God's grace): 'For the sake of Christ, then, I am content with weaknesses, insults, hardships, persecutions, and calamities; for

---

11   Marmion, Columba, "Conference, Maredret, July 21st, 1916," quoted in Philipon, M. M., *The Spiritual Doctrine of Dom Marmion*, trans. Matthew Dillon (London: Sands & Co., 1956), p. 118.
12   Marmion, "Conference, Maredret, December 1922," quoted in Philipon, p. 120.
13   Marmion, Columba, *Christ, The Ideal of the Priest*, trans. Matthew Dillon (San Francisco: Ignatius, 2005), pp. 363–64.

when I am weak, then I am strong' (2 Cor. 12:10). The problem is that we turn to God more in hardships than in daily life, too often saying to God, 'I've got this.' Sadly, this addiction to self continues until each of us passes through the dark night of the spirit (i.e., the harder of the two dark nights).

It is only after passing through the second dark night, by way of deep passive purifications of the spirit, that God liberates us from our addiction to ourselves. Let us consider Marmion on this point:

> In your letter there is a phrase which pleases me very much, because I see in it the source of great glory for Our Lord. You say, 'There is nothing, absolutely nothing in me upon which I can take a little security. Therefore I do not cease to cast myself with confidence into the heart of my Master.' That, my daughter, is the true way, for all that God does for us is the result of His mercy which is touched by the avowal of this misery; and a soul that sees her misery and presents it continually to the gaze of Divine Mercy, gives great glory to God by leaving Him the opportunity of communicating His goodness to her. Continue to follow this attraction, and let yourself be led, in the midst of the darkness of trials, to the nuptials of the Lamb to which He destines you.[14]

Yes, we must be emptied until we reach our misery, our sheer nothingness, for it is only then that we rely entirely, with the deepest confidence, upon God's mercy and transformative power, rather than our own. We may say that we are not called to that depth of self-emptying, but the Church's definition of the Universal Call to Holiness reveals that to be a lie. We may indeed need a lot of healing and maturing to reach that point, to desire this transformation, and to make it through it, but that simply brings us back to Ghandi's insight.

You may say that you cannot make it. Of course you can't, on your own power. Yet Marmion is going to call you out on that spiritual immaturity. So, note as you read this extended

---

14 Marmion, *Union with God*, p. 102.

quote the ways in which he, in Thérèsian fashion, combines absolute confidence in God with a complete knowledge of our insufficiency:

> From this teaching are born the feelings that ought to animate us in seeking to be holy: a deep humility because of our feebleness, and an absolute confidence in Christ Jesus. Our super-natural life wings backwards and forwards between two poles: on the one hand, we should have an inner conviction of our powerlessness to attain perfection without the help of God; on the other hand, we should be filled with an unshakeable hope of finding everything in the grace of Christ Jesus.
>
> Because it is super-natural, because God—sovereignly Master of His designs and of His gifts—has placed it above what the whole of our created nature requires, above the rights of that created nature, the holiness to which we are called is inaccessible without divine grace. Our Lord said to us: 'without me you can do nothing' (Jn 15:5). St Augustine remarks that Christ Jesus did not say, 'without me you cannot do great things'; He said: 'without me you can do nothing that will lead you to life eternal.' St Paul has explained in detail this teaching of our Divine Master. Paul has assurance through Christ, but he adds: 'not that we are sufficient of ourselves to think anything, as from ourselves, but our sufficiency is from God' (2 Cor. 3:5). 'Our sufficiency is from God': it is He who gives us the power of willing and brings all things to that super-natural end: 'It is God who of his good pleasure works in you both the will and the performance' (Phil. 2:13). And so, we cannot, for our holiness, do anything without divine grace.
>
> Should we, therefore, be disheartened? Quite the contrary! The inner conviction of our powerlessness should neither drive us to discouragement nor serve as an excuse for sitting back and not making an effort ourselves. Though we can do nothing without Christ, with Him we can do everything: 'I can do all things in Him who strengthens me' (Phil. 4:13). I can do all things (it is Paul again who tells us), not by myself

but 'in Him who strengthens me.' Whatever be our trials, our difficulties, our weaknesses, we can, through Christ, reach the highest sanctity.

Why is it? Because in Him are amassed 'all the treasures of wisdom and knowledge' (Col. 2:3) because 'in Him dwells the fullness of the Godhead bodily' (Col. 2:9); and because being our head, He has the power to make us sharers in all this. It is 'of His fullness'—fullness of life and holiness—'that we draw' (Jn 1:16), so much so that we 'lack no grace' (1 Cor. 1:7)!

What great assurance is engendered in us by faith in these truths! Christ Jesus is ours, and in Him we find everything: 'How can He (the Father) fail to grant us [...] all things with Him' (Rom. 8:32). What, then, can prevent us from becoming saints? IF, on the day of the Last Judgment God asks us: 'Why have you not reached the height of your vocation? Why have you not attained the holiness to which I was calling you?' we shall not be able to reply: 'Lord, my weakness was too great, the difficulties were insurmountable, the trials beyond my strength.' God would reply to us: 'On your own, it is but too true that you could do nothing. But I have given you my Son; in Him you lacked nothing of what was necessary for you. His grace is all-powerful, and through Him you could have united yourself to the very source of life.'[15]

So, we are called, perhaps after healing and maturing, to holiness, and we have what it takes, by God's design and help, to obtain it. These two saints clearly reveal that nothing lacks to us if we follow St Thérèse's way of childlike confidence in God's design and help.

Now, the following advice is merely an aid to accepting those passive purifications and their lessons most efficiently. The fundamental spiritual problem of self-reliance blocks many Christians, even mature ones who pray constantly for help, from becoming new monuments of God's mercy. Here is some spiritual direction from Marmion on the topic:

---

[15] Marmion, Columba, *Christ in His Mysteries*, trans. Alan Bancroft, British edition (Leominster: Gracewing, 2009), pp. 455–56.

> One must not, before beginning any action, give in to nature, but first unite one's self to Our Lord. Before taking up an occupation, kneel down at Christ's feet and say to Him: 'My Jesus, I leave there my natural activity, I want to do this thing solely for You, and I unite myself to You.' And if during the occupation, you feel that you are letting yourself be carried away by nature, go back to Our Lord. It must not be A—[name of the religious] who is acting, for that would be good for nothing; but it must be Jesus who acts through A—, then it will be excellent.
>
> There are some people who have a great deal of activity; they pray, mortify themselves, and give themselves up to good works; they advance but rather limpingly, because their activity is partly human. There are others whom God has taken in hand, and they advance very quickly, because He Himself acts in them. But before reaching this second state, there is much to suffer, for God must first make the soul feel that she is nothing and can do nothing; she must needs be able to say in all sincerity, 'I am brought to nothing, and I knew not. I am become as a beast before Thee' (Psalm 72:22–23).[16]

The technical term for the error here described is semi-Pelagianism, and it is rampant in our time. St Thérèse's little way and Marmion's integration of that little way into a greater systematic whole are the answers to it.

Permit me to draw one more paragraph from my book in the hope that I can bring home the damaging effects of going down the path of semi-Pelagianism:

> In a related way, those struggling with self-reliance can also struggle with attributing God's graces to themselves. In attributing God's action to ourselves, we produce a distorted sense of self-worth; this distorted sense of self-worth produces a sense of entitlement; from this sense of entitlement, we seek to possess some desired object. When we fail to obtain our desired object, we often judge ourselves harshly

---

16 *Union with God*, p. 35.

by the world's standards and lose the peace that leads to union with God. In a subtle reorienting of the Christian path, we develop, perhaps unconsciously, new motives for our external conformity to Christ's actions. In this reorienting process, we thwart the action of grace in our lives even more, and after long periods of forestalling grace, we become enmeshed in an ever-deeper self-reliance that eventually leads to bitter, discouraging feelings.[17]

Such is the path of trying to acquire spiritual importance.

The paths of semi-Pelagianism and the little way / becoming a monument of God's mercy do indeed diverge significantly. On the surface level, at least initially, the practitioners of each can look very similar, since the divergences are interior. Yet, the latter leads to greater peace and transformation. The former may seem to lead to saintliness—or so goes the hope of the self-reliant one—but it is the 'generalized pride', common to so many spiritual persons, against which Blessed Marie Eugene recommended St Thérèse's little way. Those sisters in the garden outside of St Thérèse's deathbed were so hoping for indicators of success that they missed the spiritual revolution in their midst.

The spiritual revolution begins by deepening the dual disposition of a humble confidence in God's mercy. It is a dual disposition because humility and confidence mutually reinforce each other and restrain the possible negative effects of each other. It is a dual disposition in which one must deepen, for these must become settled aspects of one's life, not passing fads. There is much to say here—an entire book's worth of material on the topic.

On the topic of humility, Marmion was expert at showing the connections between John 15:5, 'I am the vine, you are the branches, without me you can do nothing', and the ways in which a person can develop in the spiritual life. As you may have noticed above, St Thérèse, like many saints, 'recognizes

---

17 Koenemann, *Grace of Nothingness*, pp. 90–91.

her nothingness.' So too does Marmion, but he stands out in helping us to understand the biblical and dogmatic underpinnings associated with this mystical shorthand manner of speaking. He also applies lessons from this disposition to the practical realm, such as in one's relationships to God, oneself, and others. Furthermore, in the area of asceticism, Blessed Columba and St Thérèse align in prioritizing the value of passive purifications, brought about by others or circumstances, over many of the active renunciations we choose for ourselves, at times fraught with the trap of semi-Pelagianism.

On the side of confidence in God, Marmion situates it within 1 Thessalonians 4:3, 'This is the will of God, your sanctification.' If we surrender ourselves to God's plan, say to become a monument of his mercy, then He will sanctify us. He is in fact already working on doing so, and we just need to remove our (interior) obstacles to His work. Do you know what really prompts our presumption? It is our fear of coming incomplete before God, our fear of allowing the Sacred Heart of Jesus to supply for us, our fear of just allowing God, in His mercy, to love us. It may sound trite, but this spirituality accepts God's love for each of His sons and daughters as what it is. If we, with a humble confidence, come to God 'with empty hands', rather than with gifts we want to give Him, then He will fill those empty hands, to the point of turning each of us into great monuments of His mercy.

4

CHRIST'S MYSTERIES AND IMITATING WHAT THEY CONTAIN

FR PETER MARTYR YUNGWIRTH, OP

INTRODUCTION

THE ROSARY CONCLUDES WITH A prayer about the mysteries of Christ's life and how 'we may come to "imitate what they contain and obtain what they promise."'[1] St John Paul II stated that 'the contemplation of the mysteries could better express their full spiritual fruitfulness if an effort were made to conclude each mystery with *a prayer for the fruits specific to that particular mystery*.'[2] This idea seems to have been a part of popular piety for some time. Yet, how does this happen, and how does this fruitfulness come about in the life of someone who prays the Rosary? More foundational questions also arise: do the mysteries of Christ's life still have power even now, how do they have that power, and are there particular fruits associated with particular mysteries?

Our purpose here is to analyse these questions, specifically according to the thought of Blessed Columba Marmion

---

1 Pope St John Paul II, *Apostolic Letter Rosarium Virginis Mariae* (Boston: Pauline Books and Media, 2002), § 35.
2 Pope St John Paul II, *Rosarium Virginis Mariae*, 35. Some recent Popes have developed the idea of meditation on the Rosary and the fruits of the mysteries. See: Pope Leo XIII, *Octobri mense*, 7, in Claudia Carlen, ed., *The Papal Encyclicals* (Wilmington, NC: McGrath Publishing Company, 1981), 2:273; Leo XIII, *Magnae Dei Matris*, 14–19, in Carlen, *The Papal Encyclicals*, 2:291–292; Pope Pius XI, *Ingravescentibus malis*, 11, 22, in Carlen, *The Papal Encyclicals*, 3:564, 565; Ven. Pope Pius XII, *Ingruentium malorum*, 9, in Carlen, *The Papal Encyclicals*, 4:214; Pope St John Paul II, *Rosarium Virginis Mariae*, 2, 11, 13–15.

Christ's Mysteries and Imitating What They Contain

who has a richly developed understanding of Christology, grace, and the life of Christian prayer. To accomplish this, we will examine Marmion's understanding of the 'mysteries of Christ's life' by drawing out his thoughts on what the mysteries are in general, how they have perpetual power, and how they are our mysteries. We will then look at Marmion's teachings on the mystical body of Christ and adoptive sonship. Following this, we will examine three types of causality: efficient, meritorious, and exemplary. Finally, we will see how our participation in the mysteries through various forms of prayer brings about the communication of particular graces of Christ's mysteries.

Before delving into Marmion's thought, it is worth mentioning some of Marmion's sources. In many ways, Marmion closely followed St Thomas Aquinas.[3] He also was influenced in part by the French School.[4] On top of this, Marmion added elements of Benedictine spirituality, particularly the Rule of Benedict and an emphasis on the liturgy. Marmion's more liturgically based spirituality is surely a development of Aquinas and the French School, and it comes from his own

---

3 The influence of Aquinas came from his years of study for the priesthood while he was in Rome studying under Francesco Satolli [see: Marie Michel Philipon, *The Spiritual Doctrine of Dom Marmion*, trans. Matthew Dillon (Westminster, MD: The Newman Press, 1956), pp. 16, 29; Raymond Thibaut, *Abbot Columba Marmion: a Master of the Spiritual Life, 1858–1923*, trans. Mother Mary St Thomas (St Louis: B. Herder Book Co., 1949), pp. 22–23].

4 A follower of the French School, Msgr Gay was a major influence on Marmion's spiritual ideas (Philipon, *Spiritual Doctrine*, pp. 11, 36–37). It seems that there is debate over what sort of influence Bérulle had on Marmion. While it is clear that Marmion shares much similarity in thought with the founder of the French School, some maintain that Bérulle had no real direct influence on Marmion [Marie Michel Philipon, "The Doctor of the Divine Adoption," in *More About Dom Marmion: A Study of His Writings Together with a Chapter from an Unpublished Work and a Biographical Sketch*, trans. The Earl of Wicklow (St Louis: B. Herder Book Co., 1949), pp. 111–128, here p. 126, note 31; Ephrem Boularand, "The Christocentric Quality in Dom Marmion," in *More About Dom Marmion: A Study of His Writings Together with a Chapter from an Unpublished Work and a Biographical Sketch*, trans. The Earl of Wicklow (St Louis: B. Herder Book Co., 1949), pp. 89–110, here p. 109].

experience of monastic living. All in all, considering these will lead to a more fruitful reflection on Marmion's own thought.

A. WHAT ARE THE 'MYSTERIES OF CHRIST'S LIFE' FOR MARMION?

1. 'Mystery' broadly understood

Marmion understands the mysteries to be the states of Christ's humanity.[5] He defines Christ's mysteries as the 'human and visible signs of a divine and hidden reality,'[6] and this is true of '*all* the events and circumstances of His life.'[7] Thus, Marmion's understanding of 'states' is not just limited to the historical sense of these events, but it also includes the hidden realities underlying those historical circumstances.[8]

Marmion builds on this understanding of the 'divine and hidden reality' by including the notion that the mysteries are sources of grace. He writes:

> The mysteries of Jesus are states of His sacred humanity; all the graces that He had, He received from His divinity in order that they might be communicated to His humanity, and through His humanity, to each of the members of His mystical body 'according to the measure of Christ's bestowal.'[9]

In other words, for Marmion, Christ lived out His mysteries precisely to communicate graces to us through them.[10] True, Marmion understands Christ's mysteries as models to be imitated and contemplated, but the mysteries are models *so that* they might be sources of grace.[11]

---

5 Marmion, Columba, *Christ in His Mysteries*, trans. Alan Bancroft (Bethesda, MD: Zaccheus Press, 2008), p. 29 (hereafter: *CHM*, p. 29). See: David W. Fagerberg, "Theosis in a Roman Key?: The Conferences of Columba Marmion," *Antiphon* 7, no. 1 (2002): pp. 30–39, here p. 34.
6 *CHM*, p. 32.
7 Translator's note in *ibid.*, p. 12 note 48.
8 *Ibid.*, p. 32.
9 *Ibid.*, p. 29. The inset quote is from Eph. 4:7.
10 See: John Saward, *Cradle of Redeeming Love: The Theology of the Christmas Mystery* (San Francisco: Ignatius Press, 2002), p. 66.
11 *CHM*, p. 29.

2. *The perpetual power of the mysteries*

As sources of grace, Christ's mysteries are able to communicate grace even now. Marmion connects the perpetual power of the mysteries to Christ's place in heaven now, explaining that while 'it is true that in their historical, material duration the mysteries of Christ's life on earth are now past,' nevertheless, '*their power remains*, and the grace that allows us to share in them operates always.'[12] In a sense, these mysteries '*are still living ones*' which means that they have the power to affect us even now.[13]

Marmion elucidates this in two ways. The first reason concerns Christ's work in heaven. Marmion writes: 'These mysteries have a power that is always active and efficacious. From heaven, where He is seated at the right hand of God His Father, Christ continues to communicate to souls the fruit of His states, so as to effect in those souls their divine resemblance to Him.'[14] Christ is always living to make intercession for us, and thus He continues to aid us by pouring out the graces of His mysteries upon us.[15]

Secondly, Christ is the head of the mystical body. Marmion points out that Christ's mysteries still have power and virtue and can be fruitful even now because He remains the head of the mystical body.[16] More will be said on this relationship below, but for now it suffices to point out that because Christ is still alive and because we are still connected to Him as members of His body, His mysteries can still be effective for us.

3. *Christ's mysteries are for us*

The final noteworthy aspect of Marmion's understanding of Christ's mysteries is his constant refrain about how Christ's

---

12 *Ibid.*, p. 20. See: *Ibid.*, p. 23.
13 Marmion, Columba, *Christ, The Life of the Soul*, trans. Alan Bancroft (Bethesda, MD: Zaccheus Press, 2005), p. 406 (hereafter: *CLS*, p. 406).
14 *CHM*, p. 23.
15 *Ibid.*, p. 21; Heb. 7:25.
16 Marmion, Columba, *Christ, The Ideal of the Monk*, trans. a Nun of Tyburn Convent (Ireland: The Cenacle Press, 2022), p. 360 (hereafter: *CIM*, p. 360).

mysteries are *for us*: 'the mysteries of Jesus have this characteristic: *that they are ours as much as they are His.*'[17] Marmion gives three reasons for this. First, 'Christ lived them for us.'[18] Since He became incarnate for our redemption, everything He did was for us.[19] Secondly, Christ's mysteries are ours because in each of them, He is an example for us.[20] In fact, Marmion goes so far as to say that Christ 'came on earth to be our model. It was not only to announce salvation to us, and to effect (in principle) our redemption, that the Word was made flesh; He came in order to be the ideal of our souls as well.'[21] Finally, Marmion points out that we are one with Christ in His mysteries. He writes, 'Not only has Jesus lived them for us, not only are they models for us but, as well as this, *in His mysteries Christ is but one with us.*'[22] This idea is founded on Christ's headship.[23] Furthermore, Marmion notes, 'What makes the mysteries of Jesus ours is, above all, that the eternal Father saw us when seeing his Son in each one of the mysteries Jesus lived, and that Christ accomplished them as head of the Church.'[24] In other words, because of Christ's place as the head of the Church, everything that He does is for the holiness and sanctification of the whole body of Christ and thus meant for our own sanctification and holiness.

B. INCORPORATION INTO THE MYSTICAL BODY OF CHRIST

Marmion has a deep awareness of the importance of the mystical body of Christ. Because of Christ's headship and our membership in the body of Christ, He is able to communicate

---

17 *CHM*, 12. See: Boularand, "Christocentric Quality," p. 102; Retreat at Maredsous, September 1909, quoted in Philipon, "The Doctor of Divine Adoption," p. 120.
18 *Ibid.*, p. 13.
19 *CLS*, pp. 64–65.
20 *CHM*, p. 14.
21 *Ibid.*, pp. 14–15.
22 *Ibid.*, pp. 16–17.
23 *Ibid.*, p. 17.
24 *Ibid.*, p. 18.

His graces to us.[25] At the same time, Marmion has a strong emphasis on our adoptive sonship. Just as Christ is the natural Son of God so too are we God's sons by adoption through grace. In both ways, Marmion lays the foundation for how Christ causes grace in us even now.

1. The mystical body of Christ

Like Aquinas, Marmion holds that Christ is the head of all humanity.[26] Because of this, Christ is the only one who can infuse grace into our hearts.[27] Moreover, this relationship and the communication of grace establish a connection between the head and the body that is different from a moral union which exists between the head of a state and his subjects. Rather, the union in the mystical body goes much deeper. Speaking of both, Marmion points out:

> [In human society] the influence of the authority is exterior and only goes to co-ordinating and maintaining the diverse energies of the members towards a common end. The action of Christ in the Church is more intimate, more penetrating; it attains to the very life of souls, and this is one of the reasons why "the *mystical body*" is not a fiction of our reasoning, but a reality of the profoundest kind.[28]

With this communication of grace, Christ allows us to share in His very own graces, the graces of the Head.[29]

To elaborate this, Marmion builds on the foundational idea of Christ's fullness of grace.[30] Marmion notes that Christ is given the fullness of grace for a two-fold reason: for Himself

---

25 *CIM*, p. 360.
26 *CLS*, p. 69; St Thomas Aquinas, *Summa Theologica*, trans. Fathers of the English Dominican Province (Notre Dame, IN: Christian Classics, 1981), III, 48, 1, corp. (hereafter: *ST* III, 48, 1, corp.).
27 *Ibid.*, p. 89; *ST* III, 8, aa. 5, 6.
28 *Ibid.*, p. 123, note 5.
29 *Ibid.*, p. 124; Marmion, Columba, *Christ, The Ideal of the Priest*, trans. Matthew Dillon (San Francisco: Ignatius Press, 2005), p. 155 (hereafter: *CIP*, p. 155).
30 *Ibid.*, p. 26; *CIM*, p. 36.

and for the members of the Church.³¹ In explaining this, Marmion speaks of the importance of reading John 1:14a and John 1:16 together.³² This reception of grace is for the benefit of the mystical body because 'the good of one member profits the entire body, and the glory of the body is reflected upon each of its members.'³³ This helps bring about the holiness of the whole body of Christ.³⁴ In other words, our reception of Christ's graces profits not only us but also the rest of the mystical body by making the whole more closely resemble the Head.

2. Adoptive sonship

This leads us to the topic of adoptive sonship, which can be said to be the centre of Marmion's teaching.³⁵ He states, 'We are here at the central point of the Divine plan: *the Divine adoption*... It was to confer adoption on us, says St Paul, that God sent his Son: "God sent his Son, born of a woman... to enable us to be adopted as sons."'³⁶ By this adoption, we participate in the divine nature and become by grace what the Son of God is by nature.³⁷ Because of the Incarnation and of the union of the divine and human natures in Christ, His own natural Sonship is 'meant to extend all the way to us through grace, in such a way that Christ, in the Divine thought, is but the firstborn of a multitude of brethren who

---

31 *Ibid.*, p. 123; *CHM*, pp. 29, 127; *ST* III, 48, 1, corp.
32 *CHM*, p. 19. John 1:14a: "The Word became flesh and dwelt among us, full of grace and truth." John 1:16: "From his fullness have we all received, grace upon grace." See: David L. Toups, *The Sacerdotal Character as the Foundation of the Priestly Life: Including the Contribution of Blessed Columba Marmion* (Rome: Pontificia Studiorum Universitas a S. Thoma Aq. in Urbe, 2004), pp. 207–208, note 77; Saward, *Cradle of Redeeming Love*, p. 61.
33 *CLS*, p. 127. See: *ST* I-II, 21, 3, corp.; St Thomas Aquinas, *The Apostles' Creed*, in *The Catechetical Instructions of St Thomas Aquinas*, trans. Joseph B. Collins, 3–66 (New York: J. F. Wagner, 1939), c. 13 (hereafter: *Exp. Sym. Ap.*, c. 13).
34 *Ibid.*, p. 127.
35 Justin Cardinal Rigali, "Blessed Columba Marmion: Doctor of Divine Adoption," *Josephinum Journal of Theology* 13, no. 2 (Summer–Fall 2006): pp. 132–142, here p. 134. See: Philipon, *Spiritual Doctrine*, p. 15.
36 *CLS*, p. 27. The inset quote is from Gal. 4:4–5. See: *CLS*, p. 64; *ST* III, 1, 2, corp.
37 Fagerberg, "Theosis in a Roman Key," p. 35.

are, through grace as He is by nature, sons of God.'[38] In this way, there is a resemblance between the natural Son of God and the adopted sons. Marmion writes, "'The adoption of sons of God," says St Thomas, "comes about through a certain conformity in likeness to Him who is His Son by nature.'"[39] This is the greatest gift that God can give to man.[40]

Marmion points out, however, that the adoption analogy is not perfect.[41] On the one hand, human adoption welcomes a stranger into the family, who shares the family name and inherits the family's possessions. The condition for human adoption is simply that the adopted person shares the same race, i.e. that he is also human. With divine adoption, however, God takes us in our current nature, which is not the same as His, and elevates us through grace so that we can participate in and partake of His divine nature.[42] In other words, through adoption, what Christ has by nature we are given by grace, and we really do become the sons and daughters of God. Thus, this means that we really do gain a real share in His inheritance.[43]

C. HOW ARE CHRIST'S MYSTERIES CAUSATIVE FOR US?

If Christ's mysteries are for us and still have power to effect change in us because we are members of His mystical body, how does this come about? To answer this, we will investigate Marmion's understanding of the three types of causality: efficient, meritorious, and exemplary causality.[44]

---

38 *CLS*, p. 27.
39 *Ibid.*, p. 497. See: *Ibid.*, p. 21; *CHM*, p. 56; *ST* III, 45, 4, corp.; III, 62, 1, corp.
40 Marmion, Columba, *Sponsa Verbi: The Virgin Consecrated to Christ*, trans. Francis Izard (St Louis: B. Herder Book Co., 1925), p. 12 (hereafter: *SV*, p. 12).
41 *CLS*, p. 20.
42 *Ibid.*, p. 21.
43 *Ibid.*, p. 49.
44 Marmion explicitly follows Aquinas regarding these three types of causality (*CLS*, pp. 40–41), even directly citing *ST* III, 24, aa. 3, 4; III, 48, 6; III, 50, 6; III, 56, 1, ad 3 and 4. See: Philipon, "Doctor of Divine Adoption," p. 122.

1. Efficient causality
   a. Christ's humanity as a hypostatically conjoined instrument.
Marmion describes the two-fold importance of the hypostatic union and the instrumentality of Christ's humanity. Concerning the hypostatic union, Marmion points out that it 'is at the root of all the other communications made to the sacred humanity for the divine accomplishment of its mission of redemption.'[45] Through the union of the divine and human natures in the one divine person of Christ, all of Jesus's human actions are infused with a divine efficacy.[46] He is a Divine person, and thus in Him, 'it is *a Divine Person who* acts and operates *through* the human nature.'[47] Marmion states:

> In Christ, it is always God *who* acts, but sometimes *through* His divine nature, sometimes *through* His human nature. It is therefore true to say that it is *God* who toiled, who wept, who suffered, who died—even though all these actions were carried out through the human nature. However minimal they be in their physical reality, all the actions of Christ Jesus have a divine value.[48]

Herein, we begin to see the importance of the instrumentality of Christ's humanity, an instrument which the divinity uses 'in order to spread around it every grace and every life.'[49] Marmion writes:

> In all [Christ's actions], we see the sacred humanity serve as an organ of the divinity. It is the Divine Person of the Word who cures and raises from the dead: but to work these marvels, the Word makes use of the human nature that is united to Him, it is through His human nature that Christ speaks the words and, with His hands, touches the sick. Thus, life derived from the divinity and reached bodies and souls through the humanity.[50]

---

45 *CIP*, p. 243.
46 *SV*, p. 27; *CIP*, p. 31. See: Saward, *Cradle of Redeeming Love*, p. 76.
47 *CLS*, p. 66.
48 *CHM*, p. 72–73.
49 *CLS*, p. 86. See: *CIP*, p. 243.
50 *Ibid.*, p. 86.

Here, the humanity is "'an instrument united to the Word:" *ut instrumentum conjunctum.*'[51] It is an instrument which only produces effects that flow from the principal cause through it since no instrument can act of its own power.[52]

Because of this, all Christ's mysteries work instrumentally,[53] and they possess an efficacious power to sanctify.[54] Marmion writes, 'It is therefore through the contact of His sacred humanity that Christ did His miracles and gave grace; the humanity served as instrument united to the Word. And this wonderful and moving law can be verified in all the mysteries of Jesus.'[55]

b. Sacramental instrumentality. Now, the normal instrumental means to communicate Christ's graces are the sacraments. Marmion gives particular importance to the word 'communicate' because the mysteries do not only symbolize grace but also 'contain and confer it.'[56] Just like Christ's humanity, the sacraments confer this grace as channels through which graces flow.[57] Moreover, the sacraments also cause grace: 'The sacraments, signs charged with transmitting this grace to the soul, act only in the capacity of instruments. They are a cause of grace, a real and efficient cause, but an instrumental one only.'[58]

---

51   *Ibid.,* p. 86, note 6.
52   *CIP,* p. 199.
53   *CLS,* p. 88, note 3. Here, Marmion cites *ST* III, 62, 5, ad 1. See: *ST* III, 48, 6, corp.; III 49, 1, corp.; St Thomas Aquinas, *Truth,* vol. 3, trans. Robert W. Schmidt (Chicago: Henry Regnery Company, 1954), q. 27, a. 4, corp. (hereafter: *De Veritate,* q. 27, a. 4, corp.).
54   *CIP,* p. 52.
55   *CHM,* p. 81. Marmion uses various analogies for this: Christ's humanity is an intermediary between God and us (*CHM,* p. 82); a bridge thrown over the gap between the Creator and His creatures so that God, the principal cause, can directly pass His graces to us [*CIM,* p. 29; *CIP,* p. 49; Blessed Marmion, Columba, *The English Letters of Abbot Marmion, 1858–1923* (Baltimore: Helicon Press, 1962), p. 214; see also *CHM,* p. 90 in which Marmion draws this idea from St Catherine of Siena]; and a channel through which His graces pass (*SV,* p. 29).
56   *CLS,* p. 91.
57   *CHM,* p. 298.
58   *CLS,* p. 93. Here, Marmion quotes from *ST* III, 62, 1, ad 2; III, 67, 4, ad 1. See: *CLS,* 94, note 1; *ST* III, 64, 4, corp.

BELOVED OF GOD AND MEN

This is true of each sacrament but in different ways.[59] For instance, in baptism, spiritual birth is communicated to men, a birth by which they become sons of God.[60] At a retreat at the College of the Holy Spirit in Louvain, Marmion said:

> Through Baptism, we enter into a very intimate relation with Jesus Christ. Having "put on Christ," we live by his faith, like the branches of the vine, we become by grace that which he is by nature, the children of God. Our resemblance to him is still, however, only initial and rudimentary. The work of our lives is to become more and more like him, whose image we received in baptism.[61]

The other sacraments build on this by moulding us more and more into the likeness of Christ.[62]

This idea is true particularly regarding the Eucharist, which Marmion understands as the most profound means by which Christ comes into contact with us.[63] In a conference at Maredret, Marmion stated:

> The special effect of the Blessed Eucharist consists therefore in transforming us more and more completely into Christ. The soul which receives this sacrament with the proper dispositions is united to Christ and to His divinity to the point of losing its separate existence in Him. Through faith, the thoughts of Christ become its thoughts, through love, the desires of Christ become its desires, and by an act of perfect abandonment its will is entirely subordinated to the will of Christ. It effects so complete a transformation that the soul can say: "I live now, not I, but Christ liveth in me." If I might coin the word, I would say that the effect of the Eucharist is to "Christify" us.[64]

---

59 *CLS*, p. 96.
60 *Ibid.*, p. 197. Marmion speaks of baptism as the "sacrament of our Divine adoption" (*Ibid.*, p. 196). See: *CHM*, p. 210.
61 Quoted in Philipon, "Doctor of Divine Adoption," pp. 123–124.
62 Philipon, "Doctor of Divine Adoption," p. 124.
63 *CHM*, p. 404; *CIP*, pp. 250–251.
64 Quoted in Philipon, *Spiritual Doctrine*, p. 109.

In other words, the Eucharist is a means by which the effects of the principal agent pass to the object acted upon. Through it, Christ 'establishes between [the soul's] thoughts, actions, desires, and wishes and His own, such a union that if His action is not impeded He transforms her into Himself, just as the wood acquires the qualities of the fire that consumes it.'[65] Here with the sacraments of baptism and the Eucharist, Marmion appropriates Aquinas's idea that instruments function as intermediaries which effect a likeness between the principal agent and the object acted upon.[66] In other words, as instruments, the sacraments pass on the grace of God to man by making him share in the sonship of Christ. This will become clearer when we examine Marmion's understanding of exemplary causality.

2. Meritorious causality

A second type of causality that Marmion describes is meritorious causality. Marmion points out that 'Christ, through the Incarnation, has associated the whole of humanity with His Divine mysteries and has merited, for all His brethren, the grace He has willed to attach to them.'[67] There are two important things to point out here. First, this is connected to Christ's efficient causality. As Marmion states, 'Glorified by virtue of the merits which [Christ] had acquired by His death, He became the efficient cause producing constantly in the mystical body all the grace of justification and sanctity: "I am the true vine . . . you are the branches."'[68] Secondly, this meritorious causality is connected to Christ's sacrifice on the Cross. Marmion writes, 'Christ is, for us, the source of grace, because, having paid all our debts to Divine Justice by His life, His Passion and His death, He has merited to distribute every

---

65 *SV*, p. 75. See: *CLS*, p. 365; *CHM*, pp. 404–405, 454. Aquinas uses the wood and fire example to speak of the Eucharist in *ST* III, 79, 1, ad 2.
66 See: St Thomas Aquinas, *Summa Contra Gentiles: Book 2: Creation*, trans. James F. Anderson (Notre Dame, IN: University of Notre Dame Press, 1992), II, 21, 6; Torrell, "The Image of the First-Born Son," p. 130; Gilles Emery, "A Note on St Thomas and the Eastern Fathers," pp. 200, 201.
67 *CLS*, p. 407.
68 *CIP*, p. 163. The inset quote is from John 15:1, 5.

grace to us: *Causa satisfactoria et meritoria.*[69] In other words, because Christ satisfied for the sins of men on the Cross, He merits to distribute the graces of His mysteries. Marmion even points out that all of Christ's actions are meritorious because 'each one of the actions of Christ, being the action of a Divine Person, constitutes a satisfaction of infinite worth.'[70]

Moreover, Christ not only merits the right to communicate graces to us, but He also merited the right to communicate particular graces associated with particular mysteries. Marmion notes that through the merit of all of Jesus's actions, 'He merited to produce in us the necessary graces to imitate Him and to love Him.'[71] This is particularly true regarding the Passion: 'At every stage of the Passion He merited the reproduction in us by His grace of those virtues which we contemplate in Him.'[72] In other words, Christ's saving actions are intimately connected with the particular graces that He merited in each and every one of His mysteries.

This communication of grace is also based on Marmion's understanding of the mystical body of Christ. Since Christ is the Head of the body, we are fellow heirs with him.[73] Marmion states, 'The grace of divine adoption, which makes us brethren of Jesus and living members of His mystical body, gives us the right to take to ourselves His treasures so as to give them value as our own before Himself and His Father.'[74] Because of our adoptive sonship and our incorporation into the mystical body of Christ, we can claim Christ's merits as our own and share in the inheritance of the natural Son of God.

3. Exemplar causality

Finally, there is exemplar causality, a type of causality that Marmion very strongly emphasizes. He frequently describes

---

69 *CLS*, p. 61. See: Rigali, "Blessed Columba Marmion," p. 136.
70 *Ibid.*, p. 67. See: *CLS*, p. 68; *CHM*, p. 20.
71 *CIP*, p. 326.
72 *Ibid.*, p. 127.
73 *CLS*, p. 70.
74 *CHM*, p. 172.

Christ's Mysteries and Imitating What They Contain

Christ as *'the model of all Christian living*, the model of the human activity and virtues of all those who are destined to be His brothers and sisters through divine adoption.'⁷⁵ Furthermore, 'to be a model and to be imitable are the two characteristics that are to be met with in an exemplary cause.'⁷⁶ Now, Christ is our model in two ways: 'in His *state* of Son of God and in His human *activity*.'⁷⁷ It will be helpful to draw out both of these here.

Regarding Christ's state of being the Son of God, Marmion notes that this is what is fundamental in Him, and thus it is in this regard that we should resemble Him primarily. We imitate Him, in His natural sonship, through adoptive sonship by grace.⁷⁸ Since an exemplary cause is supposed to be imitable, we ought to imitate Christ not only in His human activity, but also with regard to His being.⁷⁹ For, '*Christianus, alter Christus*, "the Christian is another Christ."'⁸⁰ What this reveals is that the Christian's participation in Christ's sonship happens through divine adoption and is an imitation of the model of sonship of which He is the exemplar.

Regarding Christ's human actions, Marmion notes that every act of Christ, even the least one, is a model for us.⁸¹ This is also true of all His virtues.⁸² In fact, each mystery shows forth Christ's virtues:

> Each of His mysteries is a revelation of His virtues. The humility of the manger, the toil and self-effacement of the hidden life, the zeal of the public life, the abasement of His immolation on the cross, the glory of His triumph—these are virtues we ought to imitate,

---

75 Rigali, "Blessed Columba Marmion," p. 136.
76 *CLS*, p. 43, note 1.
77 Ibid., p. 45.
78 Ibid., p. 49.
79 *CHM*, p. 52; Fagerberg, "Theosis in a Roman Key," p. 35.
80 *CLS*, p. 59. See: Fagerberg, "Theosis in a Roman Key," p. 31.
81 Ibid., p. 43, 100; *CIM*, p. 28.
82 *CIP*, p. 43.

feelings we ought to share, or states in which we ought to participate.[83]

Thus, we ought to imitate Christ in all His actions and even the interior feelings that He experienced throughout His life. Following the footsteps of Christ, listening to His own words, and contemplating His various actions helps us to imitate Him in our own actions.[84] Marmion states, 'Jesus, by His mysteries, has (so to say) marked out all the stages that we ought to follow—follow after Him and with Him—in our super-natural life.'[85] It is by imitating Christ in this way that we appropriate the virtues and graces that He lived out in those mysteries.[86]

D. PARTICIPATION IN THE MYSTERIES

All this being said, how do we participate in these mysteries and partake of their fruits? As Marmion puts it, 'How, above all, shall we put ourselves into life-giving contact with [Christ's mysteries], so as to draw from them those fruits that, little by little, will transform our souls and effect in us that union with Christ which is an indispensable condition for being numbered among His disciples?'[87] In other words, even though Christ has already merited all our graces, those graces still need to be applied to us: 'One can die of thirst beside a fountain of pure water. One must take the trouble to put oneself in contact with it.'[88] For Marmion, there are two main ways in which this contact comes about: liturgical worship (including reception of the sacraments) and contemplation.[89] He writes:

---

83 *CHM*, p. 15.
84 *CIM*, p. 397.
85 *CHM*, p. 15.
86 *CLS*, p. 100.
87 *CHM*, p. 24.
88 *CIP*, p. 374. See: *Ibid.*, p. 69.
89 Following Aquinas, whom he cites (*ST* III, 62, 5, ad 2; *De Veritate*, q. 27, art. 4, corp.), Marmion is explicit that faith is the foundation for this contact to be possible in the sacraments and contemplation, especially with

> It is said of Jesus that when He was here on earth there went forth from His Person a power that healed the sick: 'power went forth from Him and healed all' [Lk. 6:19]. Christ Jesus is always the same: if we contemplate His mysteries with faith, be it in the Gospels or in the liturgy presented to us by the Church, it produces in us the grace that He merited for us when He lived out those mysteries. In such contemplation we see how Jesus our Exemplar practiced the virtues, we enter into a sharing of the particular feelings that animated His divine heart in each of those sets of circumstances; but above all we draw from Him the special graces He merited for us then.[90]

Examining both of these means of participation in Christ's mysteries will help to draw this out.

1. Liturgy and Sacraments

Marmion's writings are imbued with liturgical texts, and the liturgy is one of the primary ways in which Christ's graces can be applied to us. Through the annual liturgical cycle, the Church re-lives Christ's mysteries.[91] She is, so to say, led by the hand as she follows in Christ's footsteps.[92] Marmion notes:

> Nowhere [more than in the liturgy] can we better learn the actions of Christ Jesus, the words that fell from His lips, the affections of His Divine Heart; it is the Gospel lived over again at each of the stages of the terrestrial life of Christ, the Man-God, Saviour of the world, Head of His mystical body, and

---

regard to contemplation [*CLS*, p. 58; *CHM*, pp. 32–33, 393; Blessed Columba Marmion, *Union with God: Letters of Spiritual Direction by Blessed Columba Marmion*, ed. Raymond Thibaut, trans. Mother Mary St Thomas (Bethesda, MD: Zaccheus Press, 2006), p. 82 (hereafter: *UWG*, p. 82)].
90   *CHM*, p. 29. See: *CLS*, pp. 405, 409; O. Rousseau, "Dom Marmion and the Bible," in *More About Dom Marmion: A Study of His Writings Together with a Chapter from an Unpublished Work and a Biographical Sketch*, trans. The Earl of Wicklow (St Louis: B. Herder Book Co., 1949): pp. 30–45, here p. 40.
91   *CLS*, p. 113–114; *CIM*, p. 397; *SV*, p. 71; *CIP*, p. 269.
92   *CIM*, p. 360.

> bringing with Him to our souls the virtue and grace of all His mysteries.[93]

In other words, through the liturgy, the virtues that Christ lived out on earth and the various graces that were given to those whom He encountered in His earthly life can be communicated to us too. This is because 'when we celebrate [the mysteries of Christ's life] in the sacred liturgy, we receive therefrom, according to the measure of our faith, the same graces as if we had lived at the time of Our Lord and had been present at all of His mysteries.'[94] As Philipon states,

> The virtue of the liturgy consists in perpetuating these mysteries among men and thus applying to them the redemptive merits of Christ. While the Voice of the Church, 'Vox sponsae,' is united in the praise of the Word Incarnate, a grace corresponding to each of these mysteries is infused into the souls of those assisting, in proportion to their fervour and their faith. The liturgy was for him [Marmion] "the most suitable food for the soul."[95]

Thus, in the liturgy, the Church prays in union with the Head of the mystical body, and the contact with Him that occurs through the liturgy brings His graces to her.[96] When we encounter Christ in the liturgy on a particular feast day, we also have a chance to appropriate the graces of that particular feast.

For Marmion, this is particularly the case in the celebration of the sacraments, especially the Eucharist. Regarding the sacrifice of the Mass and Holy Communion, he writes:

> Whichever mystery of Jesus we celebrate, therefore, we cannot, after having contemplated it and meditated on it with the Church—we cannot participate in it more perfectly, nor better dispose ourselves to receive

---

93 *CIM*, p. 397. See: Fagerberg, "Theosis in a Roman Key," p. 34.
94 *CLS*, p. 407. See: *Ibid.*, pp. 99–102.
95 Philipon, *Spiritual Doctrine*, p. 17.
96 Fagerberg, "Theosis in a Roman Key," p. 33.

its fruits, than by being present with faith and love at the Sacrifice of the Mass and by uniting ourselves, through holy communion, with the Divine Victim immolated for us on the altar.[97]

At Mass and in Holy Communion, the merits of Christ's Passion and death are communicated to us.[98] There is a particular connection here: 'The altar is, upon earth, the centre of the religion of Jesus, exactly as Calvary is the summit of His life... [A]ll the mysteries of Jesus's existence on earth converge upon His immolation upon the cross; all the states of His glorified life derive their splendour from the cross.'[99] In other words, when Christ's mysteries are celebrated at Mass, Christ communicates to us the graces associated with the particular mystery being celebrated. In this sense, Marmion is speaking of the Mass, 'not as a memorial but as a source of graces.'[100] It is the main font by which Christ pours out His graces upon us.

It should also be said that Marmion uses the liturgical texts as a source for his understanding of the virtues and graces associated with the various mysteries. Developing an idea from the French School, Marmion moves from just a speculative idea about what graces and sentiments are present in each mystery to something that is grounded in a *locus* of theology. Marmion points out that this becomes clear by looking at the liturgical texts for the different feasts: 'The object of these prayers, which hold a special rank among those of the Eucharistic Sacrifice, varies according to the nature of the particular mysteries then being celebrated.'[101] Furthermore, '[t]he Church, through the choice, through the setting in due order, of these bits and longer extracts taken from the sacred books [in the liturgy], *makes us enter into the very feelings*

---

97   *CHM*, p. 105.
98   *CIP*, p. 101.
99   *CHM*, p. 104.
100 *Ibid.*, p. 403. See: *Ibid.*, p. 404–405.
101 *Ibid.*, p. 406.

that animated the heart of Christ Jesus.'[102] In other words, in the liturgical celebration of Christ's mysteries, the choice of liturgical texts reveals something of what God desires to communicate to His spouse, the Church. While the Gospel authors mainly recount the historical actions and sufferings of Christ, the Church through her liturgy leads us to lift a corner of the veil of the mystery and peer into the heart of Christ to understand His sentiments. Thus, we can have a sense of Christ's interior sentiments as well as the graces particular to each mystery because of the understanding that the Bride, the Church, has of her Divine Bridegroom, and in meditating upon them, we can appropriate their fruits.[103]

For instance, Marmion states that Christ's recitation of Psalm 22 on the Cross reveals the inner feelings of His soul during the crucifixion:

> "'I am a worm, not a man: the scorn of men, despised by the people. All they who see me scoff at me; they mock me with parted lips, they wag their heads,' saying: "He relied on the Lord; let Him deliver him, let him rescue him, if He loves him!"' ... 'Many bullocks'—raging bullocks—'surround me.... I am like water poured out; all my bones are racked. My heart has become like wax melting away within my bosom.' ... 'But you, O Lord, be not far from me; O my help, hasten to aid me ... save me from the lion's mouth!'" These words are a revelation of the feelings of the heart of Christ during His Passion. The Church knows this well: guided by the Holy Spirit, she causes us to recite this psalm during Holy Week, so as to make our souls share in the feelings of the heart of Christ.[104]

Marmion appropriates the liturgy's depiction of Christ's sentiments—how the mocking, scorning, and scoffing affect Christ's heart—and proposes those sentiments as the ones associated

---

[102] *CLS*, p. 404. See: *Ibid.*, p. 409; *CIM*, p. 399.
[103] *Ibid.*, pp. 365, 404–405; *CIM*, pp. 359–361.
[104] *Ibid.*, p. 405.

with the various mysteries in Christ's life. This becomes the framework by which we can not only know Christ's sentiments but also begin to appropriate them in our own lives.

2. Contemplation

As mentioned above, Christ acts both in the sacraments and outside the sacraments to bring about an increase in grace in us.[105] Marmion is very clear that Christ's primary means of pouring out graces into the soul is through the sacraments, but that He also acts through 'prayer, the contemplation of His mysteries, humility, and love in all its forms.'[106] Moreover, the liturgical prayers used in the celebration of the sacraments can greatly assist contemplation, even being a fruitful source for it.[107]

In general, Marmion understands contemplation to be a means by which God acts within us.[108] God desires to see the features of Christ, the exemplary model, reproduced within us,[109] and the whole 'spiritual life consists above all in contemplating Christ in order to reproduce in us His state of Son of God and His virtues.'[110] Now, Christ is not a model who forms us only superficially and extrinsically. Rather, He is a model who shapes us intrinsically through grace.[111] This is possible because

> it is as the Head of the human race, and for the human race, that He has lived these mysteries: therefore simply by contemplating them with faith, the soul is moulded little by little upon Christ, its Ideal, and is gradually transformed in Him, by entering the sentiments felt by His Divine Heart when He lived each of His mysteries.[112]

---

105 *CIP*, p. 41.
106 *Ibid.*, p. 51.
107 *CIM*, pp. 395, 397.
108 Undated letter, found in *UWG*, p. 142.
109 *CIM*, p. 142; *CIP*, p. 37.
110 *CLS*, p. 84.
111 *CLS*, p. 84–85.
112 *CIM*, p. 360. See: *Ibid.*, pp. 190–191.

Here again, we see the importance of the mystical body for Marmion. Because Christ is the head and we are the members, He can shape us to be more and more like Him as we encounter the mysteries He once lived on earth. In His virtues and in His sentiments, Christ shapes the members of His mystical body so that they become like Him.

Ultimately for Marmion, the purpose for this communication and appropriation of Christ's virtues and sentiments is so that Christ's features can be reproduced in us.[113] He points out that we ought to contemplate all the stages of Christ's life 'so as to conform our own lives to this model who makes God accessible to us, so as to draw on Him for divine life, in order that our thirst be fully quenched.'[114] Moreover, for Marmion, it is 'true to say that when we contemplate in their successive order the different mysteries of Christ,' this is not only for a mental recollection nor for a means of imitating Him, but it is also a means for our souls to 'participate in a special set of circumstances of the sacred humanity' so that we 'may draw forth, from each of those circumstances, the specific grace it has pleased the Divine Master to attach to it by meriting that grace as head of the Church, for His mystical body.'[115] In other words, just as the liturgy reveals to us the sentiments, graces, and fruits of Christ's various mysteries, the continued contemplation of these mysteries can deepen our appropriation of them. Meditating upon the Gospels, the Stations of the Cross, or the mysteries of the Rosary are primary means to be shaped and moulded by the graces flowing from Christ's mysteries.

E. PARTICULAR GRACES FOR PARTICULAR MYSTERIES

From what has been said already, it seems clear that for Marmion each of Christ's mysteries contains a particular grace. He explicitly states this: 'For everything in the life of Jesus

---

[113] *CIM*, p. 142.
[114] *CHM*, p. 9. See: *CIP*, p. 287.
[115] *Ibid.*, p. 30. See: *Ibid.*, pp. 403–404.

Christ's Mysteries and Imitating What They Contain

the Incarnate Word is full of significance... And that is true of all Jesus's circumstances, of every one of His deeds... and to each of His mysteries He attaches a grace that is there to help us reproduce in ourselves His divine traits, so as to make us resemble Him.'[116] Furthermore, 'each mystery... constitutes for our souls a new manifestation of Christ; each has its special beauty, its particular splendour, as also its own grace.'[117] Here, this will become clear if we look at specific examples of both the virtues and the graces communicated by various mysteries.

1. Particular virtues communicated by the mysteries

Following the French School's emphasis on the Incarnation, Marmion develops a strong notion of the imitability of both the Incarnation and the Nativity. Following the Rule of St Benedict, Marmion sees that in the Incarnation, Christ is a model of humility.[118] It is important to note that, here, Marmion takes his source as the Rule of St Benedict rather than Aquinas, and thus we see the importance that the Rule gave to forming Marmion's thought. While the principle about the mysteries might come from Aquinas, the French School, or some combination of the two, it was the Rule that actually gave the foundation for Marmion's treatment of this specific mystery's exemplarity in this case.

Secondly, like Aquinas, Marmion is clear that Christ's victory over the devil is an example that we should follow in the midst of our own temptations.[119] Marmion, though, adds some depth to Aquinas's idea. Marmion points out that Christ did this as Head of the Church, and that it is through our connection to Him now that we are able to continue triumphing in the face of the devil's temptations.[120] This

---

[116] *Ibid.*, p. 270.
[117] *Ibid.*, p. 27.
[118] *CIM*, p. 277.
[119] For Aquinas: *ST* III, 41, 1, corp.; III, 41, 4, ad 6; *Ad. Haeb.*, ch. 2, lect. 4, n. 154; ch. 4, lect. 3, n. 237. For Marmion: *CHM*, p. 215, 221, 224.
[120] *CHM*, p. 221.

is possible because Christ merited this grace for us: 'Christ Jesus has merited that those who are united to Him share in His impeccability—and share in the same measure as that of their union with Him.'[121] Marmion continues, 'In the measure that, through faith, we live a life of contemplation of God and remain united to Jesus Christ, in that same measure we become invulnerable to temptation.'[122] The more that we are united to Christ by faith and contemplation, the more we will share in His impeccability and invulnerability to temptation. Thus, through a contemplative gaze upon Christ's triumph during His temptation, we can become more resistant to temptations when they arise.

The final mystery worth noting is the Passion. Here, following Aquinas's lead, Marmion points out that the Passion is the 'perfect model of all virtues.'[123] Both authors speak specifically of love of neighbour,[124] patience,[125] obedience,[126] humility,[127] charity,[128] and forbearance.[129] In a similar but

---

[121] Ibid., p. 221.
[122] Ibid., p. 224.
[123] CIP, p. 127. See: *Exp. Sym. Ap.*, art. 4, no. 920; St Thomas Aquinas, *Commentary on the Letter of Saint Paul to the Hebrews*, trans. Fabian Larcher, ed. J. Mortensen and E. Alarcón, vol. 41 of *Latin/English Edition of the Works of St Thomas Aquinas* (Lander, WY: The Aquinas Institute for the Study of Sacred Doctrine, 2012), ch. 12, lect. 1, n. 667. (hereafter: *Ad Haeb.*, ch. 12, lect. 1, n. 667).
[124] For Aquinas: *Ad Haeb.*, ch. 12, lect. 1, n. 667. For Marmion: *CHM*, p. 320; *CIP*, p. 127.
[125] For Aquinas: *Ad Haeb.*, ch. 12, lect. 1, n. 667; *ST* II-II, 108, 1, obj. 4; III, 14, 1, corp.; III, 51, 2, ad 1; St Thomas Aquinas, *Expositio in Psalmos David*, in *Opera Omnia*, volume 14, pages 148–353 (Parma: Typis Petri Fiaccadori, 1863; photographic reprint, New York: Musurgia Publishers, 1949), psalm 28, n. 6; *Exp. Sym. Ap.*, art. 4, no. 920–924. For Marmion: *CLS*, p. 53; *CHM*, pp. 311, 320; *CIM*, p. 262; *CIP*, pp. 127, 189.
[126] For Aquinas: *Ad Haeb.*, ch. 12, lect. 1, n. 667; *ST* III, 46, 3, corp.; *Exp. Sym. Ap.*, art. 4, no. 920–924. For Marmion: *CHM*, pp. 314, 324; *CIM*, pp. 285–286, 311–312; *CIP*, p. 127.
[127] For Aquinas: *ST* III, 46, 3, corp.; *Exp. Sym. Ap.*, art. 4, no. 920–924. For Marmion: *CHM*, p. 316; *CIM*, pp. 188, 278.
[128] For Aquinas: *Ad Haeb.*, ch. 12, lect. 1, n. 667; *Exp. Sym. Ap.*, art. 4, no. 920–924. For Marmion: *CHM*, p. 311, 320; *CIP*, pp. 127, 185.
[129] For Aquinas: *ST* III, 46, 3, corp.; III, 46, 4, corp.; III, 51, 2, ad 1. For Marmion: *CHM*, p. 320.

slightly different manner, Aquinas speaks of the Passion as an example of contempt for earthly things,[130] while Marmion speaks of it as a model for hatred of sin: 'By meditating on the interior sufferings of Jesus we learn to share His hatred for sin and we offer with Him His sacrifice to make good the abyss of the iniquities of the world.'[131]

Where the distinctions between Aquinas and Marmion begin to be most notable is with Marmion's treatment of the Stations of the Cross, most of which he specifically describes as exemplar causes.[132] While Aquinas does not specifically draw out each of the mysteries in the various Stations of the Cross, Marmion does point out their various virtues, especially humility and obedience.[133] It would seem that this is most likely the result of Marmion's deep appropriation of the Benedictine way of life and its emphases on both obedience and humility.

This is very clear in Marmion's explanation of Christ's complaining on the Cross.[134] Here, Marmion makes a distinction between murmuring and complaining. He points out that murmuring comes from an ill will, while complaining can come from a pure heart and thus be an expression of suffering. When complaining is seen in this light, complaints can be prayers that are ultimately connected with a resolution to obey the Lord's will. In other words, Marmion sees Christ's cry on the Cross as a prayer and thus as related to

---

130 *Exp. Sym. Ap.*, art. 4, no. 920–924.
131 *CIP*, p. 127.
132 *CHM*, pp. 312–327.
133 Marmion discusses humility in connection with the Incarnation (*CIM*, pp. 277–278), the Nativity (*CHM*, pp. 146–147, 406), Christ's thirty years in Nazareth (*CIM*, pp. 88–89), the Baptism of the Lord (*CHM*, pp. 205–206), the Last Supper (*CHM*, p. 15), the Passion (*CIM*, pp. 188, 278), and Christ's falls while carrying the Cross (*CHM*, p. 316). He discusses obedience in connection with the Nativity (*CHM*, pp. 146–147), Christ's thirty years in Nazareth (*CHM*, p. 195; *CIM*, pp. 285–286), Christ's following the precepts of the Law (*CLS*, p. 53), the Passion (*CIP*, p. 127), the agony in the garden (*CIM*, pp. 313–314), the condemnation by Pilate (*CHM*, pp. 314), and the Crucifixion (*CHM*, p. 324; *CIM*, pp. 285–286).
134 *CIM*, p. 322. Marmion held the position that Christ recited the whole of Psalm 22 while on the Cross (*CLS*, pp. 404–405).

the virtue of obedience, which he then explicitly connects to the Benedictine ideal of obedience.

2. Particular graces communicated by the mysteries

Marmion also points out that all of Christ's mysteries have particular graces for the soul. In this way, he seems to build on Aquinas and the French School while using liturgical sources as his theological support. While virtues communicated by means of the liturgy and contemplative prayer are indeed graces, Marmion also associates other graces with the mysteries. Examining two of Christ's mysteries should clearly show this.

With the Nativity, not only are we given the grace to imitate Christ's virtue of poverty,[135] but He also gives us other graces, such as sharing in His divinity and being born to divine life: 'To be made sharers in the divinity to which our humanity has been united in the Person of Christ, and to receive this divine gift through that very humanity—such is the grace attached to the celebration of the mystery of this day, Christmas Day.'[136] To draw this out, Marmion makes reference to key liturgical texts for Christmas:

> Let the oblation of the festival we are celebrating today be acceptable to you, we beseech you, Lord; so that by your bountiful grace, by means of this most holy exchange, we may be found like unto Him in whom our substance is united to you.[137]

> May our offerings, we beseech you, Lord, prove suitable to the mysteries of the Nativity of which we sing today; that as this man who has been born into our human nature has at the same time shone gloriously upon us as God, so this earthly substance... may communicate to us that which in Him is divine.[138]

> The great grace of the Nativity is one which will deliver you from all your troubles. "That new birth

---

[135] *CHM*, pp. 146–147, 406; *CIM*, p. 229.
[136] *Ibid.*, p. 133. See: *Ibid.*, pp. 29, 148.
[137] *Secretum* of the Mass during the Night; see: *CHM*, p. 133.
[138] *Secretum* of the Mass at Dawn; see: *CHM*, p. 133.

will deliver you from the yoke of the old bondage." It is the grace of being born with Jesus, to that liberty of the *children of God*. 'Unless you become as little children, you shall not enter into the Kingdom of Heaven.'[139]

In other words, Marmion not only sees the liturgical texts as presenting Christ as a virtuous model to be imitated, but he also understands the three Masses of Christmas Day as a means of communicating these other particular graces that are also bound up with the mystery of the Nativity.

Secondly, there is Marmion's treatment of the Resurrection as presented in the Easter liturgies. Marmion lists a variety of graces associated with the Resurrection, such as freedom,[140] interior joy,[141] hope,[142] transformation into a new creature,[143] and detachment from worldly things.[144] Marmion sees Easter particularly as 'a mystery of joy.'[145] He writes:

> The Church shows this during Eastertide by multiplying the *Alleluia*, a cry of elation and happiness, borrowed from the liturgy of heaven. She had excluded it during Lent, so as to manifest her sadness and commune with the sufferings of her Spouse. Now that Christ is risen, she rejoices with Him, she takes up again, with a new fervour, this joyous exclamation that sums up all the ardour of her feelings.[146]

> Let us also, with our Mother the Church, say the *Alleluia* often, to show Christ our joy at seeing Him triumph over death, and to thank the Father for the glory He gives His Son. The *Alleluia* which the Church tirelessly repeats during the fifty days of the Pascal

---

139 Letter to Sœur Pauline Antoinette d'Outrepont, December 21, 1922, in which Marmion quotes from the *Oratio* for the Mass during the Day, found in *UWG*, pp. 27–28.
140 *CLS*, p. 408; *CHM*, pp. 30, 334.
141 *CHM*, pp. 27, 346.
142 Ibid., p. 346.
143 Ibid., p. 343.
144 Ibid., pp. 346, 407.
145 Ibid., p. 346.
146 Ibid., pp. 346.

> season is like an ever-renewed echo of that prayer with which she ends Easter Week: "Grant us, we beseech thee, O Lord, ever to rejoice in these Paschal mysteries, that the work of our renewal may continue and bring us to everlasting bliss."[147]

In other words, the liturgies throughout the whole Easter season beseech the Lord to fill the hearts of His people with the same joy that He has in His Resurrection. This is clearly not just an imitation of the Lord's virtuous living. Rather, the mystery offers us a participation in a particular grace which Christ desires to communicate to us.

In summary, Marmion clearly understands the mysteries of Christ's life to be means of communicating particular graces that reflect the mystery as it was lived by Christ. Using St Thomas, the teachings of the French School, the Rule of St Benedict, and the texts of the Church's liturgy, Marmion has a well-developed understanding of the power of the mysteries. This is the case regarding both the communication of Christ's imitable virtues and other graces particularly associated with Christ's various mysteries. Regarding the former, Aquinas and Marmion use similar principles, even if they come to different conclusions about which virtues are communicated. Regarding the latter, while Aquinas does not describe these other types of graces in his treatment of Christ's mysteries, Marmion seems to develop a position that can be seen in harmony with Aquinas's own explanation of the power of the mysteries to communicate graces.

CONCLUSION

From what has been said, it is clear that Marmion holds that particular mysteries in Christ's life communicate particular graces. He describes how Christ's mysteries have power, even now, to communicate graces. While the mysteries are moral examples of virtue, they are not just that. They are also saving

---

147 *Ibid.*, p. 346; here, Marmion quotes the *Secretum* of the Saturday of Easter Week.

Christ's Mysteries and Imitating What They Contain

actions which give life, conform us to Christ, and bring about our redemption.[148] Marmion clearly states that Christ's mysteries were lived for us so that He could communicate grace to us through them.[149]

This is all possible because of the mystical body of Christ and our place within it. Marmion emphasizes that the unity between the head and the body helps bring about this communication of the graces from Christ to us.[150] From this union with Christ through our incorporation into the mystical body and our right to Christ's inheritance because of our divine adoption, it follows that Christ's mysteries can have a causative effect on us.

Practically, this occurs through the liturgy, sacraments, and contemplative prayer. Marmion clearly uses liturgical texts as a source of theological reflection and insight. He posits that the liturgical texts themselves can help us to understand what are the particular virtues and graces of each mystery, and that as we pray about those mysteries on particular feasts, we can partake of the very fruits of those mysteries.

Ultimately, for Marmion, the mysteries in Christ's life are powerful and life-giving. With particular virtues and graces associated to them, Christ's mysteries are a means for the transformation of the whole person so that in thought, word, and deed, he may be conformed to Christ. His mysteries provide us not only the examples but also the causes of grace so that we who 'imitate what they contain' may also 'obtain what they promise'[151] as we follow in the footsteps of the Saviour, the very One who guides us by the hand along the path of salvation.

---

148   *CLS*, pp. 64–65.
149   *CHM*, p. 29.
150   *CLS*, p. 123, note 5; *Ibid.*, p. 124.
151   Pope St John Paul II, *Rosarium Virginis Mariae*, §35.

5

MEDITATIONS FOR THE ROSARY FROM THE WRITINGS OF BLESSED COLVMBA MARMION

TEXTS SELECTED BY SR CLAIRE WADDELOVE OF ST CECILIA'S ABBEY, RYDE

THE JOYFUL MYSTERIES

1. The Annunciation

In order that the exchange which God willed to contract with humanity should be possible, it was necessary that humanity should consent to it...

'Behold the handmaid of the Lord; be it done to me according to thy word': *Ecce ancilla Domini, fiat mihi secundum verbum tuum.*

In this solemn moment, the exchange is concluded. When Mary pronounces her *fiat*, all humanity says to God by her mouth: 'Yes, O God, I consent, so be it.' And immediately the Word is made Flesh: *Et Verbum caro factum est*. At this instant, the Word becomes incarnate by the operation of the Holy Spirit; the Blessed Virgin becomes the Ark of the New Covenant between God and man.[1]

2. The Visitation

Mary refers to the Lord the glory of the marvels wrought in her. She sings within her heart a canticle full of love and gratitude. With her cousin Elizabeth, she lets the innermost

---

[1] Marmion, Columba, *Christ in His Mysteries* (Ireland: Cenacle Press, 2022), pp. 151–152.

feelings of her heart overflow; she sings the *Magnificat* which, throughout the centuries, her children will repeat after her in praise of God for having chosen her out of all women: 'My soul doth magnify the Lord...because He hath regarded the humility of His handmaid...because He that is mighty, hath done great things to me,' *Magnificat anima mea Dominum: quia fecit mihi magna qui potens est.*[2]

3. The Nativity

By this exchange, God again gives us His friendship, He restores to us the right of entering into possession of the eternal inheritance; He looks anew upon humanity with love and complacency.

Therefore, joy is one of the most marked characteristics of the celebration of this mystery. The Church constantly invites us to it, remembering the words of the angel to the shepherds: 'Behold, I bring you tidings of great joy...for this day is born to you a Saviour.' It is the joy of deliverance, of the inheritance regained, of peace found once again, and, above all, of the vision of God Himself given to men: *Et vocabitur nomen ejus Emmanuel.*[3]

4. The Presentation

In the same way as she had given her consent in the name of the whole human race when the Angel announced to her the mystery of the Incarnation, so upon this day, Mary offered her Son Jesus in the name of the human race. She knew that her Son is 'the glorious King of the new Light...begotten before the day-star...the Lord of life and death.' And so she presents Him to God in order to obtain for us all the graces of salvation that Jesus, according to the Angel's promise, is to bring to the world: *Ipsa enim portat Regem gloriae novi luminis; subsistit Virgo adducens manibus Filium ante lucifernum genitum.*[4]

---

2 *Ibid.*, p. 153.
3 *Ibid.*, p. 126.
4 *Ibid.*, p. 158. 'She herself bears the glorious King of new light; she remains a virgin, bearing in her hands the Son begotten before the day-star.'

5. The Finding in the Temple

And what was the object of the Child Jesus in thus questioning the doctors of the Law? He wished, doubtless, to enlighten them, to lead them, by His questions and His replies, by the quotations that He made from the Scriptures, to speak of the coming of the Messias; to direct their search towards this point, so that their attention should be awakened as to the circumstances of the appearing of the promised Saviour. This is, apparently, what the Eternal Father willed of His Son, the mission that He gave Him to accomplish, and for which He caused Him to interrupt, for a short space of time, His hidden and silent life. And the doctors of Israel 'were astonished at His wisdom and His answers': *Stupebant...prudentia et responsis ejus.*[5]

THE LUMINOUS MYSTERIES

1. The Baptism in the Jordan

Whenever Christ undergoes humiliation, for us, He must be glorified.

Jesus stoops so low as to mingle with the multitude of sinners, and forthwith the heavens are opened to magnify Him; — He asks for the baptism of penance, of reconciliation, and behold, the Spirit of Love testifies that He abides in Jesus with the plenitude of His gifts of grace; — He acknowledges Himself worthy of the strokes of divine justice, and behold, the Father declares that He takes all His delight in Him: *Humiliavit semetipsum...propter quod et Deus exaltavit illum.*[6]

2. The Wedding at Cana

The Gospel, as you know, has only preserved a very few words of the Blessed Virgin. I have just reminded you of one of these words, that which was said to the servants at the marriage feast at Cana: 'Whatsoever my Son shall say

---

Antiphon *Adorna* after the Blessing of the Candles on the Feast of the Presentation.
5 *Ibid.*, p. 162
6 *Ibid.*, p. 176.

to you, do ye', *Quodcumque dixerit vobis, facite*. This word is like an echo of the word of the Eternal Father: 'This is my beloved Son, in Whom I am well pleased: hear ye Him': *Ipsum audite*. We can apply to ourselves this word of Mary: 'Do all that my Son shall say to you'... It will be the best form our devotion towards the Mother of Jesus can take. The Virgin Mother has no greater wish than to see her Divine Son obeyed, loved, glorified and exalted. Jesus is the Son in whom she, like the Eternal Father, is well pleased.[7]

3. The Proclamation of the Kingdom and Call to Conversion

There are obligations every Christian must fulfil: the exact keeping of God's commandments, of the precepts of the Church(...); daily fidelity to the duties of one's state, to the law of labour; watchfulness in order constantly to shun the many occasions of sin; all this often involves acts of renunciation, and sacrifices costly to nature.

There is next the struggle against the special defects that may beset and weaken the Divine life. In one it is self-love; in another, levity of mind; in this one, jealousy or anger; in that one sensuality or sloth. These defects, if not resisted, are the occasion of a thousand sins and voluntary infidelities that hinder God's action in us... He expects us to take no respite until the roots of these vices are so weakened that they can no longer spring up and bear fruit. For the more these roots decrease, the more the Divine life grows strong within us, because it has great liberty to unfold.[8]

4. The Transfiguration

Whence then came this wonderful radiance? From the Divinity. It was an overflowing of the Divinity upon the holy Humanity, an irradiation from the furnace of eternal life which was ordinarily hidden in Christ, and now at this hour caused

---

7 Marmion, Columba, *Christ, The Life of the Soul* (Tacoma, WA: Angelico Press, 2012), pp. 354–355.
8 *Ibid.*, p. 194.

His sacred body to shine with marvellous splendour. This was not a borrowed light, coming from without, but rather a reflection of that incommensurable majesty which Christ contained within Himself.... [A]t the Transfiguration, the Word gave full liberty to His eternal glory; He allowed it to throw its splendour upon the humanity which He had taken.[9]

5. The Institution of the Eucharist

It is as if He said: My desire is to communicate My Divine life to you. I hold My being, My life, all, from My Father, and because I hold all from Him, I live only for Him; I desire with an intense desire that you, likewise, holding all from Me, live only for Me. Your corporal life is sustained and developed by food; I will to be the food of your soul, so as to preserve and develop its life which is Myself.[10] He that eats Me, lives by My life; I possess the fulness of grace, and those to whom I give Myself as food partake of this grace.[11]

THE SORROWFUL MYSTERIES

1. The Agony in the Garden

If you contemplate with faith and devotion the sufferings of Jesus Christ you will have a revelation of God's love and justice; you will know, better than with any amount of reasoning, the malice of sin. This contemplation is like a sacramental causing the soul to share in that Divine sadness which invaded the soul of Jesus in the Garden of Olives—Jesus, the very Son of God, in Whom the Father, Whose exigencies are infinite, was well pleased. And yet His heart was full of sorrow—'sorrowful even unto death': *Tristis est anima mea*

---

9 Marmion, *Christ in His Mysteries*, p. 237.
10 *Sumi autem voluit sacramentum hoc tamquam spiritualem animarum cibum quo alantur et confortentur viventes vita illius qui dixit: et qui manducat me et ipse vivet propter me.* (His will was that this sacrament be received as the soul's spiritual food which would nourish and strengthen those who live by the life of him who said: 'He who eats me wll live because of me.') Concil. Trid. Sess. XIII, cap. 2.
11 Marmion, *Christ, The Life of the Soul*, p. 261.

usque ad mortem. Great cries arise from His breast, as tears arise from His eyes; *cum clamore valido et lacrymis.* Whence come this sadness, these sighs and tears? They come from the weight of the burden of the world's crimes: *Posuit Dominus in eo iniquitatem omnium nostrum.*[12]

2. The Scourging at the Pillar

Moreover, we should love to meditate upon the Passion because it is also therein that Christ's virtues shine forth with such brilliancy. He possesses every virtue within His soul, but the occasions of manifesting them especially arise in His Passion. His immense love for His Father, His charity for mankind, hatred of sin, forgiveness of injuries, patience, meekness, fortitude, obedience to lawful authority, compassion, all these virtues shine out in a heroic manner in these days of sorrow.[13]

3. The Crowning with Thorns

Isaias had foretold of the suffering Jesus: 'There is no beauty in Him, nor comeliness, and we have seen Him, and there was no sightliness, that we should be desirous of Him': *Non est species ei, neque decor, nec reputavimus eum.* The Gospel tells us that during those terrible hours after His apprehension the soldiers had dealt Him insolent blows, that they had spat in His face; the crowning with thorns had caused the blood to trickle down His sacred countenance. Christ Jesus willed to suffer all this in order to expiate our sins; He willed that we should be healed by the bruises that His Divine Face received for us: *Livore ejus sanati sumus.*[14]

4. The Carrying of the Cross

We shall never sound the depths of the abyss of afflictions to which our Divine Saviour consented in receiving His Cross.

---

12 Marmion, Columba, *Christ, The Ideal of the Monk* (Ireland: The Cenacle Press, 2022), pp. 190–191; Isa. 53:6. 'The Lord has laid on him the iniquity of us all.'
13 *Christ in His Mysteries*, p. 263.
14 *Ibid.*, p. 272.

At this moment, too, Christ Jesus Who represented us all, and was going to die for us, accepted the cross for all His members, for each one of us: *Vere languores nostros ipse tulit, et dolores nostros ipse portavit.*[15] He then united to His own sufferings all the sufferings of His mystical body, causing them to find in this union their value and price.

Let us, therefore, accept our cross in union with Him, like Him, so that we may be worthy disciples of this Divine Head; let us accept it without reasoning, without repining... In the generous acceptance of this cross, we shall find peace. Nothing brings such peace to the soul that is in suffering as this utter self-surrender to God's good pleasure.[16]

5. The Crucifixion

'And Jesus crying with a loud voice said: Father, into Thy hands I commend My spirit. And saying this, He gave up the ghost.' After three hours of indescribable sufferings, Jesus dies. The only oblation worthy of God, the one sacrifice that redeems the world, and sanctifies souls is consummated: *Una enim oblatione consummavit in sempiternum sanctificatos....*

Let us implore Him to draw us to His Sacred Heart by the virtue of His death upon the Cross; to grant that we may die to our self-love and our self-will, the source of so many infidelities and sins, and that we may live for Him Who died for us. Since it is to His death that we owe the life of our souls, is it not just that we should live only for Him? *Ut et qui vivunt, jam non sibi vivant, sed ei qui pro ipsis mortuus est.*[17]

THE GLORIOUS MYSTERIES

1. The Resurrection

Christ, as I have often said, is our Head; we form with Him a mystical body. If Christ is risen—and He is risen in His human nature—it is necessary that we, His members,

---

15   Isa. 53:4. 'Truly he has borne our griefs and carried our sorrows.'
16   Marmion, *Christ in His Mysteries*, pp. 267–268.
17   *Ibid.*, pp. 276–277.

should share in the same glory. For it is not only in our soul, it is likewise in our body, it is in our whole being that we are members of Christ. The most intimate union binds us to Jesus. If then He is risen glorious, the faithful who, by grace, make part of His mystical body, will be united with Him even in His Resurrection.[18]

2. The Ascension

Our Lord Himself said to His Apostles before leaving them: *Si diligeretis me, gauderetis utique quia vado ad Patrem,* 'because I go to the Father.' To us too Christ repeats those words. If we love Him, we shall rejoice in His glorification; we shall rejoice in that, having finished His course, He ascends to His Father's right hand, to be there exalted to the highest heaven, there to taste, after His labours, sufferings, and death, eternal repose in incommensurable glory. Bliss, such as is incomprehensible to us, envelops and penetrates Him for ever in the bosom of the Divinity. Supreme power is given to Him over every creature.[19]

3. The Descent of the Holy Spirit at Pentecost

Because He is the Spirit of truth, this Consoler assuages the needs of our intelligence; because He is the Spirit of love, He satisfies the desires of our heart; because He is the Spirit of strength, He sustains us in our toils, trials and tears: the Holy Spirit is eminently the Consoler.

> *Consolator optime,*
> *Dulcis hospes animae,*
> *Dulce refrigerium!*[20]

Oh! Come and dwell in us, Father of the poor, Giver of heavenly gifts, Thou best Consoler, sweet Guest, and Refreshment full of sweetness for the soul.[21]

---

18   Ibid., p. 292.
19   Ibid., p. 306.
20   Sequence of Pentecost, *Veni Sancte Spiritus*.
21   Marmion, *Christ in His Mysteries*, p. 326.

4. *The Assumption*

A whole crown of graces adorns Christ's Virgin Mother, all due to her Divine maternity...

To fill up the measure, there is her *Assumption into Heaven*. Mary's virginal body, whence Christ took the substance of His human nature, is not to know corruption; upon her head is to be placed a crown of inestimable price; she will reign as queen at her Son's right hand, adorned with the vestment of glory woven for her by all these privileges: *Adstitit regina a dextris tuis, in vestitu deaurato*.[22]

5. *The Coronation of Our Lady and the Glory of All the Saints*

In Heaven we shall *see* God. To see God as He sees Himself is the first element in this participation in the Divine nature that constitutes the life of blessedness. It is the first vital act of glory.... The soul will be confirmed in grace by 'the light of glory' which is the unfolding of grace in Heaven. We shall see God with all His perfections; or, rather, we shall see that all His perfections are but one infinite perfection, which is the Divinity. We shall contemplate the inner life of God. We shall enter, as St John says, into fellowship with the Holy and Blessed Trinity, Father, Son, and Holy Spirit. We shall contemplate the fulness of Being, the fulness of all truth, of all holiness, all beauty and all goodness. We shall contemplate, and that for ever, the Humanity of the Incarnate Word; we shall see Jesus Christ, in whom the Father is infinitely well pleased... We shall see the Blessed Virgin Mary, the choirs of angels, all that multitude of the elect which St John declared to be innumerable, surrounding the throne of God.[23]

---

[22] *Christ, The Life of the Soul*, pp. 343-344.
[23] *Ibid.*, p. 359.

+ PART · II +
ESTOTE · ERGO · VOS · PERFECTI

6

BLESSED COLVMBA MARMION

GUIDE FOR THE MONASTIC LIFE

BY A BENEDICTINE MONK

THE OPPORTUNITY TO WRITE ABOUT Blessed Columba Marmion as a guide for the monastic life is, for me, the fulfillment of a personal debt of gratitude. I first heard the name of Marmion mentioned by then-Archbishop Justin Rigali of Saint Louis when, as a university student, I attended a retreat which he preached for prospective seminarians in early 2003. In reply to a question from one of the young retreatants, the future Cardinal mentioned Abbot Columba Marmion (then quite recently beatified) as one of the spiritual writers who had most influenced him. I continued to hear the name of Marmion during the course of my seminary studies and early priesthood.

Then, as a doctoral student in Rome, a providential series of circumstances led to my presence at the dedication of the monument, commissioned by His Eminence Raymond Cardinal Burke, to commemorate Marmion's ordination in the church of Sant'Agata dei Goti, formerly the home of the Irish College. During this event, I heard the story of Marmion's own years in Rome related by Monsignor Joseph Murphy, postulator of Marmion's cause. In the year or two that followed, I gradually became more familiar with Marmion's work, and with the story of his own journey from a happy and fruitful priestly ministry in Dublin to the surprising choice to bury himself in a continental monastery. In time, as my own sense of a religious vocation began to develop, I naturally turned to Marmion. Reading *Christ, The Ideal of the Monk* provided the answer to my search and pointed me definitively towards Benedictine life. In the years to come, Marmion's teachings would guide me, and his example and prayers sustain me, leading me eventually to embrace Benedictine life in his own native country.

I cannot lay claim to the expertise in Marmion's life and works possessed by other contributors to this volume. But as a priest and a monk whose life has been profoundly shaped by Marmion's own monastic journey, I hope that these reflections will be of some help to other sons and daughters of Saint Benedict, and indeed to all who draw inspiration from the monastic ideal in their following of Christ.

I. BLESSED COLUMBA MARMION, A LUMINARY OF THE BENEDICTINE REVIVAL

At the beginning of the nineteenth century, Benedictine monasticism was at one of the lowest points of its history. Already in the eighteenth century, the secularizing influence of the Enlightenment had led to the closure of many monasteries, or at least to drastic changes in monastic observance. The French Revolution and the ensuing Napoleonic wars resulted in the suppression of virtually all monastic life in France and many other parts of Europe. At a time when the Church's very survival as an institution seemed precarious, monasticism seemed to be a spent force belonging decisively to the past.

Few could have foreseen, then, the flowering of monastic life that would occur over the course of the coming century. Yet as the Church began to recover from the devastation left by the Revolution and its aftermath, monastic life quickly began to re-emerge. The vision of Dom Prosper Guéranger, a young priest of the Diocese of Le Mans, to save the ancient priory of Solesmes in his native village of Sablé-sur-Sarthe, led to the formation of what would eventually become the Benedictine Congregation of France (now the Congregation of Solesmes). In Italy, Pietro Casaretto would draw inspiration from Dom Guéranger in bringing about a return to monastic observance in what would become the Congregation of Subiaco. At about the same time, Père Jean-Baptiste Muard's decision to adopt the Rule of Saint Benedict for his missionary preachers led to the foundation of La-Pierre-qui-Vire and the beginnings of the French province of the Subiaco Congregation. In the German-speaking world, similar revivals took hold in Bavaria and Switzerland, and the brothers Maurus and Placid Wolter drew inspiration from Dom Guéranger and Solesmes in the revival of monastic life at Beuron, from which Placid Wolter would depart for Belgium to found Maredsous.

While Benedictine life was blossoming again in Europe, Ireland seemed largely unaffected by this movement. Once the most thoroughly monastic country in the Western Church, Ireland had been bereft of monastic life since the Reformation, and only with the arrival of exiled Cistercians from France to Mount Melleray did monasticism return to Ireland. The revival of the 'black monks' remained a foreign phenomenon. Yet Providence arranged that the land of Saint Patrick, Saint Colm Cille, and Saint Columbanus would provide the European Benedictine revival with its greatest spiritual master and its first *beatus* in the person of Abbot Columba Marmion.

Marmion's earliest influences were in the soil of nineteenth-century Irish piety. His years as a student in Rome, however, put him in contact with influences in the wider Church that would shape his spiritual and intellectual development. His studies at the College of Propaganda allowed him to learn from some of the leading figures of the revival of Thomism, and the clarity of the Angelic Doctor's theological vision would mark the young Irishman's intellectual work in the decades to come. The same period of studies also gave him a thorough grounding in the writings of Saint Paul, whose vision of the mystery of Christ would be at the heart of Marmion's spiritual doctrine. Most significant, however, although its significance would only become apparent with time, was his visit in September 1880 to Monte Cassino, which first put him in contact with monastic life under the Rule of Saint Benedict. The desire for Benedictine life seized Marmion instantly, and would continue to pursue him after his ordination to the priesthood in 1881. He considered various ways of realizing this desire, initially carrying out a correspondence with Bishop Rosendo Salvado about the possibility of joining his foundation at New Norcia in Western Australia. Yet he finally decided to enter the abbey of Maredsous in Belgium, where his friend Joseph Moreau had preceded him, and where, during a brief visit in 1881, he had been captivated by 'the peace and silence of the vast cloisters, the chant of the divine office, and the feeling of complete separation from the world which reigned there.'[1] After years of negotiations with the diocesan authorities in Dublin, Joseph Marmion departed for Maredsous in November 1886, and received as a novice the name Columba.

The Irish sapling, once transplanted, quickly took root in the Benedictine soil. Amidst the many trials of his novitiate, Marmion's spiritual life deepened and matured. The early years of his monastic life afforded the opportunity for him to synthesize the fruits of his theological formation and his early years of priesthood with the Rule of Saint Benedict which was now the foundation of his life as a Christian and a monk. In time, circumstances led Dom Columba, simply professed in 1889 and solemnly professed in 1891, to take up responsibilities of preaching and teaching both in his community and in the wider Church. Elected abbot of Maredsous in 1909, Marmion nourished his community with spiritual teaching in conferences which would eventually be disseminated in his 'trilogy': *Christ, The Life of the Soul*, *Christ in His Mysteries*, and *Christ, The Ideal of the Monk*. Even as Abbot, he continued to serve as a spiritual guide to religious, priests, devout lay faithful, and even high-ranking prelates in Belgium and beyond. His writings were disseminated throughout the Catholic world and received praise from the Supreme Pontiffs. By the time of his death in 1923, he was perhaps the most renowned spiritual teacher of the Benedictine order.

---

1 *The Belvederian*, 1908, p. 13, cited in Mark Tierney OSB, *Dom Columba Marmion: A Biography* (Dublin: The Columba Press, 1994), p. 32.

II. MARMION'S CHRISTOCENTRIC DOCTRINE OF THE MONASTIC LIFE

While Marmion's teaching on the monastic life is distilled most clearly in *Christ, The Ideal of the Monk*, in its essence it is one with his general teaching on the spiritual life. In the Preface to that work, Marmion writes that 'in the eyes of the Patriarch of monks, the religious state, taken in what is essential, does not constitute a particular form of existence on the borders or at the side of Christianity: it is this same Christianity lived in its fulness in the pure light of the Gospel: *Per ducatum Evangelii pergamus itinera Christi.*' [2] For Marmion, as for Saint Benedict, the monastic life is simply the Christian life lived with a particular intensity, and so to grasp his understanding of monastic life one must look at his understanding of the Christian life itself.

II.A. Marmion's teaching on the Christian life

For Marmion, the fundamental truth of the Christian life is the divine plan for our adoption as sons of God in Christ. It is this plan, set forth by Saint Paul especially in the Letter to the Ephesians, which Marmion expounds in *Christ, The Life of the Soul* (1917). He maintains that the difficulty which many Christians encounter in striving for holiness is caused by a failure to grasp this divine plan:

> It is therefore extremely important, as St Paul says, to run in the race, "not as at an uncertainty", as one beating the air, but so as to obtain the prize... to know as perfectly as possible the Divine idea of holiness.... In a matter so grave, so vital, we ought to look at and weigh things as God looks at and weighs them.... If we leave the Divine idea full freedom to operate in us, if we adapt ourselves to it with love and fidelity, it becomes extremely fruitful and may lead us to the most sublime sanctity.[3]

---

2 *Christ, The Ideal of the Monk*, trans. by a Nun of Tyburn (Ireland: Cenacle Press, 2022), p. x.
3 Marmion, *Christ, The Life of the Soul*, trans. Mother M. St Thomas (London: Sands & Co., 1925), p. 4.

Marmion proceeds to sum up this divine plan: from all eternity, God the Father begets His Son, and in His goodness He chooses to bestow adoption as sons on His creatures, an adoption which is communicated through the Only-Begotten Son in His Incarnation. 'Hence all holiness consists in this: to receive the Divine life from Christ and by Christ, Who possesses its fulness and Who has been constituted the One Mediator; to keep this Divine life and increase it unceasingly by an ever more perfect adhesion, an ever closer union with Him Who is its source.'[4]

The following fundamental chapters of *Christ, The Life of the Soul* present the various aspects of Christ's place in the divine plan for our sanctification, using the scholastic concepts of causality. First, as the *causa exemplaris*, Christ is the model of all holiness—first in His status as Son, and then in all of His works: the Christian is called to imitate Christ both by sharing through sanctifying grace in His Divine Sonship and by imitating His works. Then, as the *causa satisfactoria et meritoria*, Christ is the source of our holiness, since by His Sacrifice on the Cross He atones fully for our sins and merits all grace for us: conscious of his own weakness, the Christian should place all his trust in these infinite merits of Christ. Finally, as the *causa efficiens*, Christ is the agent of our sanctification, Whose Sacred Humanity produces grace in us: first through the official channels of the Church's sacraments, but also whenever we come into contact with Him through faith.

Having shown how Christ is the model, the source, and the agent of man's sanctification, Marmion completes his overview of the Divine plan by presenting the role of the Church, Christ's Mystical Body, and of the Holy Spirit, Who is inseparable both from Christ and from the Church.

These foundations having been laid, Marmion presents the unfolding of the Christian life in three distinct sets of chapters. First, he presents the starting point of the Christian life: its essential foundation is the theological virtue of faith, above all

---

4 *Ibid.*, p. 7.

faith in the Divinity of Christ: 'Whoever... accepts the Divinity of Christ embraces the whole of revelation.... Therefore the intimate conviction that Our Lord is truly God constitutes the first foundation of our supernatural life.'[5] Faith, however, must be accompanied by baptism, the sacrament of Divine adoption, by which we become members of Christ's Mystical Body.

As baptism involves both death to sin and new life in Christ, the remainder of *Christ, The Life of the Soul* unpacks this twofold dynamic of the Christian life. First, a section on 'Death to Sin' presents the nature of sin (*'Delicta quis intelligit?'*) and its remedy ('The Sacrament and the Virtue of Penance'). This is followed by 'Life for God', the longest section of the work, which treats of the nature of good works and growth in grace, the Most Holy Eucharist, the Sacred Liturgy, prayer, fraternal charity, and the Blessed Virgin Mary, concluding with a chapter on the blessedness of Heaven (*'Coheredes Christi'*).

Marmion's fundamental teaching on Christ as the model, source, and agent of all our sanctification is applied in the second part of his 'trilogy', *Christ in His Mysteries* (1919). Marmion introduces that work by restating the thesis of his earlier work: 'The Christian life is essentially supernatural, and can only be found in Christ, the supreme Model of perfection, the infinite Treasure of grace and the efficient Cause of all holiness.' This being so, 'the mysteries of the God-Man are not only models which we must consider: they contain moreover within themselves treasures of merit and grace. By His almighty virtue, Christ Jesus, ever-living, produces the inward and supernatural perfection of His states in those who are moved by the desire of imitating Him and placing themselves in contact with Him by faith and love.'[6]

In the opening chapters of *Christ in His Mysteries*, Marmion shows how 'Christ's mysteries are our mysteries'.[7] Marmion

---

5   *Ibid.*, p. 130.
6   *Christ in His Mysteries*, trans. Mother M. St Thomas (Cenacle Press, 2022), p. ix.
7   *Ibid.*, p. 8.

gives three reasons for this, which seem to correspond to the three types of causality presented in *Christ, The Life of the Soul*. First Christ lived His mysteries for us, meriting for us all grace (*causa satisfactoria et meritoria*). Second, He shows Himself in them as our exemplar (*causa exemplaris*). Finally, in His mysteries 'Christ makes but one with us', that is, He acts as Head of His Mystical Body, and thus while the mysteries are past as historical events, their virtue, or power, remains and is constantly communicated to us (*causa efficiens*). We come into contact with the sanctifying power of Christ's mysteries by contemplating them in faith, above all in the celebration of the Church's holy orders. Christ is not simply given to us as a human model to be imitated, as it were, from the outside, by seeing what He did and trying to do the same. Rather, He is a Divine model, and thus 'the Holy Spirit alone—*Digitus paternae dexterae*—is capable of reproducing within us the true image of the Son, because our imitation must be of a supernatural order. Now this work of the Divine Artist is wrought above all in prayer based upon faith and enkindled by love.... This is why the contemplation of the mysteries of Jesus is so fruitful in itself.'[8]

The remainder of *Christ in His Mysteries* is a contemplation first of the Person of Christ—in His Eternal Sonship, in His Incarnation, and in His office as Saviour and High Priest—and then of the mysteries of His life as they are celebrated in the Church's liturgical cycle. In each of the mysteries, Marmion shows how they communicate to the Christian a particular grace of sanctification. Concluding with a chapter on the feast of All Saints, he shows how all of the celebrations of the sanctoral cycle lead back to Christ: 'Christ is the very principle of our perfection. As the vine pours forth its nourishing sap into the branches so that they may bear fruit, so Christ Jesus ceaselessly pours forth His grace into all those who abide in Him.'[9] Thus all the work of man's sanctification redounds to the glory of the Father's Beloved Son: 'It is to

---

8   *Ibid.*, p. 24.
9   *Ibid.*, p. 394.

this last end that all the mystery of Christ tends. God wills that His Son Jesus shall be for ever exalted, because He is His own Only-Begotten Son, the object of His complacency.'[10]

Together, these first two collections of Marmion's conferences present a comprehensive vision of the Divine economy. Christ, the Father's Beloved Son, is the model to which man is meant to be conformed, the High Priest and Mediator Who obtains all the grace needed for our perfection in His image, and the Head of the Mystical Body Who communicates His life to us through our contact with Him by faith, by the Church's sacraments and by prayer. The Christian life is death to sin and life to God in imitation of Christ, thanks to the merits of Christ, and in total dependence on Christ as our Head. This doctrine, fruitful in itself for the sanctification of Christians in any state of life, will be presented by Marmion in his third volume as the foundation of the monastic life.

II.B. Marmion's spiritual teaching applied to the monastic life

Since, as mentioned above, Marmion considers the religious and monastic life to be simply 'Christianity lived in its fulness', his teaching in *Christ, The Ideal of the Monk* follows very closely that of his earlier volumes, even in the organisation of the material. He himself admits in his Preface that the plan of the work 'closely follows the one adopted in *Christ, The Life of the Soul*. This is not to be wondered at, since religious perfection is so essentially akin to Christian holiness.'[11] Thus, Marmion's presentation of the monastic life begins by stressing the monk's complete dependence on Christ as the cause of all holiness, and upon His Mystical Body made concrete in the monastic community. He proceeds to show how the monk's pursuit of perfection is founded upon faith and the 'second baptism' of monastic profession. Then in the latter portion of the work he shows how the monk participates in Christ's Death and Resurrection by his life of abnegation and of union.

---

10   *Ibid.*, p. 395.
11   *Christ, The Ideal of the Monk*, p. xi.

II.B.1. The monk's dependence on Christ and His Mystical Body. *Christ, The Ideal of the Monk* opens with a distinctively 'monastic' chapter, 'To Seek God', in which Marmion identifies the pursuit of union with God through faith and love as the exclusive end of the monk's life. The second chapter, 'The Following of Christ', then charts the path of this seeking in terms that follow very closely the opening chapters of *Christ, The Life of the Soul.* Since man has departed from God by sin, his seeking for God now has the character of a return to God. How are we to make this return? As in his earlier work, Marmion here again stresses the need of knowing and following the Divine plan:

> Now, by what path are we 'to return to God?' It is extremely important that we should know it. In fact if we do not take this path, we shall not come to God, we shall miss our end. For we must never forget that our holiness is a supernatural holiness, we cannot acquire it by our own efforts.... a man's most finished perfection in the merely natural domain has of itself no value for eternal life.... Now, as God is the sole Author of the supernatural order, He alone, 'according to His good pleasure,' *secundum beneplacitum ejus*, can show us the road whereby to arrive at it; hence we must seek God as God wishes us to seek Him, otherwise we shall not find Him.[12]

As in the previous work, Marmion observes that the lack of understanding of or attention to the Divine plan is the cause of many souls' lack of spiritual progress:

> They imagine a holiness for themselves, they want to be the architects of their own perfection, built up according to their personal conceptions; they do not understand God's plan as it concerns them, or else they do not adapt themselves to it... they do not fly in the way that leads to God, they go haltingly all their life. The more I come in contact with souls, the more assured I am that it is already a most precious grace to know this Divine plan; to have recourse to it is a

---

12   *Ibid.*, pp. 24–25.

Guide for the Monastic Life

source of continual communication of divine grace; to adapt oneself to it is the very substance of sanctity.[13]

Marmion then presents in a condensed form the doctrine of the opening four chapters of *Christ, The Life of the Soul*. The Divine plan is summed up in four words of Saint Paul: *Instaurare omnia in Christo*.[14] In the previous work, Marmion identified the three aspects of Christ's role as the exemplary, meritorious, and efficient cause of our sanctification. Here Marmion presents similar concepts, although this time, rather than the technical vocabulary of causality, He uses more evocative scriptural language, speaking of Christ as the Way, the High Priest, and the Fountainhead of grace:

> He is the Way by His doctrine and example; He is the supreme High Priest, Who was [sic] merited for us, by His sacrifice, the power to follow in the way which He has established; He is the Fountain of grace wherefrom we draw strength to persevere in the path that leads to 'the holy mountain'.[15]

Marmion proceeds to discuss these aspects of Christ's work, as usual bringing together a variety of scriptural texts and this time also drawing on the teaching of the Benedictine Abbot Blosius.[16] First, by His teaching and His example, Christ is the Way: as God made Man, He makes God accessible to us, and allows those seeking perfection to arrive at union with God by following Him:

> All that Jesus did, even His least actions, were the actions of a God and infinitely pleasing to His Father: they are consequently for us examples to be followed, models of perfection... Let us then contemplate in the Gospel the example of Jesus: it is the norm of all human sanctity. If we remain united to Jesus by faith in

---

13 *Ibid.*, p. 25.
14 Eph. 1:10. 'To re-establish all things in Christ'.
15 *Christ, The Ideal of the Monk*, p. 26.
16 Louis de Blois, or Blosius (1506–66) was Abbot of Liessies in Belgium, and a renowned spiritual author. Abbot Marmion cites him frequently throughout *Christ, The Ideal of the Monk*.

His doctrine, by the imitation of His virtues, especially His religious virtues, we shall surely attain to God.[17]

Christ not only is the Way by which we are to arrive at union with God: He is the High Priest and Mediator Who obtains for us the power to follow this way. As God and Man, Christ, our 'Elder Brother', effects a perfect reconciliation with God, and His merits provide us with an infinite treasury of grace to supply for our failings: 'So our confidence ought to be boundless. All the graces that adorn the soul and make it blossom forth in virtues ... have their inexhaustible source on Calvary: for this river of life gushed forth from the Heart and Wounds of Jesus.'[18] Since Christ's merits are a treasury from which we can draw 'to expiate our faults, repair our negligences, provide for our needs, perfect our deeds, supply for our shortcomings,' Marmion says that those seeking perfection should 'unite all their actions to those of Jesus.'[19]

Finally, Christ is the Fountain of grace Who, as the Head of the Mystical Body, distributes and communicates to His members all of the grace which He merited: 'Bear this truth well in mind: there is no grace of which a soul can have need that is not found in Jesus, the Fount of every grace.... If we can sing that only Jesus Christ is holy: *Tu solus sanctus*, it is because no one is holy except by Him and in Him.'[20]

Only after having shown how all holiness is modeled on Christ, merited by Christ, and communicated by Christ does Marmion turn his attention to the religious vocation, since, as he explains,

> He [Christ] is 'the Religious' pre-eminently, the Example of the perfect religious; more than that, He is the very source of perfection, and the consummation of all holiness.... Our religious "holiness" is but the plenitude of our Divine adoption in Jesus.... All that God

---

17 *Christ, The Ideal of the Monk*, pp. 28–29.
18 *Ibid.*, p. 34.
19 *Ibid.*, p. 35.
20 *Ibid.*, p. 37.

enjoins upon us and asks of us, all that Christ counsels us, has no other end than to give us the opportunity of showing that we are God's children and the brethren of Jesus; and when we attain this ideal in everything, not only in our thoughts and actions, but even in the motives from which we act, then we reach perfection.[21]

Marmion sums up perfection as 'this inward disposition of the soul seeking to please the Heavenly Father by living habitually and totally in the spirit of its supernatural adoption.' The perfect soul 'lives *habitually* and *totally* according to grace.'[22] But such a life, whose actions are completely rooted in supernatural charity, is only possible through the grace that comes from Christ as its Source, through abiding with Him, as branches on the Vine, through faith and love.

While this definition of perfection applies to a Christian in any state of life, the religious seeks explicitly to put aside all that could be an obstacle to perfection, in order that his life may be more completely dominated by faith and love which unite Him to Christ. It is Christ Who initiates, models, and consummates this perfection:

> We must be perfect as our Heavenly Father is perfect... but it is God alone Who can make us perfect and He does so by giving us His Son. Therefore all is summed up in constant union with Jesus, in ceaselessly contemplating Him in order to imitate Him, and in doing, at all times, for love, as He did... the things that please the Father.... This is the secret of perfection.[23]

Marmion concludes this fundamental chapter of his monastic doctrine by showing how this conception of the religious life—a life patterned completely on that of Christ, and lived in constant union with and dependence on Christ—is the same which underpins the Rule of Saint Benedict. He cites Saint Benedict's description, given at the beginning of the

---

21 *Ibid.*, p. 38.
22 *Ibid.*, pp. 38–39.
23 *Ibid.*, p. 41.

Prologue to the Rule, of the aspiring monk as one who would 'fight for the Lord Christ, our true King' (*Domino Christo vero Regi militaturus*), a phrase which for him is a key to understanding the entire Rule:

> It is not a mere formula with St Benedict; this idea impregnates the entire Rule and gives it [its] eminently *Christian* character.... The holy Legislator points out by these opening words of his Rule that he intends to take Christ fundamentally as Example and to consider Him as the source of perfection. His Rule is 'Christocentric.'[24]

Marmion points out how Saint Benedict introduces Christ and the love of Christ at the most significant points in the Rule, culminating in the admonition of Chapter 72, 'Let nothing whatever be preferred to Christ, Who deigns to bring us all alike to everlasting life.' (*Christo OMNINO nihil praeponant qui nos pariter ad vitam aeternam perducat.*) The Rule thus ends as it began: 'Christ is the Alpha and Omega of all perfection.' The 'epilogue' to the Rule in Chapter 73 likewise concludes with the phrase *adjuvante Christo*, showing 'that it is by His grace alone we can fulfil the Rule traced out, and thus attain the end proposed at the head of the first page: "to seek God."'[25] Throughout the Rule, especially when proposing difficult things to his disciples, Saint Benedict continually proposes Christ and His love as the motive force for the monk's self-denial, obedience, struggle against temptation, and patience.[26] And Christ is continually spoken of as the inspiration for relations within the monastic community.[27] 'You see how for St Benedict Christ must be everything to the monk. In all things he would have the monk think of Christ, lean upon him.'[28]

---

24 *Ibid.*, pp. 42–43.
25 *Ibid.*, p. 43.
26 *Ibid.*, pp. 43–44, citing Rule of St Benedict [= RSB] Prologue and Chapters 4, 5, and 7.
27 *Ibid.*, p. 44, citing RSB Chapters 2, 4, 36, 53, and 63.
28 *Ibid.*

Guide for the Monastic Life

These truths about the place of Christ in the life of the monk may seem too obvious to need stating, yet in fact Marmion himself sees this Christocentric character as a distinctive feature of Saint Benedict's Rule, somewhat in contrast with other important sources of the ascetical tradition. In an important note at the end of this chapter on 'The Following of Christ', he draws attention to the fact that Saint Benedict, in concluding Chapter VII of the Rule, *De humilitate*, quotes the words of Cassian, but adds *amore Christi*, 'for love of Christ':

> It is a remarkable fact that these two words have sufficed to change essentially the 'physiognomy' and the bearing of the quotation, and to open out a special perspective, unknown to Cassian but revealing the thought of the great Patriarch.[29]

Marmion cites his confrere at Maredsous, Dom Festugière, in support of the idea that Saint Benedict's 'originality' lies in his understanding of grace, as a result of which 'he repudiates rationalistic tendencies and entirely subjects the natural to the supernatural.'[30]

Thus, for Marmion, the genius of the Rule of Saint Benedict lies in its Christocentric character. He sees this trait reproduced in the greatest Benedictine spiritual writers—'the ardent aspirations of St Anselm towards the Word Incarnate, the tenderness of St Bernard's love for Christ, the astonishing familiarities of St Gertrude and St Mechtilde with the Divine Saviour, the burning outpourings of Ven. Blosius to the Sacred Humanity of Jesus.' Ultimately, this is the reason for the Rule's success, for '[t]his way of making everything converge to Christ Jesus... makes the life of the soul powerful.... It renders it attractive, for nothing can more delight the mind and more easily obtain the necessary efforts from the heart than to view the Adorable Person of Christ Jesus.'[31]

---

29 *Ibid.*, p. 44.
30 *Ibid.*
31 *Ibid.*, p. 45.

Having established the centrality of Christ in the life of the monk, first on the basis of Scripture and dogma and then on the testimony of Saint Benedict, Marmion proceeds to show how the monk lives the life of Christ. As mentioned above, his presentation of the monastic life follows the same logic as that of the Christian life in general in *Christ, The Life of the Soul*. Thus, as the opening chapters on Christ in that work were followed by a treatment of the Church as Christ's Mystical Body, so too, having established the place of Christ in the monk's life, Marmion proceeds to speak of the monastic community, which, like the Church, is 'a supernatural society.'[32] He devotes two chapters to the subject of the community. First, he treats of 'The Abbot, Christ's Representative', whose authority lies at the foundation of the community in a way analogous to the position of St Peter and his successors in the Church as a whole: just as 'the first time Christ speaks of His Church it is to indicate its foundation' in Peter, so too, '[a]fter a preliminary chapter where he sets aside the different forms of religious life in order to retain only the cenobitical form, [St Benedict] at once and before all speaks of the Abbot.'[33] Nonetheless, the abbot is not considered as an isolated figure, or as an absolute monarch, but as organically connected to the community. The following chapter, 'The Cenobitical Society', stresses that as '[t]he Sovereign Pontiff, in his teaching, must follow Christ's doctrine and the spirit of tradition', so too 'the Abbot... must not teach ordain, or command anything contrary to the Divine precepts', and as the Pope relies upon the counsel of the Cardinals, so the abbot is to make use of the counsel of his *seniores*, and indeed of the entire community.[34]

However, for Marmion the likeness between the Church and the monastic community does not consist merely in the similarity of their hierarchical structure. Just as the Church,

---

32 *Ibid.*, p. 49.
33 *Ibid.*, pp. 49–50.
34 *Ibid.*, pp. 74–75.

while a visibly ordered society, is at the same time Christ's Mystical Body which gives supernatural life to His members, so also the 'singular graces' intended by God for the religious 'only reach our souls in the same measure that we live by the organic life of the Society whereof we are members.'[35] Thus, as the Christian must remain united to the Church in order to live the life of Christ, so the monk must remain united to the community in order to profit by the grace of his vocation: 'If we put aside the common life, which is the sign of our particular divine election, we shall be like wrecks stranded on the riverbank, doubtless still lapped by the tide, but no longer lifted up and borne along on its impetuous living waters.'[36] The monk must thus guard at all costs against being separated from the common life, either by explicitly withdrawing from it or by making himself 'singular' and despising the community's customs: 'The true monk, whose gaze is ever fixed upon the Divine Model, follows with simplicity and uprightness the customs common to the Community he has entered and which are a sign of the unity that Christ wishes to see reigning among the members of His Mystical Body.'[37]

Marmion thus establishes his presentation of monastic perfection on the same foundation as that which he had previously laid for the supernatural life of every Christian: complete dependence on Christ as the exemplary, meritorious, and efficient cause of all grace, which is communicated to us through our union with Him in His Mystical Body.[38]

---

35 *Ibid.*, p. 86.
36 *Ibid.*
37 *Ibid.*, p. 89.
38 There is an apparent difference between the plan of these opening sections in that in *Christ, The Life of the Soul* the chapter on the Church, the Mystical Body, is followed by that on 'The Holy Spirit, the Spirit of Jesus', while *Christ, The Ideal of the Monk* has no corresponding chapter on the Holy Spirit. However, it is noteworthy that the chapter on 'The Cenobitical Society' concludes with an encomium on the Holy Rule, ending with the Collect for the Votive Mass of Saint Benedict: 'Raise up, O Lord, in Thy Church the spirit that animated our Blessed Father Benedict, Abbot, that being replenished with this same spirit, we may strive to love what he loved

II.B.2. The starting point of monastic perfection: faith and profession.

In *Christ, The Life of the Soul*, Marmion's initial section on 'The Divine Economy' is followed by the treatment of the 'Foundation and Double Aspect of the Christian Life'. The same plan is followed in the second part of *Christ, The Ideal of the Monk*, 'Starting Point and Twofold Character of Monastic Perfection'. Having given a general overview of the monastic life as a following of Christ, united to His Body through the monastic community under its abbot, Marmion describes the origin and progress of monastic holiness in a manner analogous to that of the Christian life as a whole. The first two chapters of this second part correspond exactly to those in the earlier work, on faith and the sacrament of baptism.

In *Christ, The Life of the Soul*, the theological virtue of faith was presented as 'the foundation of the Christian life'. In *Christ, The Ideal of the Monk*, Marmion presents faith, in the words of Saint John, as 'the victory over the world' (1 Jn 5:4). It is faith in Christ that makes us children of God; the same faith is at the foundation of monastic perfection, for Christian perfection and monastic perfection 'both intrinsically belong to the same supernatural order.... A simple Christian is a child of God; a monk is likewise a child of God, but one who seeks, in the largest possible degree and by especially adapted means, to develop this condition of a child of God.'[39]

Thus, since the Christian life is based upon faith, the monk seeks in a particular and very practical way to base his life on that same faith:

> The monastic life, like the Christian life, is the practical consequence of an act of faith.... Why have we become monks? Because we have said to Jesus Christ:

---

and in our actions to practise what he taught.' (*Excita, Domine, in Ecclesia tua, spiritum cui Beatus Pater noster Benedictus abbas servivit, ut eodem nos repleti, studeamus amare quod amavit et opere exercere quod docuit.*) While 'spirit' is not capitalised in the text as quoted by Marmion, the Collect concludes in the Missal with the formula *in unitate ejusdem Spiritus Sancti*, showing that the 'spirit' in question is understood to be the Holy Spirit.

39 *Christ, The Ideal of the Monk*, p. 107.

'Thou art the Christ... Thou art the Fountainhead of all life, of all good, of all perfection, of all beatitude.' And this initial act of faith explains the whole of our conduct.[40]

Indeed, without faith in the Christ, the choice of the monastic life appears to be foolishness. Only faith gives it sense, both when considered as a whole and in the everyday details of monastic life. As Christ's Beatific Vision of the Father was the light in which His human Soul saw all of created reality, so for the monk faith, which gives a participation in God's own knowledge, is the 'deifying light' (*deificum lumen*) spoken of by Saint Benedict, which 'illumines and uplifts our whole life.'[41] While 'the soul that has faith leads outwardly the ordinary existence of the rest of mankind', its human activity is carried out 'in the higher light of Divine truth.'[42]

Once again, Marmion supports his teaching, based as it is on the principles of theology, with the teaching of Saint Benedict, showing how throughout the Holy Rule Saint Benedict demands that the monk act from the supernatural viewpoint of faith. It is thus that monks are to reverence Christ in their abbot, in the guests, and in the sick, and that even the most ordinary objects of the monastery are to be treated with the reverence due to sacred vessels: '[Saint Benedict] understood that all things are only of any value in God's sight according to the measure of our faith.'[43]

And since faith is the foundation upon which the monastic life rests, a monk's spiritual life will be strong and firm in proportion to the degree to which faith is the motivating power of his life:

> [W]hen faith is living, strong, ardent, when we live by faith... when faith is the root of all our actions... then we become strong and steadfast in

---

40 *Ibid.*, p. 108.
41 *Ibid.*, p. 110; cf. RSB Prologue.
42 *Ibid.*, p. 111.
43 *Ibid.*, pp. 112–13; cf. RSB Ch. 2, 31, 36, and 53.

spite of difficulties within and without.... Why so? Because, by faith, we judge, we estimate all things as God sees and estimates them: we participate in the Divine immutability and stability.[44]

Such a living faith preserves the monk from the danger of routine, and gives him the supernatural joy which Saint Benedict promises to the monk whose heart is enlarged with the sweetness of love as he progresses in faith: *Processu vero conversationis et fidei, dilatato corde, inenarrabili dilectionis duldecine curritur.*[45]

However, just as the Christian life requires not only the inward virtue of faith, but incorporation into the visible organism of the Church through the sacraments, so too the monastic life requires not only living according to Saint Benedict's spirit, but being bound to the monastic community by profession. Marmion sees this as the completion of faith through charity: 'Faith brought [the monk] to the threshold of the cloister, love expressed by solemn engagement will attach him to the monastic life: that will be the work of his Profession.'[46] Following an ancient tradition, Marmion likens monastic profession to baptism: 'Baptism places the neophyte in God's family and seals him with the character of Christian; the Profession or emission of vows places the novice in the monastic family and consecrates him to God's service that he may become a perfect disciple of Christ Jesus.'[47] Like baptism, profession renders the soul pleasing to God and makes her a new creation: 'At this blessed hour, the soul is given to Jesus as the bride to the bridegroom.... The Heavenly Father can say of this soul as of the newly baptized who has just "put on Christ": "This is my Beloved child in whom I am well pleased."'[48]

In *Christ, The Life of the Soul*, Marmion had stressed that the grace of baptism consists especially in participating in

---

44 *Ibid.*, p. 114.
45 *Ibid.*, p. 117; RSB Prologue.
46 *Ibid.*, p. 121.
47 *Ibid.*, p. 122.
48 *Ibid.*, p.131.

Guide for the Monastic Life

Christ's Death and Resurrection.[49] Now, in presenting monastic profession, Marmion likewise focuses on profession as a participation in Christ's Sacrifice.[50] Thus, it consists first in a death, a renunciation of creatures, in order then to live for God: 'Separation from all that is earthly... is the first aspect of holiness; the donation of oneself to God is the second. But it is necessary to be "separated" in order to be "consecrated."'[51]

This twofold aspect of death and life found in profession will structure the remainder of Marmion's monastic conferences, as the same aspects of baptism also structured the treatment of the life of grace in his earlier work, for the entirety of the Christian and monastic life consists in the development of what is contained in these foundational acts. Marmion earlier stated that '[a]ll Christian asceticism proceeds from baptismal grace', and aims 'to cultivate the Divine germ cast into the soul by the Church on the day of her children's initiation.'[52] So too, while '[t]he act of profession itself only lasts a few moments... its effects are permanent and its fruits eternal', and the remainder of the monk's life is 'like the gradual developing of an initial act of immense weight.'[53] Thus, as the Christian should often 'renew the virtue of [the] sacrament of adoption and initiation by renewing the promises made in Baptism',[54] the monk should often renew the promises of his profession, for 'there is no state so precious in [God's] sight as that of constancy in the dispositions wherein the soul was

---

49 See *Christ, The Life of the Soul*, p. 149; cf. Rom. 6: 3–13; St Thomas, ST III, q. 66, a. 2 and q. 69, a. 2.
50 As Marmion notes towards the beginning of his chapter on monastic profession, the texts and images which he uses in speaking of profession highlight primarily its character as an oblation, rather than as a second baptism. However, since, following Saint Paul and Saint Thomas, he present baptism itself primarily in terms of a share in Christ's Death and Resurrection, the chapter on profession in fact is still intimately related to Marmion's understanding of baptism.
51 *Christ, The Ideal of the Monk*, p. 129.
52 *Christ, The Life of the Soul*, p. 153.
53 *Christ, The Ideal of the Monk*, p. 131.
54 *Christ, The Life of the Soul*, p. 154.

at that moment.'⁵⁵ Borrowing words of Saint Paul regarding ordination, Marmion describes both the renewal of baptismal promises and the monk's renewal of profession as means to 'stir up' the grace of God received in those initial moments.⁵⁶

Yet while in one sense the entire grace of the Christian life and the monastic life are contained in these initial moments, Marmion reminds the reader that these graces are given as a seed whose development will be long and laborious. Thus, in the final section of his chapter on baptism, he states that 'in Baptism God does not give us back at once all the integrity of the Divine gift.' Concupiscence remains for the Christian to struggle with, so that the work of death to sin and life to God must continue throughout the Christian's life:

> Therefore our whole existence ought to be the realisation of what Baptism inaugurates. By Baptism, we communicate in the mystery and divine virtue of Christ's death and risen life... but on account of the concupiscence remaining in us, we must maintain this death by continual renunciation.... Grace is the principle of life in us, but it is a germ we must cultivate.... Our work therefore is to guard and develop this germ until at the last day we arrive at the fulness of the age of Christ.... *Christian life is nothing else but the progressive and continuous development, the practical application, throughout our whole life, of this double supernatural result of 'death' and of 'life' produced by Baptism.* There is all the program of Christianity.'⁵⁷

In turn, the grace of profession is likewise a seed that must be cultivated: 'religious Profession is only the beginning of our real monastic life.... The faith that gave us up to Christ when we pronounced our Vows ought to continue to be a daily principle of action in us; it ought, if it is to be perfect, to blossom into love and... set all our energies in motion, in

---

55 *Christ, The Ideal of the Monk*, p. 135.
56 2 Tim 1:6; *Christ, The Life of the Soul*, p. 155; *Christ, The Ideal of the Monk*, p. 135.
57 *Christ, The Life of the Soul*, p. 153 (emphasis original).

order that we may work out our union with Christ Jesus.'[58]

Marmion thus proceeds in subsequent chapters to speak about the progressive development, through the practice of good works and the virtues, of the initial grace given in baptism and profession. In *Christ, The Life of the Soul*, this occurs in two chapters, 'The Truth in Charity', and 'Our Supernatural Growth in Christ'. The first of these succinctly sums up the nature of the good works we are called to: 'the supernatural life must be maintained in us by human acts, animated by sanctifying grace and referred to God through charity.'[59] Marmion reminds his readers that a Christian must first of all fulfill the precepts of the natural law, acting in accord with right reason, lest '[one's] religion spoil his morality'.[60] Nonetheless, for such acts to have supernatural value they must be done in charity, that is, for love of God, which springs from the grace of Divine adoption. The following chapter describes how the supernatural life which is expressed in such good works is called to grow and become perfect through the life of the virtues, all of which are ruled by charity: 'It is charity that, properly speaking, rules the measure of the Divine life in us.'[61] And thus the Christian should seek, as much as possible, to renew in every act the charity which should be his constant intention.[62]

As the supernatural life begun in baptism is expressed and perfected through good works and the virtues, so too the life of perfection to which the monk is committed by his profession requires the exercise of the 'instruments of good works', and thus Marmion follows his chapter on profession with a discussion of good works in the monastic life. His presentation again closely follows his general treatment of good works

---

58 *Christ, The Ideal of the Monk*, pp. 139–40.
59 *Christ, The Life of the Soul*, p. 198.
60 Words of William Gladstone, cited in *Christ, The Life of the Soul*, p. 199–200.
61 *Christ, The Life of the Soul*, p. 221.
62 *Ibid.*, p. 226–27.

and the life of virtue in *Christ, The Life of the Soul*.⁶³ Noting that Saint Benedict's catalogue of instruments of good works includes many elements addressed to all Christians, Marmion says that the monk must be 'first of all a man who observes the natural law, and then fully practices the Christian law.' As in his previous work, however, Marmion stresses above all that it is only the grace of Christ which confers supernatural value on a monk's works: 'We must be convinced... that our works are only of value by reason of our union with Jesus.'⁶⁴ And for the monk, as for every Christian, this union with Jesus is above all seen in the charity which must be the motive for a monk's works, and which he should renew frequently in all of his actions: 'O Jesus, I wish to live by Thy life, through faith and love; I wish Thy desires to be my desires, and, like Thee, out of love for Thy Father, I wish to do all that may be pleasing to Thee.'⁶⁵

II.B.3. Death to Sin—Leaving All Things. Having established the foundation of the monastic life in faith and profession, which is to be lived out in good works performed in charity, Marmion devotes the second half of *Christ, The Ideal of the Monk* to a fuller exposition of the twofold dynamic contained in monastic profession, and which is expressed in the words of Saint Peter to Our Lord: *Ecce nos reliquimus omnia et secuti sumus te*: 'Behold we have left all things and have followed

---

63 It should be noted that the placement of the subject of good works is somewhat different in the two books: in *Christ, The Life of the Soul* the chapters just discussed are separated from that on baptism by the section on 'Death to Sin', while in *Christ, The Ideal of the Monk* the chapter on 'The Instruments of Good Works' immediately follows that on profession, before the section on 'The Way of Abnegation'. Nonetheless, it is clear from the content that 'The Instruments of Good Works' is the monastic counterpart of the chapters 'Truth in Charity' and 'Our Supernatural Growth in Christ'. The lack of complete parallelism can perhaps be explained by the fact that the rejection of sin (at least mortal sin) is necessary in order to practice good works and virtue in a supernatural way, while the chapters on the way of abnegation deal not so much with the rejection of sin itself as with the ways in which the monk dies to any remaining attachments to creatures.
64 *Christ, The Ideal of the Monk*, p. 151.
65 *Ibid.*, pp. 158–59.

Guide for the Monastic Life

Thee.'⁶⁶ Marmion cites this text at the beginning of the chapter on good works, to explain what happened in profession; he proceeds to use the two parts of the verse to structure the remainder of his conferences. *Reliquimus omnia* sets the theme for 'The Way of Abnegation', while *et secuti sumus te* sets the theme for 'The Way of Union'.

In presenting the entire monastic life as a development of the twofold movement of profession—leaving all things created, in order to cling to Christ—Marmion again patterns the monastic life on the Christian life received in baptism. As described above, the second part of *Christ, The Life of the Soul* presents the Christian life in terms of the death to sin and life to God which are contained in baptism, and *Christ, The Ideal of the Monk* will do the same with the life of Christian perfection pursued by the monk.

The section of 'Death to Sin' in *Christ, The Life of the Soul* is fairly brief, consisting of two chapters on sin and penance. Perhaps because the perfection sought by the monk requires a more complete renunciation of all that could hinder the life of God, the 'negative' section of *Christ, The Ideal of the Monk*, 'The Way of Abnegation', is much longer. It begins, however, in the same place: with the rejection of sin, this time with a chapter on 'Compunction of Heart', defined as 'an abiding state of habitual contrition.'⁶⁷ Marmion considers compunction to be the secret of stability in the spiritual life, and laments the neglect of this virtue in modern spirituality. Far from destroying joy and confidence, true compunction, says Marmion, by purifying the soul, 'strengthens our confidence in God's forgiveness and confirms our soul in peace.'⁶⁸

From compunction follow the other acts and virtues of abnegation, including those which are more particular to the

---

66   Matt. 19:27. This Gospel text, used in the Roman Missal in the Common of Abbots, is also used in the monastic Propers for the feasts and votive Masses of Saint Benedict. It would thus have been very familiar to Abbot Marmion and his monastic audience.
67   *Christ, The Ideal of the Monk*, p. 173.
68   Ibid., p. 182.

monastic life. Marmion treats of these, as it were, beginning from the outside and working his way into the interior. Thus, the chapter on compunction is followed by 'Self-Renunciation', which speaks of practices of mortification. Characteristically, Marmion presents these above all as a means of union with Christ's expiation, from which they derive all their value, and he affirms Saint Benedict's concern that all personal practices of mortification be submitted to obedience. Next comes 'Poverty': while treating of the obvious material implications of this virtue, Marmion presents it above all as an imitation of the inner life of Christ, Who even in His Divinity had nothing that He had not received from the Father.

The way of abnegation concludes with the chapters on the virtues that most cut to the heart of the old man: humility and its inseparable companion, obedience. In 'Humility', which stands at the centre of *Christ, The Ideal of the Monk* and is by far its longest chapter, Marmion explains that pride is the principal obstacle to God's desire to communicate Himself to the soul, and thus humility is the key to union with God. He examines Saint Benedict's twelve degrees of humility in the light of the teaching of Saint Thomas, and concludes by presenting Christ's humiliation and exaltation as the law which 'touches all the members whereof He is the Head.'[69] And since 'the practical expression of humility, with the monk, is obedience,'[70] in '*Bonum Obedientiae*' Marmion presents the implications of this most monastic virtue, patterned upon the obedience of Christ, 'the means preordained by God for saving the world and restoring to it the heavenly inheritance.'[71]

II.B.4. Life for God—Following Christ. Just as in the Holy Rule Saint Benedict's ladder of humility in Chapter 7 leads directly to the presentation of the Divine Office and prayer in Chapters 8 through 20, so Marmion's chapters on humility and obedience are followed by three chapters on prayer: two on liturgical prayer and one on personal prayer. A somewhat

---

69 *Ibid.*, p. 281.
70 *Ibid.*, p. 283.
71 *Ibid.*, p. 287.

Guide for the Monastic Life

similar approach was followed in *Christ, The Life of the Soul*, where, after the chapters on good works and virtue, Marmion had devoted two chapters to the Holy Eucharist as Sacrifice and Sacrament, then one chapter each to the Divine Office and to personal prayer.

The centrality of the Divine Office in a monk's life is seen in the fact that Marmion devotes two entire chapters to it: 'The *Opus Dei*, Divine Praise', and 'The *Opus Dei*, Means of Union with God'. The first focuses on the primary purpose of the Office, to give God glory for His own sake. Further developing ideas presented in the chapter '*Vox Sponsae*' in his earlier work, Marmion sets the Church's liturgy on the foundation of the Eternal Son's praise of the Father: 'The Word is the Canticle that God inwardly sings to Himself... the Living Canticle wherein God eternally delights, because it is the infinite expression of His perfection.'[72] In the Incarnation, and then in the Church's liturgy, this eternal praise enters creation, as Christ associates us to His own praise of the Father: 'Such is the fundamental reason of the transcendency of the *Opus Dei*.'[73] But the Divine Office, as it glorifies God, also sanctifies man. Marmion cites the words of Pius X, written not long before, that the Sacred Liturgy is 'the first and indispensable source whence is drawn the true Christian spirit.'[74] If this be true for all Christians, then in light of Saint Benedict's teaching that 'among all the positive works of piety that his monks are to perform, none is to take precedence of the Divine Office', the monk must realize that 'the Divine Praise constitutes one of the most infallible means of realizing in ourselves the eternal and special idea that God has of our perfection.'[75] Accordingly, Marmion devotes his second chapter on the liturgy to the necessary dispositions for the monk to pray the Divine Office fruitfully, in union with Christ.

---

72   *Ibid.*, p. 333.
73   *Ibid.*, p. 337.
74   *Tra le sollecitudini*, 22 November 1903, cited in Marmion, *Christ, The Ideal of the Monk*, p. 352.
75   *Christ, The Ideal of the Monk*, p. 353.

Then, just as Saint Benedict follows his chapters on the Divine Office with the precious Chapter 20, *De reverentia orationis*, Marmion's teaching on the *Opus Dei* is followed by a substantial chapter on 'Monastic Prayer', tracing its development through the purgative, illuminative, and unitive ways. While this framework, also used in the corresponding chapter of *Christ, The Life of the Soul*, is common to the entire spiritual tradition of the Church, Marmion places at the centre of the chapter an emphasis that is characteristically Benedictine and also in keeping with the fundamental idea of his work. For Marmion, mental prayer is fundamentally a contemplation of Christ, Who is 'the great revelation of God ... God interpreted to our souls.'[76] And since Christ's mysteries are best set forth for us in the Church's liturgy, the liturgy is the best source for the monk's prayer, in order that He can appropriate all the fruits of Christ's mysteries. This liturgical approach to prayer leads a monk's prayer to become, 'not exclusively but mostly, affective.'[77] The Divine Office disposes the monk to pour out his heart to God in prayer without words: 'we stay looking at Him, praising Him, adoring Him, were it only by a humble attitude, full of reverence and confidence.' Thus, the Divine Office leads the soul to 'the fountainhead of a life of intense union.'[78] Marmion concludes with a description of the unitive state: while ordinarily God does not grant this 'until the evening of life, when the soul has proved, by a constant fidelity to the inspirations of grace, that it belongs wholly to God', nonetheless 'it is to this life of union that the monk's whole existence should tend; otherwise it is useless.'[79] Nourished by the practice of silence, solitude, and holy reading—living habitually in the presence of God, even while setting aside specific times for the formal exercise of prayer—'monastic life necessarily becomes an ascending pathway towards God.' Such a life of continual prayer is 'the normal state of a religious

---

76   *Ibid.*, p. 396.
77   *Ibid.*, p. 402.
78   *Ibid.*, pp. 402–03.
79   *Ibid.*, p. 405.

Guide for the Monastic Life

in his monastery... the necessary expansion of our grace of adoption, of our monastic vocation.'[80]

The three chapters on prayer are followed by three concluding chapters which illustrate the dispositions which result from a monk's union with God: 'The Spirit of Abandonment to God's Will', 'Good Zeal', and 'The Peace of Christ'. Marmion describes the spirit of abandonment as embodied in the *Suscipe* sung by the monk at his profession, with its confident cry: *Non confundas me ab exspectatione mea!*[81] Closely related to the spirit of faith spoken of at the beginning of the work, the spirit of abandonment 'inspires all the acts that are derived from [our] profession as from their point of departure', and 'gives them their supreme fecundity,' for 'holy abandonment is one of the purest and most absolute forms of love... when the spirit of abandonment to God animates a monk's whole life, that monk has attained holiness.'[82] The objective basis for this abandonment is, not surprisingly, the Divine plan revealed in Christ, which assures us of the Father's love: 'To make us His children, God gives us His Son Christ Jesus: that is love's supreme gift.... God grants us to find in the Son of His delight the well spring of *all* grace and *all* perfection.... Shall we not, therefore, abandon ourselves in all confidence to this all-powerful Will, which is love itself...?'[83] The spirit of abandonment brings 'peace and deep joy' to those who practice it, 'because they know they are in the hands of the best of fathers, the most faithful of friends, the most tender of spouses.'[84]

The next result of the life of union is the fraternal charity that Marmion, following Saint Benedict in Chapter 72 of the Rule, describes as 'good zeal'. He describes how this zeal is manifested both in fraternal life in the monastery, especially in patiently bearing one another's infirmities, and also in such works of apostolate which a monastery or a monk may

---

80   *Ibid.*, p. 416.
81   'Do not disappoint me in my hope', Psalm 118:116.
82   *Christ, The Ideal of the Monk*, p. 420.
83   *Ibid.*, pp. 423–24.
84   *Ibid.*, p. 444.

undertake with the blessing of obedience. As Saint Benedict's description of good zeal culminates with the command *Christo nihil omnino praeponant* (Let them prefer nothing whatsoever to Christ), so Marmion's chapter concludes by bringing the focus back directly to the '*absolute* love which we ought to bear to the Person of Christ Jesus.'[85]

Finally, as in *Christ, The Life of the Soul* Marmion had concluded with a meditation on the eternal beatitude to which our Divine adoption is meant to lead ('*Coheredes Christi*'),[86] he concludes *Christ, The Ideal of the Monk* with a vision of the peace that Christ bestows on those who truly seek God in all things: 'In the centre of the soul that loves God there rises up the *civitas pacis* which no noise of earth can trouble, that no attack can surprise.'[87] Marmion says that the entire Rule is ordered towards this peace, for peace is the 'tranquillity of order', and Divine order is reestablished in the soul that seeks God alone, and does so through Christ:

> Such is, in brief, the whole of the Divine order shown forth by the holy Legislator with an admirable simplicity of outline. To return to God by Christ, to seek God in Christ, to tend towards God in the footsteps of Christ.... Happy the monk who walks in this

---

[85] *Ibid.*, p. 474.
[86] The parallels between *Christ, The Life of the Soul* and *Christ, The Ideal of the Monk* are admittedly somewhat harder to discern in the final chapters. While 'Love One Another' bears a fairly clear relation to 'Good Zeal', it is harder to discern a counterpart to 'The Mother of the Incarnate Word' and '*Coheredes Christi*'. As suggested here, Marmion's description of the peace of Christ does in some way mirror the earlier work's chapter on beatitude, both of them describing the fruit of the life of grace in the soul. One might well regret, on the other hand, that *Christ, The Ideal of the Monk* does not have any significant treatment of Our Lady's place in the monk's life. It is nonetheless interesting to note that, towards the beginning of 'The Spirit of Abandonment to God's Will', Marmion describes holiness as 'the *fiat* full of love, whereby the whole creature responds, unceasingly and unfalteringly, to all of the Divine Will.' (p. 420) The use of the term *fiat* (cf. Luke 1:38), which appears only here in *Christ, The Ideal of the Monk*, suggests that 'The Spirit of Abandonment' could indeed be considered implicitly as the 'Marian' chapter of Marmion's monastic teaching.
[87] *Christ, The Ideal of the Monk*, p. 492.

path! Even in the greatest sufferings... he will find light, peace, and joy. Everything is ordered in his soul as God wills it, and all his desires are unified in the one sole Good for Whom he is created.'[88]

With this recapitulation of his opening themes, Marmion concludes *Christ, The Ideal of the Monk*. It would be hard to identify any work which provides a better synthesis of the theology and spirituality of Benedictine life. While he does not aim to provide a systematic commentary on the Rule of Saint Benedict, Marmion's vision of our life in Christ enables him to set forth the theological foundations of Saint Benedict's teaching in a manner that is intellectually coherent, stirs up the affections to love the ideals he proposes, and provides clear direction for the soul that desires to put these ideals into practice.

III. CONCLUSION: MARMION AS A GUIDE FOR MONASTIC LIFE TODAY

A hundred years have passed since Abbot Marmion's death; a hundred years which have witnessed radical changes in the world, in the Church, and in monastic life. Yet Marmion's monastic teaching remains as fresh and relevant to monastic life today as it did in his own time. What is the secret of his continued appeal, and what does Marmion have to teach monastics in the early twenty-first century?

III.A. A timeless message rooted in Christ

Throughout the preceding sections, we have seen again and again that for Marmion the monastic life is the Christian life writ large, and thus the central truths of the Christian life are also the central truths of monastic life. Marmion's enduring significance for monastic life in our time is thus, in the end, based on the same reasons that make his work continually relevant for all Christians seeking holiness. Marmion's genius lies in the way in which he grasped the heart of the Divine plan of salvation—our adoption as sons in Christ—and consistently

---

88 *Ibid.*, p. 497.

viewed all of the Christian life in the light of this simple but infinitely rich truth. The result is a spiritual vision which nourishes contemplation and at the same time inspires the soul in the practice of virtue.[89] It is a vision which, because it is based upon the essential truths of Revelation, can never be out-of-date, which Pope Benedict XV aptly characterized as 'the pure doctrine of the Church'.[90] This same simple and profound vision of our life in Christ can and must be the source of renewal for monastic life in the Church today, and thereby be a source of renewal for the entire Church, which draws her spiritual strength from the hidden springs of the cloister.

As was pointed out at the beginning of this article, Marmion's own monastic life was shaped by the revival of the nineteenth century which gave new life to monasticism after the devastation it had suffered in early modern times. Marmion was the heir of this revival as it had expressed itself, for instance, at Solesmes, at Subiaco, and at Beuron. But his own vision of life in Christ, grounded in his study of Saint Paul and of Saint Thomas, and nourished in his own life of monastic observance and prayer, allowed him to articulate in a unique way the Christological foundations of the monastic life as it is found in the Rule of Saint Benedict. Thus, on the one hand, Marmion reminds monastics that their life must be based on nothing more nor less than the central truths of the Christian faith. On the other hand, he reminds the entire Church that it is the monastic life which embodies most fully in this life the truths which should animate every Christian life. We might sum up Marmion's value for understanding monastic life by saying that Marmion can remind monks that they should above all be Christians, and can help Christians understand why they should be, or at least in some way aspire to be, monks!

---

89 See the observations of Marmion's confrere, Dom Bernard Capelle, 'Marmion's Place in the History of Spirituality', in *Abbot Marmion: An Irish Tribute*, ed. by the Monks of Glenstal (Cork: Mercier Press, 1948), pp. 10–20.
90 Words of Pope Benedict XV to Archbishop Szeptickij, cited in Dom Raymond Thibault, *Abbot Columba Marmion: A Master of the Spiritual Life*, trans. Mother Mary St Thomas (London: Sands, 1932), p. 353.

III.B. Marmion's message for monastics

With regard to the first point, Marmion challenges monks never to forget that their life has no other foundation than faith in Jesus Christ, the one Mediator between God and man, the unique Source and Model of holiness. It is a teaching which is echoed by the principal pronouncements of the Magisterium on consecrated life in our time. The Second Vatican Council set forth as the first principle of renewal of the religious life that 'the ultimate norm of religious life is the following of Christ set forth in the Gospels'.[91] Several decades later, John Paul II, in an exposition which seems to owe much to Marmion's vision, proclaimed:

> [C]onsecrated persons not only make Christ the whole meaning of their lives but strive to reproduce in themselves, as far as possible, "that form of life which he, as the Son of God, accepted in entering this world".... His way of living in chastity, poverty and obedience appears as the most radical way of living the Gospel on this earth, a way which may be called divine, for it was embraced by him, God and man, as the expression of his relationship as the Only-Begotten Son with the Father and with the Holy Spirit.... The consecrated life truly constitutes a living memorial of Jesus' way of living and acting as the Incarnate Word in relation to the Father and in relation to the brethren.[92]

This Christocentric vision of the religious life, and of the monastic life in particular, may seem basic and self-evident. Yet in fact it is precisely these basic truths which are sometimes forgotten by monks themselves, and which must be continually recalled if monastic life is to be renewed at its authentic sources. Otherwise, monastic life easily risks deviating along paths which take it away from Christ Who is the only source of its fruitfulness—a deviation which can happen in several ways—for instance, through relativism, through activism

---

91 *Perfectae caritatis* 2.
92 *Vita consecrata* 16, 18, 22.

and worldliness, or through semi-Pelagianism and formalism.

III.B.1. Against relativism: Christ the only Way. With regard to relativism, a notable phenomenon in Catholic monastic life over the past decades has been the establishment of many forms of dialogue with monastic traditions outside the Church, even with non-Christian monastics. While such dialogues, if carried out with due regard to avoid any form of syncretism, can offer certain potential benefits, they undeniably pose real dangers, not least the possibility that those things which are distinctive to Christian and Catholic faith could come to be seen as of secondary importance.

Marmion's monastic teaching provides a bracing antidote to any such religious relativism. For Marmion, Christian monasticism is based upon and modeled upon the Christian life, which is founded upon faith in Jesus Christ's divinity, has its starting point in baptism, and presupposes living membership in Christ's Mystical Body, the Catholic Church. Were he writing today, Marmion would surely remind us, serenely but clearly, that any form of monastic life that is not based upon faith in Christ may indeed possess many of the same external features as Benedictine life, but will lack its very soul, since Saint Benedict's spirit is marked by nothing so much as his constant focus on Christ: 'for St Benedict Christ must be everything for the monk.'[93] Non-Christian monasticism, like other vestiges of truth found in non-Christian religions, may indeed bear a certain outward similarity to Christian monasticism, yet it differs from it essentially as the shadow does from the reality, and only through faith in Christ can it be purified from human error and demonic deception in order to attain union with the Triune God.

III.B.2. Against activism and worldliness: Seeking God alone. Even where faith in Christ is clearly affirmed as the foundation of the monastic life, the temptation of activism can easily take a monk's focus from Christ. In an age where many ancient monastic communities are aging and declining in

---

93 Marmion, *Christ, The Ideal of the Monk*, p. 44.

numbers, while newer communities are facing the challenges of foundation and initial growth, monks are probably busier than ever before. The general decline of religious and priestly vocations in the developed world can lead to increasing pressure being made upon monastic orders to become involved in seemingly urgent works of apostolate. The desire to respond to the needs of our times can cause monastics, like religious in general, to become involved in social action on behalf of the innocent unborn, of migrants and refugees, or of the protection of the environment.

Due to these trends, along with the ever-increasing presence of means of instant communication even in the cloister, the temptation to activism is probably greater than ever before. The Second Vatican Council concluded its principles for the renewal of religious life with the reminder that 'even the best adjustments made in accordance with the needs of our age will be ineffectual unless they are animated by a renewal of spirit', which 'must take precedence over even the active ministry'.[94] Yet the decades since the Council have, if anything, witnessed an even greater tendency towards activism and the adoption of a worldly mentality, not only in the Church in general but even in monastic communities, seen, for instance, in the dramatic reductions made to the Divine Office, the loss in many communities of effective separation from the world, and the incursions of modern means of communication on the spirit of silence.

In the face of all of these temptations to activism and worldliness, Marmion proposes to us a clear vision of why the monastery exists: to seek God through the following of Christ:

> 'To attain to God,' this is the end that St Benedict wishes us to have ever before our eyes. This principle, like a life-giving sap, circulates through all the articles of the monastic code. We have not come to the monastery then, in order to devote ourselves to science, nor the arts, nor the work of education ... the end is

---

94 *Perfectae caritatis* 2.

> higher: it is in God, it is God sought for Himself, as the Supreme Beatitude.... St Benedict will have us seek God,—seek Him for His own glory, because we love Him above all things. He would have us seek to unite ourselves to Him by charity. There is not, for us, any other end, or any other perfection.[95]

And since Christ alone is the Way to union with God, the monk's single-minded pursuit of God means a single-minded focus upon Christ: 'So throughout our life, whatever be the state of our soul and the circumstances that may arise, we ought never to turn our gaze away from Christ.'[96]

The monk who allows himself to be imbued with Marmion's understanding of our life in Christ will find in this truth a lasting safeguard against temptations to activism and a worldly mentality. At the same time, monastic communities which are formed by his vision, who make faith in Christ truly the foundation of their life, will be moved to order their lives in ways that consciously give primacy to the monastery's supernatural end, even when this may defy what the world considers useful. In particular, a monk or a community whose focus is on seeking God and whose foundation is faith in Christ will follow faithfully Saint Benedict's injunction to 'prefer nothing to the work of God', that is, to the worship of God in choir.[97] Marmion himself makes it clear that the primacy given to the Divine Office follows from the very nature of the monastic life:

> Now we, as religious, are seeking God; it was for this that we came to the monastery; what is more natural therefore than to adopt the Divine Office as our principal work, by which we especially devote ourselves to God's service? How are we 'to seek Him truly'... unless we occupy ourselves first of all with Him, with His perfections and His works?'[98]

---

95 Marmion, *Christ, The Ideal of the Monk*, pp. 7–8.
96 *Ibid.*, p. 43.
97 RSB Ch. 43.
98 *Christ, The Ideal of the Monk*, p. 331.

The primacy given to the *Opus Dei*, then, shows that a monk and a monastery are truly seeking God. It likewise shows that they desire to be united as fully as possible to Christ, Who is our only Way to the Father, for '[t]hrough the Divine Praise, we associate creation and ourselves, as intimately as possible, with the eternal praise that the Word gives to His Father.'[99] Marmion's Christocentric vision of the monastic life thus provides the best possible inspiration for monks and monasteries to ward off the temptation of activism and worldliness and remain focused on what the Church describes as their principal duty, 'to offer a service to the divine majesty at once humble and noble within the walls of the monastery'.[100]

III.B.3. Against semi-Pelagianism and formalism: The primacy of grace and charity. Finally, however, even for monks and communities which resist the errors of relativism and the pressure of activism and worldliness, there remains perhaps a more subtle danger: that of semi-Pelagianism in the spiritual life and formalism in monastic observance. The past two decades have seen a new generation embracing many aspects of the Church's liturgical and ascetical tradition which had been forgotten in initial post-Conciliar period, a movement which has led many to embrace traditional forms of monastic life marked by strict observance of the Rule and careful attention to the Sacred Liturgy. Marmion himself, drawn as he was to join the Benedictine revival of his time, would certainly have

---

99   *Ibid.*, p. 341.
100 *Perfectae caritatis* 9. The text cited acknowledges that monks offer this service 'whether they dedicate themselves entirely to divine worship in the contemplative life or have legitimately undertaken some apostolate or work of Christian charity'. Marmion himself, towards the end of his chapter on 'Good Zeal' (Christ, The Ideal of the Monk, pp. 466-474), praises the various forms of monastic apostolate on behalf of souls. Such apostolic efforts, already present in the life of Saint Benedict and developed by the succeeding Benedictine tradition, very much characterised Marmion's own monastic life. Nonetheless it is clear that for Marmion all such works are of secondary importance. This can be seen in the plan of *Christ, The Ideal of the Monk*, whose section on 'The Life of Union' begins with two substantial chapters on the *Opus Dei*, chapters which establish its primacy on the basis of the fundamental principles with which the book began.

sympathized with the aspirations of these young religious. But his spiritual vision and his deep knowledge of the human soul would also have cautioned them to be on guard against the subtle ways in which, in any such movement, human activity (semi-Pelagianism) and external observances (formalism) can easily become substitutes for the grace and charity of Christ.

It is fundamentally to the ever-present temptation of semi-Pelagianism that Marmion speaks when, both in *Christ, The Life of the Soul* and *Christ, The Ideal of the Monk*, he laments the lack of progress made by souls who rely on their own conceptions of holiness rather than on the Divine plan of our sanctification in Christ. It is thus that, in his discussion of the place of good works in the progress of the spiritual life, he ever echoes Saint Benedict's insistence that all be referred to the action of Divine grace: 'We must be convinced... that our works are only of value by reason of our union with Jesus.'[101] The remembrance of this fundamental truth of the Christian life, far from making the soul complacent, will enable it to persevere by inspiring boundless confidence in God, thus warding off the discouragement and scrupulosity which handicap so many souls who desire perfection:

> The devil delights... in urging us to sadness, to discouragement, because he well knows that when the soul is sad it is led to abandon the exercise of good works.... When therefore a like sadness arises in our heart, we may be assured that it comes from the devil or from our own pride.... Could a movement of distrust, of despair, come from God? Never, *nunquam*.... As long as we are here below we must never lose confidence: because the satisfactions and merits of Christ Jesus are infinite... because Jesus prays and pleads for us with His Father.[102]

In addition to warning against semi-Pelagianism, whose attitude of pride so easily leads to discouragement, Marmion is also on guard against a formalistic approach to outward observances, which he censures in some of his strongest language:

---

101 Marmion, *Christ, The Ideal of the Monk*, p. 151.
102 *Ibid.*, pp. 154–55.

> Praiseworthy though it be ardently to seek God by good works and especially by works of the Rule, we must yet be forearmed against a certain erroneous conception of perfection, which is sometimes to be met with in not very enlightened souls. It may happen that these place the *whole* of perfection in the *merely outward and material observance*. Although the word I am going to use is severe, I do not hesitate to pronounce it: the abovesaid prejudicial idea would border upon pharisaism...[103]

Just as the Christian life itself does not consist principally in outward observances, however necessary these may be, Marmion stresses that the outward observances of the monastic life do not constitute its essence:

> It may happen that a monk succeeds by force of will and energy in keeping all the rules, and yet has no monastic spirit, no true inner life: there is the body, but not the soul. And in fact it is not so rare to find religious whose spiritual progress is very slow, although their outward exactitude lends itself to no reproach. It is because there is often only self-seeking and self-complacency in this exactitude, or because they look down on their brethren who do not appear to be so faithful; or else because they put their perfection in the exterior observance itself.[104]

Thus, for all his devotion to the Holy Rule, Marmion reminds the monk that it is 'a means of arriving at holiness.... What is important in our observance is the *inner principle* that animates us.'[105] Echoing the evangelical primacy of love found in Saint Benedict's catalogue of instruments of good works, Marmion declares: 'Love it is that measures, in the last resort, the value of all our actions, even the most ordinary.'[106] And so he calls the monk to 'the exactitude of love', which will never make light of the Rule, but which at the same time gives 'a

---

103 *Ibid.*, p. 155.
104 *Ibid.*, p. 157.
105 *Ibid.*, p. 158.
106 *Ibid.*, p. 159.

great liberty of spirit in regard to observances', knowing, like Christ, how to evaluate all prescriptions in light of the great commandment of charity.[107]

III.C. Marmion's monastic message for all Christians

In many ways, then, Marmion's teaching on the monastic life can provide monks and communities today with a coherent vision of monastic holiness, based on the essentials of the Christian faith, safe from relativistic distortions, from activist and worldly compromises, and from semi-Pelagian and formalistic counterfeits. At the same time, his monastic doctrine is a challenge to the entire Church to give the monastic vocation its due place in the understanding of the Christian life.

This is quite timely in an era that has seen much confusion regarding the Church's traditional doctrine regarding the states of the Christian life and their relation one to another. The Church's Tradition, based on Our Lord's own words and example, has always recognized the religious life, and monastic life in particular, to be an objectively superior way of living the Gospel, and one which can procure a greater degree of heavenly glory. Saint Thomas, following the teaching of the Fathers, was not afraid to draw practical consequences from this truth regarding the legitimacy and desirability (*in se*) for every Christian of pursuing the path of the counsels.[108] Throughout the Christian centuries, this conviction that the

---

107 *Ibid.* pp. 160–161.
108 See ST II-II, q. 189, esp. a.10: 'Long deliberation and the advice of many are required in great matters of doubt... while advice is unnecessary in matters that are certain and fixed. Now with regard to entering religion three points may be considered. First, the entrance itself into religion, considered by itself; and thus it is certain that entrance into religion is a greater good, and to doubt about this is to disparage Christ Who gave this counsel.... Secondly, the entrance into religion may be considered in relation to the strength of the person who intends to enter. And here again there is no room for doubt about the entrance to religion, since those who enter religion trust not to be able to stay by their own power, but by the assistance of the divine power... Yet if there be some special obstacle (such as bodily weakness, a burden of debts, or the like) in such cases a man must deliberate and take counsel with such as are likely to help and not hinder him.'

monastic life was indeed the 'best portion' (Luke 10:42) caused cloisters to be filled with people of all backgrounds intent on seeking God. Yet modern times have seen a growing reluctance on the part of Christians to proclaim these truths or to act upon them. No doubt this is in part due to a reaction against possible abuses of an overly simplistic approach to the question of vocation. Yet it also seems to betray a loss of confidence in the Church in our time in the truth of Christ's words, a hesitancy to propose or to accept the radical terms of the call to perfect discipleship. While as recently as 1996 John Paul II affirmed the *'objective superiority of the consecrated life'*,[109] the modern and post-modern aversion to any concept of an objective hierarchy of states seems to hinder even many devout Catholics today from openly affirming or acting upon this perennial Christian truth. At the same time, an overly subjective approach to the spiritual life can lead to a view of vocational discernment which is preoccupied with inner experiences, resulting in a great deal of indecision and hesitancy in making decisions which Christians in former times made much more readily.

I believe that here Abbot Marmion's doctrine, and perhaps above all his example, have an important message for all Christians today, especially for young people considering their vocation in life. Marmion's own monastic vocation was certainly the fruit of a remarkable encounter with divine grace. Yet his theology of the monastic vocation, if one may use the phrase, does not view the life of the counsels as something extraordinary or as a specialized vocation open only to a few privileged souls. Rather, from the beginning of *Christ, The Ideal of the Monk* Marmion makes it clear, as we have said several times above, that the Rule of Saint Benedict is presented 'only as an abridgement of Christianity, and a means of practising the Christian Life in its fulness and perfection.'[110] Saint Benedict's opening invitation in the Prologue of the Rule, as

---

[109] *Vita consecrata* 18; cf. *VC* 32.
[110] Marmion, *Christ, The Ideal of the Monk*, p. 3.

well as his concluding exhortation in Chapter 73, bear this out: 'he only addresses those who wish to return to God under Christ's leadership... he proposes the accomplishment of this rule to whomsoever, through the help of Christ, hasteneth to the heavenly country.'[111]

Marmion proceeds to examine the great aim of the monastic life—'to seek God'—and shows that this is in fact the great aim of human life, because 'a man is worth what he seeks.'[112] The monk is one who seeks God through faith and love, always, in all things, and exclusively. Yet this search is in fact the only thing that can satisfy the human heart: Marmion is speaking not just of monks but of all men when he says that 'when we seek anything apart from God or from His will, we do not find stable and perfect happiness.'[113] The motives which, according to Marmion, bring a man to the monastery are in the end the only ones worthy of human life.

Likewise, in speaking of the following of Christ which is at the centre of the life proposed by Saint Benedict in the Rule, Marmion's doctrine, as we have seen above, does not propose to the monk a goal which is essentially different from that to which every Christian is called by virtue of his baptism: 'The religious life is not an institution created on the borders of Christianity; plunging its roots in the Gospel of Christ, it aims only at expressing the Gospel in all its integrity.'[114]

Marmion does not, of course, mean to say that all of the baptized must become religious or monks. As we have seen, he often stresses that the outward observances of monastic life are simply a means for allowing the life of grace and charity to develop in the soul. Marmion's own experience as a monk and as a priest made him very aware of the manifold paths by which Divine grace draws souls to God.[115] Yet his

---

[111] *Ibid.*
[112] *Ibid.*, p. 5.
[113] *Ibid.*, p. 15.
[114] *Ibid.*, p. 38.
[115] This emerges clearly throughout Marmion's letters. Writing to a young person whose attempt at religious life had been unsuccessful, Marmion writes:

clear understanding of the monastic life's purpose and of its intrinsic connection to the fundamental aim of the Christian life would seem to imply that the monastic vocation, while it is certainly a grace not given to all, is something which any Christian can legitimately desire and pray for, and which, in a spiritually healthy Church, should be pursued by a great number of the faithful. Indeed, the holiness of the Church requires that many of her children would embrace a way of life aimed at allowing the grace of their baptism to reach the fullest possible development. In so doing, those who embrace monastic life offer to the entire Church an irreplaceable witness, calling all Christians to seek God above all things, to prefer nothing to the love of Christ, to live as fully as possible the life of Christ begun in them in baptism.[116]

Abbot Marmion's teaching on the monastic life thus has a powerful message for all Christians today, whatever their state. He challenges those already living the monastic life, whether in the first fervour of their conversion or after long years of experience, to remember that their life is meaningless if it is not spent in the pursuit of union with God, a union which can only be brought about through believing in Christ and following His teaching, in complete dependence on His

---

'The fact of living in a cloister is a mere accident and cannot effect or diminish your love.' He memorably concludes, 'Neither Our Lady, nor many of the holy virgins and spouses of Jesus, Thecla, Agatha, Agnes, lived in a convent, yet they were perfect spouses of Jesus.' Letter of 6 February 1921, quoted in Thibault, *Union with God according to the letters of direction of Dom Marmion*, trans. Mother Mary St Thomas (London: Sands, 1934), pp. 225–27.

116 The role of the consecrated life in witnessing to the holiness demanded of all Christians by the sacraments is well articulated in *Vita consecrata* 33: 'A particular duty of the consecrated life is to remind the baptized of the fundamental values of the Gospel.... The consecrated life thus continually fosters in the People of God an awareness of the need to respond with holiness of life to the love of God poured into their hearts by the Holy Spirit (cf. Rom 5:5), by reflecting in their conduct the sacramental consecration which is brought about by God's power in baptism, confirmation or holy orders. In fact it is necessary to pass from the holiness communicated in the sacraments to the holiness of daily life. The consecrated life, by its very existence in the Church, seeks to serve the consecration of the lives of all the faithful, clergy and laity alike.'

grace. Marmion would remind monks that any spirituality, ideology, activity, or pious observance—however impressive in the world's sight—which does not lead them to God through Jesus Christ, true God and true Man, our only High Priest and Way to the Father, will simply be a dead end and lead to spiritual sterility. At the same time, he would assure us that the monk who is intent on seeking God, in complete dependence upon Christ to Whose love he prefers nothing else—even if in the eyes of the world his life may seem to be a waste or even a failure—will find life in abundance and bear great fruit for souls. And to all of Christ's faithful, already made sharers in His life through their baptism, Marmion holds up the monastic life as traced by Saint Benedict in the Rule as a sure path for arriving at perfect maturity as children of the heavenly Father. This is a message needed by all Christians in our age, and in every age, for its foundation is the plan hidden in God from before the foundation of the world, but now made known through His Son and taught in every age by the Church, His Mystical Body, ever ancient, ever new.

7
BLESSED COLVMBA MARMION

SPIRITUAL FATHER TO THE SPOUSES OF THE WORD

MOTHER MARIA REGINA OF THE EUCHARISTIC HEART OF JESUS, FLM

INTRODUCTION: RELIGIOUS SISTERS IN THE LIFE OF BLESSED COLUMBA

BLESSED COLUMBA MARMION HAD A great zeal for souls. As one of his spiritual sons, Dom Francis Izard, OSB, writes in the preface to the 1924 edition of *Sponsa Verbi*, 'For souls he had a great passion. He gave himself entirely for them that they should be all for Christ. But if his affection embraced all, like his Divine Master, he was specially attracted by two classes: the sinners, and those consecrated by vows of chastity.'[1]

Divine Providence prepared Blessed Columba for his service to religious sisters. His parents were blessed with nine children, four girls and five boys, but the two boys older than Blessed Columba died before his own birth. Two boys were born after him, but Blessed Columba, who received the name Joseph, grew up primarily in the company of his older sisters. From his early childhood with his four older sisters, he must have come to understand women quite well. His siblings were:

1. Mary (1848–1924).—She married Stephen Joyce and their marriage was blessed with eight children, five

---

[1] Dom Francis Izard, OSB, 'Editor's Preface', *Sponsa Verbi: Spiritual Conferences on Saint Bernard's Sermons on the Canticle of Canticles* by Dom Columba Marmion, OSB, trans. Dom Francis Izard, OSB (Minneapolis, MN: Joannes Press, 2022), p. 1.

girls and three boys. Of the girls, Joséphine became a Canoness of Saint Augustine at Jupille (Liége, Belgium), receiving the name Dame Scholastique[2]; Cécile entered the Abbey of Saint Scholastica at Maredret (Belgium) and received the name Dame Caecilia.[3]

2. Elizabeth (1849–1918).—She entered the Convent of the Sisters of Mercy, receiving the name Sister Columba. She was a regional superior of the Sisters of Mercy and made a new foundation of a convent in Dunmore East (Ireland) and also one in Waterford (Ireland).[4]

3. John Sebastian (1851–1853)[5]

4. Philip (1852–1853)[6]

5. Flora (1853–1892).—She entered the Convent of the Sisters of Mercy at Clonakilty (Ireland), receiving the name Sister Lorenzo.[7]

6. Rosie (1855–1930).—She entered the Convent of the Sisters of Mercy, receiving the name Sister Peter. She was assigned as superior in Clonakilty a number of times.[8]

7. Joseph (1858–1923) (Blessed Columba)[9]

8. Frank (ca. 1860?)[10]

9. Matthew (1863–1927).—He became a surgeon who married Rosa and had three sons.[11]

Dom Raymund Thibaut, who served as Blessed Columba's assistant during the latter's abbacy, and who became his first biographer, remarks that Joseph was particularly close to his older sister, Rosie:

---

[2] In some orders, a solemnly professed nun is called 'Dame.'
[3] Marmion, Columba, *Correspondance 1881–1923*, ed. Mark Tierney, R.-Ferdinand Poswick, and Nicolas Dayez. (Paris: François-Xavier de Guibert, 2008), "Index: Marmion, Mary," p. 1300.
[4] *Ibid.*, "Index: Marmion, Lizzie," p. 1300.
[5] *Ibid.*, "Index: Marmion (Famille)," p. 1300.
[6] *Ibid.*, p. 1300.
[7] *Ibid.*, "Index: Marmion, Flora," p. 1300.
[8] *Ibid.*, "Index: Marmion, Rosie," p. 1300.
[9] *Ibid.*, p. 11.
[10] http://www.marmionfamilytree.com/DomColumbaMarmion.html.
[11] Columba Marmion, *Correspondance 1881–1923*, "Index: Marmion, Matthew," p. 1300.

It was with Rosie, the youngest girl, though three years older than himself, that Joseph from his childhood and ever afterwards was bound by a special affection. The same meditative character, the same constant zest for spiritual things, later in the case of each to be developed in the cloister, had very early drawn these two together—twin souls despite their difference in age, and of the self-same candour. Rosie was Joseph's favourite companion in his games and walks, the safe confidante of his sorrows, joys and plans, and it was always her advice he was most ready to follow.[12]

When Joseph was twelve years old, on 4 August 1870, his older sister Elizabeth, who was called Lizzie at home, entered the Convent of Mercy in Clonakilty. In religion, she received the name of Sister Columba, a patron whom her brother would come to share in religion. Three years later, on 2 July 1873, Flora entered the same Convent of Mercy. Another three years later, on 12 February 1876, his sister Rosie entered the same convent. Having been at home as three of his four sisters prepared to enter the convent, one imagines that Joseph spoke with them about their intentions and desires in entering religious life. There do not appear to be any written records of conversations or correspondence which Joseph had with his sisters who were preparing to enter religious life, but his intimate understanding of the religious life, even before he himself was a religious, suggests that he came to know the life through his sisters.

Religious sisters were entrusted to Father Marmion throughout all of his life as a priest and as a monk, from his first assignment up to his death. His work with religious sisters increased substantially during the period when he was serving at Louvain (Belgium) (1899–1909) and remained a key part of his ministry, even during his years as Abbot of Maredsous (1909–1923) and even when his health began to decline. His

---

12   Dom Raymund Thibaut, *Abbot Columba Marmion: A Master of the Spiritual Life: 1858–1923*, trans. Mother Mary St Thomas (St Louis, MO: B. Herder Book Co., 1949), pp. 9–10.

contacts with religious sisters are so numerous throughout his life that it is difficult to establish a complete list of his ministry to sisters. The list is the more impressive when we consider that it was always the case that sisters were entrusted to him *in addition to* other tasks. In general, there were three ways he served religious sisters: through spiritual direction in person and through letter; through the giving of conferences and retreats; and through his service as chaplain.[13]

BLESSED COLUMBA AS A SPIRITUAL DIRECTOR

The long list of letters written and retreats directed for religious sisters gives witness to Blessed Columba's indefatigable pastoral charity for religious sisters. Even during the years when he was, as he himself phrased it, 'eaten up' by others,[14] he continued to direct retreats and to write letters of direction, in addition to his many other duties. Of the 1,880 extant letters of Blessed Columba, 512 are written to religious sisters.[15] If there are some years in Blessed Columba's mature life in which we notice fewer letters and fewer retreats, the reason for the limited apostolate is to be found in unavoidable circumstances, such as the impossibility of travel or communication during the years of the First World War or a serious undermining of his health toward the end of his life.

The list also underscores the universality of Blessed Columba's solicitude for sisters. Although he wrote many letters to Benedictine nuns and directed many retreats for Benedictines,

---

13 A long list of Blessed Columba's service to religious sisters based on extant correspondence can be found in the Appendix. It serves to illustrate his devotion to religious sisters as a spiritual father, the universality of his spiritual solicitude, and his commitment to their sanctification. Note that the list begins with the year of his ordination to the priesthood and concludes with the year of his death.
14 See Thibaut, *Abbot Columba Marmion: A Master of the Spiritual Life: 1858–1923*, p. 136 and p. 349
15 Marmion, *Correspondance 1881–1923*, p. 11 for the total number of extant letters. Total letters directed to religious Sisters calculated based on the letters indicated in "*Chronologie des Lettres et de la vie du Bienheureux Columba Marmion*," pp. 1319–1361.

Blessed Columba Marmion

his care for sisters extended far beyond the spirituality of his own religious order. On the basis of what is published in *Correspondance 1881–1923*, Blessed Columba wrote to sisters or gave retreats to members of twenty-nine different communities.[16] He directed a total of twenty-two retreats for religious sisters of various communities: Carmelites, Augustinians, Benedictines, Poor Clares, and others.

Like Saint Paul, Blessed Columba sought to be 'all things to all men' (1 Cor. 9:22) in the sense that he sought to help each sister live fully according to the spirituality of *her* community. In 1899, Blessed Columba was assigned to serve as the ordinary confessor of the Carmel at Louvain. Dom Raymund describes the manner in which Blessed Columba undertook his assignment:

---

16 Based on information available in Columba Marmion, *Correspondance 1881–1923*, "Chronologie des Lettres et de la vie du Bienheureux Columba Marmion," pp. 1319–1361, the communities are: Adorers of the Sacred Heart of Jesus at Montmarte (France); Adorers of the Sacred Heart of Jesus of Montmarte at Ganshoren (Belgium); Adorers of the Sacred Heart at Tyburn, London (Great Britain); Benedictine Nuns of the Abbey of St Scholastica at Maredret (Belgium); Benedictine Nuns of Douai at Reading (Great Britain); Benedictine Abbey at Stanbrook, Allow End, Worcester (Great Britain); Benedictines of La Paix Notre Dame at Liège (Belgium); Benedictine Monastery of Saint Cecilia at Ryde on the Isle of Wight (Great Britain); Benedictine Convent of Ventnor, Isle of Wight (Great Britain); Benedictine Nuns at Oosterhout (the Netherlands); Benedictine Nuns of Saint-Louis-du-Temple Abbey at Paris (France); Benedictine Irish Ladies of Ypres, established first in Macmine Castle, Co. Wexford then in Kylemore (Ireland); Canonesses of Saint Augustine at the English Convent of Bruges (Belgium); Canonesses of Saint Augustine at Hayward's Heath, East Sussex (Great Britain); Canonesses of Saint Augustine at Jupille (Belgium); Carmelite Nuns of Louvain (Belgium); Carmelite Nuns at the Carmel of Saint-Joseph at Virton (Belgium); Carmelite Nuns of Dijon (France); Congregation for Christian Education (Ireland); Dominican Convent of Sion Hill at Dublin (Ireland); Dominicans at Louvain (Belgium); Filles du Coeur de Jésus (Daughters of the Heart of Jesus); Poor Clares of Cork (Ireland); Redemptoristine Convent, Drumcondra, Dublin (Ireland); Servantes du Sacrement at Binche (Belgium); Sisters of the Assumption, Kensington, London (Great Britain); Nuns of the Sacred Heart, Mt. Anville (Ireland); Ursulines of Toldonk at Wespelaer (Belgium) (at least a visit, but not sure whether there was additional contact); Visitation Nuns of Troyes (France)

> [E]ach week Dom Columba traversed on foot the long distance which separates the two monasteries to give a conference to the nuns and hear their confessions.
>
> This apostolate was dear to him for two reasons. In the same way that his functions as professor gave him occasion to review theology as a whole, so the obligation of leading contemplative souls to perfection made him go deeply into the spiritual works of St John of the Cross and of St Teresa. This was for him the foundation of a wealth of ascetical and mystical lore whereof other souls were to benefit. The knowledge gained in this matter was so much the more valuable in that, from day to day, he was able to put to experimental proof the theoretical notions brought before him quite naturally by his contact in this cloister with souls who had reached a high state of prayer and had confided their direction to him.[17]

Recognizing that the diversity of religious communities is a gift from God, Blessed Marmion guided each religious sister according to the spirituality of *her* order, not of *his* order. A Carmelite nun reflected on the service of Blessed Columba to her Carmel:

> As director of our Carmel, he was the Church's representative. He so well understood that, being delegated by the Church for the spiritual direction of a Carmel in a town where there was no convent of Carmelite Fathers—the authorised directors of Carmelite nuns and generally delegated for this ministry—he ought to guide his spiritual daughters as the Church wills, and as the Order has the right to expect, *in the spirit of Carmel*. Certain people said: "He will make the Carmelites semi-Benedictines." ... He wished us to be, he kept us Carmelites, even exaggerating the fact in the precautions he took, such was his respect for the diversity of vocations.[18]

---

17 Thibaut, *Abbot Columba Marmion: A Master of the Spiritual Life: 1858–1923*, pp. 133–134.
18 *Ibid.*, p. 267.

In his role as spiritual director, Blessed Columba was particularly outstanding for two qualities which, even though they may *appear* at first sight to be incompatible, are actually two sides of the same coin of loving after the Heart of Jesus: detachment and affection.

Even before he himself was a monk, Blessed Columba recognized that Christian detachment is a keystone to the spiritual life. Early in his priesthood, having been ordained just four years, in the second extant letter he is known to have written to a religious sister, he speaks of the importance of detachment:

> Holy Cross College, 29 April, 1885. My dear child, . . . I will pray very specially for you that you may receive the grace of resembling your holy patron, especially in the generous oblation she made of herself to her Divine Spouse. Your life at present should be a perpetual oblation of yourself to the Sacred Heart, and as the Holy Sacrifice is being offered at every moment during the day, you can unite yourself with our Lord at every moment and thus be sure your offering will be accepted. When you have got the habit of thus living in a state of perpetual oblation, it becomes a matter of absolute indifference to you, what you are engaged at, as your only desire then, is to accomplish the Will of God, which is manifested to you at every moment by obedience. The more generous you are in endeavouring to arrive at this state of holy indifference and detachment from your own inclinations, the more perfectly you will taste that peace, which is the "hundredfold" which our Lord promises to those who have left all things for His love.[19]

There are various aspects of detachment; detachment from one's occupation is but one aspect. As a novice, Blessed Columba reflected in his spiritual journal on the degrees of detachment:

---

19 Cited in Thibaut, *Abbot Columba Marmion: A Master of the Spiritual Life: 1858–1923*, p. 37. See *Correspondance*, p. 36, letter of 29 April 1995 to Sister Alphonsus Waddock.

> September 10, 1887—I was greatly struck to-day while those words, *Vos qui reliquistis omnia et secuti estis me* were being sung in the Communion of the Mass. I understood that this "leaving all things" has many degrees. There is (a) material leaving of all things which is very pleasing to God but yet very imperfect; (b) the spiritual leaving of all things which is detachment; (c) there is entire leaving of all things which consists not only in abandoning all that we hold dear, but in denying ourselves the joys of memory and imagination in their regard. As spiritual mortification transcends corporal, as spirit transcends materiality, so does this spiritual abandon of all things transcend the merely bodily absence.[20]

Only a few weeks later, on October 5th of the same year, the novice writes similar reflections in his notebook:

> If I would but "leave all things" I would soon receive the "hundredfold" but the material "leaving" of all things is but little, as long as our minds and hearts are not detached. "Where your treasure is there will your heart be also. . . ." *Conversatio nostra in coelis est.*[21]

Concerning the period immediately after Blessed Columba's solemn profession of vows, Dom Raymund writes that Blessed Columba's detachment from seeking his own ways and his own will in the apostolate served to give him a liberty of spirit:

> From that day forth, his activity was to be exerted in many and various directions, but obedience and zeal for souls were to ensure its unity, whilst the very diversity of its nature contributed towards that total detachment which gives full inward liberty and prepares the heart to rise to heavenly things.[22]

'Full inward liberty' is the mark of Christian detachment; true detachment has nothing in common with a stoic indifference.

---

20 *Ibid.*, p. 58.
21 *Ibid.*, p. 59.
22 *Ibid.*, p. 82.

In 1891, Blessed Columba wrote to Sister Peter (his blood sister), in response to her request for counsel about her desire to search out during recreation certain sisters who desire to speak of God and who are fervent. Blessed Columba counselled his sister that it is more perfect and more pleasing to Our Lord to associate with whomever is near, not to choose one's companions. He explained to his sister that "this practice will have a great power of detaching your heart from all merely human consolation and fixing it in the S. Heart." He continued: "However in all this there must be nothing strained or violent, no closing yourself up in yourself, but every day as you advance in love of Jesus Christ and in union with Him your heart must expand more and more in love towards all your sisters."[23] Detachment, then, serves to *free* and to *expand* the heart. Genuine Christian detachment *permits* a free and appropriate affection and love for other human persons.

In 1902, Blessed Columba reflected in a letter to Dom Hildebrand de Hemptinne about his own state of detachment:

> I feel great detachment of heart from all the persons and gifts of this world, and I have only one desire, that of belonging to God unreservedly, occupying myself only with Him alone with the persons and labours which He wills to confide to me, ready to leave them and to occupy myself with other persons and other things, according as He makes this known to me by obedience. Such is, truly at present, my disposition of heart, and I consider it as one of the most precious graces that God has ever given me.[24]

In a letter of the same year, Blessed Columba wrote to Dame Cécile de Hemptinne about the relationship between detachment and affection:

---

23 Marmion, Columba, *Spiritual Writings*, Letter to his Sister Rosie of 17 October 1891, p. 986. Cf. *Correpondance 1881–1923*, p. 55.
24 Cited in Thibaut, *Abbot Columba Marmion: A Master of the Spiritual Life: 1858–1923*, p. 154: Letter of 2 June 1902 to Dom Hildebrand de Hemptinne. Cf. *Correpondance 1881–1923*, pp. 139–140.

> On the feast of the Espousals of the Blessed Virgin, at the end of my prayer, which had been altogether dry, I received a very clear light on the love of Mary and Joseph. Never did two creatures love one another as did this espoused pair, and never was love so purified from all human element. I saw, but with great peace and calm, that my affections are supernatural, and that I am very detached, but there still remains much progress for me to make before arriving at perfect purity, and I have taken the resolution of striving for it with calm and generosity.[25]

Genuine Christian detachment is not a cold, distant reserve, but rather, after the example of Christ Himself, is filled with warmth and with affection. Genuine detachment provides the inward freedom for an affection that is truly directed to the other, which is not self-seeking. To Evelyn Bax, a young girl, Blessed Columba explains:

> The angels must love God *angelically*, that is without heart, sentiments, affections, for they have none of these things. But He expects man to love Him *humanly* that is with all his heart, soul, strength and mind, and *his neighbour in the same way.* We are neither spirits nor ghosts, but human beings; and we cannot go higher than perfect humanity elevated by grace. Now Jesus is perfect humanity, perfect Deity. He loved His Mother as a child should love, not only with His Head, but with His Heart. He kissed her and was fondled by her, and liked it. He loved all men: a) for their souls, in view of eternity; b) for their *entire persons*, humanly; c) He loved some with a special human love. He wept when Lazarus died. Where did these tears come from? Not from His soul, but from His Heart. He did not love angelically, because He was not an angel but the Son of Man; no one was ever so human as Jesus. His Father found all His delights in Him. Amongst the creatures which

---

25 Cited in Thibaut, *Abbot Columba Marmion: A Master of the Spiritual Life: 1858–1923*, p. 250: Letter of 30 January 1902 to Dame Cécile de Hemptinne. Cf. *Correpondance 1881–1923*, p. 125.

God has given us to lead us to Him, and to *render our exile here possible*, there is the love and affection of those who surround us.[26]

He continues:

> Now, my dear child... just act *simply*, and ask Jesus to give you the gift of loving with detachment; that is, so that no human affection *be necessary*. "One thing is necessary." [Lk 10:42] Use affections as you do other creatures. You will not *rest* in creatures, if you desire to use them according to God's Will. See St Teresa keeping her niece in the convent with her; St Francis de Sales and St Chantal; St Augustine weeping for his mother... without a scrap of attachment.[27]

It is precisely a *warm detachment* that characterized Blessed Marmion's relations with people. Dom Raymund, who knew him so well, confirms that, 'to the very end he cherished a warmth of charity which nothing could diminish, a freshness of soul which long intercourse with men had been powerless to impair.'[28] And:

> With those nearest to him his heart absolutely refused to admit the possibility of coldness or even to be resigned to indifference. Indeed, in Dom Marmion reigned that real affective love which makes a man count as his own all the good or evil which befalls those given him to love. He espoused the interests

---

26 Marmion, *Spiritual Writings*, Letter to a young girl of 4 December 1919, p. 1078. Cf. *Correpondance 1881–1923*, p. 1036. See *Correspondance*, "Index: Bax, Evelyn," p. 1269: "Young Protestant friend of Dom Marmion, who also calls her 'Eva' or 'Mousie'. She was an actress and theater actress in London. He received her into the Catholic Church on December 23, 1900, as mentioned in the Annals of Mont-Cesar. He mentions her, it seems, in his letter of December 16, 1902. Dom Marmion's spiritual daughter, she was unable, for health reasons, to realize a religious vocation that she tried to implement in Carmel and other orders. During a stay in England in 1915–1916, Dom Marmion stayed with her aunt and uncle in Hampstead."
27 *Ibid.*, pp. 1078–1079.
28 Thibaut, *Abbot Columba Marmion: A Master of the Spiritual Life: 1858–1923*, p. 210.

of others, sympathized with their moral or physical state, shared their joys, their troubles, their anxieties, their family losses. And the moment having come, the occasion being given, this love was translated into self-forgetfulness and gift of self.[29]

It was to a true Christian detachment which opens the way not only to warm affection with our neighbour but also to union with the Blessed Trinity that Blessed Columba called his spiritual daughters.

DETACHMENT FOR UNION: SPONSA VERBI

During the summer of 1918, Dom Columba was ordered by physicians to take a number of weeks of rest. He went to Luxembourg and, during his long walks, he read and pondered over Saint Bernard's *Commentary on the Canticle of Canticles*. Upon his return to Belgium, he gave a series of conferences to the Benedictine Nuns at Maredret in which he shared the fruit of his reflections on Saint Bernard's works. The conferences were transcribed by one of the nuns, and, before he died in January of 1923, Dom Columba approved the text which the nuns had prepared from his conferences. The text of *Sponsa Verbi* was published posthumously, as the fifth and last of his published texts.

As the editor of *Sponsa Verbi* points out, '[T]hese conferences were given to Benedictine nuns, [but] they are not specifically monastic.'[30] The text is directed rather to each woman who, consecrated by profession of vows, is a spouse of Christ. *Sponsa Verbi* is the fruit of Dom Columba's long experience of guiding women in the religious life.

The opening line of *Sponsa Verbi* reminds the reader of the main theme of Dom Columba's spirituality: 'The greatest gift made by God to the human creature is that of his supernatural adoption by grace into Jesus Christ the Word Incarnate.'[31]

---

29 *Ibid.*, pp. 210–211.
30 Izard, Dom Francis, OSB, 'Preface,' to Marmion, Columba, *Sponsa Verbi*, p. 3.
31 Marmion, *Sponsa Verbi*, p. 5.

Man's supernatural adoption in Jesus Christ is the keystone of Dom Columba's spirituality. It would be difficult to enumerate all his references to supernatural adoption, because they are so numerous. Dom Raymund Thibaut writes the following about Blessed Columba's final years of life: '[W]hen his malady had already undermined his health, he was apt to return rather more frequently and more willingly to certain subjects: the Divine Filiation of Jesus, our supernatural adoption, unshaken confidence in Christ's merits...'[32] The elderly Blessed Columba returned to the subjects which were most important to him. *Christ, The Life of the Soul* explains the whole spiritual life in terms of our supernatural adoption in Jesus Christ.

In the first chapter of *Sponsa Verbi*, Blessed Columba uses Our Lord's image in which He compares the Kingdom of Heaven to a nuptial banquet.[33] Following the example of Our Lord, Blessed Columba explains the supernatural reality of heaven by comparing it to a reality which is nearer at hand, namely, a nuptial banquet.

Given the emphasis which Blessed Columba gave to the filial nature of our spiritual life, it is somewhat surprising to read in the first chapter of *Sponsa Verbi* the enumeration of the different classes of persons who are called to the banquet of Divine union. There are the *servants* who obey God but have no intimacy with Him, and the *friends* who have an intermittent relationship with Him. The next class is that of *children*, the adopted children of God. 'To these souls who are His children, God gives Himself as the supreme good which satisfies all their desires.'[34] Given Blessed Columba's emphasis on our filial adoption in Christ, one would expect the *children* to be highest class. But it is not so.

---

32 Thibaut, *Abbot Columba Marmion: A Master of the Spiritual Life: 1858–1923*, p. 177.
33 Cf. Marmion, *Sponsa Verbi*, pp. 5–6. Cf. Mt. 22:1ff.; Mt. 25:1ff.; Lk. 14:16ff.
34 *Ibid.*, p. 7.

There is *more* than the spirituality of our supernatural adoption as children: some are called to a *spousal* relationship with Jesus: 'Those who are espoused, said our Lord, "shall leave father and mother, and shall cleave to one another": *Dimittet homo patrem et matrem et adhaerebit uxori suae* (Mt. 19:50) no union surpasses this in intimacy, tenderness and fecundity. Now it is to contract an union of this sort that the Word invites the soul who is consecrated to Him by the vows of religion.'[35]

Blessed Columba responds to the question: Is not every baptized soul in some measure espoused to the Word? 'Yes,' *but* 'the union is much closer, the quality of spouse shines with a much greater brilliance in the case of the souls consecrated to God by the vows of religion. It is to these souls that in all verity can be applied the title of spouse of the Word; in them this sublime condition is realized in its plenitude.'[36]

The reality of spousal union is the portion of *every* consecrated religious; it is not reserved to those who receive special mystical gifts. Blessed Columba emphasizes that it is 'not, however, of these [mystic] states, to which no one has the right by his own actions, that we speak here.'[37] He emphasizes that *every* faithful religious is a spouse: 'Every soul vowed to God by the religious consecration is called to this position of spouse of the Word; she carries the title; if she is faithful, she enjoys the rights which are attached to it; she is loaded with marks of tenderness by her divine Spouse, and her union with Him becomes the source of a wonderful fecundity.'[38]

In explaining the nature of the spousal union in the second chapter of *Sponsa Verbi*, Blessed Columba does not choose a likeness to something which is *nearer* to our everyday experience, as he did in the first chapter. He does not compare

---

35 Ibid., pp. 7–8. See Thibaut, *Abbot Columba Marmion: A Master of the Spiritual Life: 1858–1923: Dom Columba Marmion*, pp. 164–165, for a passage from Dom Columba's notebook of 1906 in which he delineates different classes of persons at the banquet of the King: servants, friends, and the bride.
36 Ibid., p. 8.
37 Ibid., p. 13.
38 Ibid., p. 12.

the spousal quality to human marriage, but he rather compares it to a union infinitely elevated beyond our experience: the union of the sacred Humanity with the Word. '[I]f we carefully observe the sacred Humanity in this union with the Word,' he explains, 'we shall see that it marvellously and most fully realizes those characteristics that St Bernard wished to see in a spouse of the Word.'[39] The qualities of the union which Blessed Columba highlights are the freedom from self-seeking, *'relictis omnibus'*,[40] and the absolute *poverty* of the humanity of Jesus which 'possessed nothing of its own, it had no personality in itself, it remained stript of that which in us is the inmost center,'[41] so that it received *all* from the Word. Having nothing and belonging to nothing, then, the human nature in Jesus adhered fully to the Word: *Verba votis omnibus adhaerere.*[42] Blessed Columba describes the union of the humanity and the Word:

> What an absolute possession of the humanity by the Word, yet also what an absolute surrender of itself by the human nature, and in its free acts, what a transport of love towards the Word! Between the human nature and the Word, there was a perfect and unceasing community of thought, sentiments, will and action.[43]

Blessed Columba places this highest of realities before religious sisters as 'at the same time, the model and source of the union of the Word with consecrated souls.'[44] For women who have given themselves entirely to a supernatural vocation of spousal union with Christ, Blessed Columba does not use earthly realities to explain the splendour of the vocation, but he rather draws them higher by showing them the sublime reality of the union which is both the reality and the aspiration of their vocation.

---

39 *Ibid.*, p. 16.
40 *Ibid.*, p. 17.
41 *Ibid.*
42 *Ibid.*
43 *Ibid.*, p. 18.
44 *Ibid.*, p. 21.

The religious sister's life of elected poverty, chastity, and obedience makes no sense on a natural level; it makes sense only on a supernatural level. She lives her vocation fully when she keeps the eyes of her soul fixed on the supernatural realities: *sub specie aeterni*. It is fitting, then, that, in addressing religious sisters, Blessed Columba does not draw the eyes of the spouses of Christ *down* to earth, not even to learn from earthly realities, but that he draws their eyes *up* to the supernatural. Contemplation of supernatural mysteries is fitting because, as Blessed Columba explains, quoting the Pontifical for the Consecration of Virgins, in the religious life 'one does not imitate what is accomplished in earthly unions.'[45] In marriage we find 'the symbol and the shadow; here the profound and luminous reality.'[46]

A comparison between the approach taken in *Christ, The Ideal of the Monk* and *Sponsa Verbi*, both written for religious, will highlight how masterfully Blessed Columba addresses religious women *as women* in *Sponsa Verbi*. *Christ, The Ideal of the Monk*, as the title makes plain, is directed, above all, to monks, and the text is based on the Rule of Saint Benedict. It is by no means the case that *Christ, The Ideal of the Monk* is not helpful to women, but only that *Sponsa Verbi* is directed to them in a particular manner.

In *Christ, The Ideal of the Monk*, Blessed Columba explains the meaning and end of the monastic life in terms of 'seeking God'. In the monastic life, he explains, 'God [is] sought for Himself, as the Supreme Beatitude.... St Benedict will have us seek God,—seek Him for His own glory, because we love Him above all things. He would have us seek to unite ourselves to Him by charity.'[47] Our model in seeking God is Jesus Himself. 'And we see Christ Jesus, like a giant, rejoice to run the way in the pursuit of the glory of His Father.'[48] Jesus

---

45 *Ibid.*, p. 26.
46 *Ibid.*
47 Marmion, Columba, *Christ, The Ideal of the Monk*, trans. by a Nun of Tyburn (Ireland: The Cenacle Press, 2022), p. 8.
48 *Ibid.*, p. 19.

seeks His Father's glory with constancy, with persistency, even through His Passion and death itself. Blessed Columba urges the monk to imitate Jesus: '[I]n the same way as Christ Jesus rejoices "to run the way" *ad currendam viam* [Ps 18:6], let us run in His train since He is Himself the *way*.... [C]arried along by the holy desire of reaching the Kingdom where our heavenly Father awaits us, let us press forward unceasingly in the practice of good deeds'.[49]

The manner of presentation in *Sponsa Verbi* is quite distinct: rather than placing before the consecrated religious the end of seeking God and encouraging them to have 'the motive and *ambition* of possessing God',[50] Blessed Columba places before the religious the splendour 'of the divine nuptials of the Word with human nature.'[51] Blessed Columba recognizes that a man is more often motivated by a challenge, by a mission, by 'running in His train', whereas a woman's desire is enkindled by loving and being loved, by the longing for 'complete union'.

In both works, Blessed Columba speaks of the necessity of detachment, quoting, as is his wont, the Biblical phrase, '*relictis omnibus*',[52] as the means for arriving at union. In *Christ, The Ideal of the Monk*, Blessed Columba explains monastic profession by comparing it to the immolation of Jesus Christ in the Holy Sacrifice of the Mass: 'St Benedict links this profession to the Sacrifice of the Altar' in the sense that the monk 'unites his immolation with that of Jesus Christ.'[53] He summarizes: 'Monastic Profession is indeed an immolation, and this immolation derives its value from its union with Christ's holocaust.'[54] At the heart of monastic profession is the total gift of one's will: 'The vows give us the power of reaching the highest possible

---

49   Ibid., p. 20.
50   Ibid., p. 5. Emphasis added.
51   *Sponsa Verbi*, p. 21.
52   See *Christ, The Ideal of the Monk*, chapter 8, A.: The Way of Abnegation (*Reliquimus omnia*), p. 169; Marmion, *Sponsa Verbi*, chapter 3: *Relictis Omnibus*, p. 23.
53   *Christ, The Ideal of the Monk*, p. 123.
54   Ibid., p. 124.

degree of separation from the creature, since we renounce our own will. We can truly say: "We have left all," *Reliquimus omnia*. But we must not delay to add: "that we may follow Thee," *Et secuti sumus te*. Such is the formula of union with God.'[55]

In *Sponsa Verbi*, Blessed Columba develops the same theme in a manner suited to women. Blessed Columba emphasizes that attachments are an obstacle to union: 'it is the separation from all that could divide, all that could constitute an obstacle to perfect union'.[56] In addressing nuns, 'we regard specially the obstacles which hinder the complete union of the soul with the Word, considered as Spouse'.[57] Whereas chastity is hardly mentioned in *Christ, The Ideal of the Monk*, it is the main theme of *Sponsa Verbi*.[58] Blessed Columba explains to nuns that the essence of the total gift of self is the gift of chastity:

> The vow of virginity, then, marks the absolute separation from any creature, which is a necessary requisite for that soul which desires to be united with the Word as spouse. On the day of your religious profession, you fulfilled this condition; then it was that you not only said good-bye to that home in which you were born and nurtured, but freely responding to the divine call, you renounced of your own free will all earthly union, and the legitimate right to found a family: you became detached from all things: you then realized the most complete abandonment even of yourselves, *relictis omnibus*, so that you might consecrate yourself, soul and body, to the Word. This complete donation of yourself, inspired and realized by the help of grace, is the great subject of your interior joy. It should also be a constant source of thanksgiving. For does it not confer upon you the magnificent faculty "of

---

55 *Ibid.*, pp. 129–130.
56 *Sponsa Verbi*, p. 23.
57 *Ibid.*, p. 24.
58 We find in the Rule of St Benedict only passing mentions of chastity: 'To love chastity' is listed as one of the Instruments of Good Works in chapter 4; 'being chaste' is mentioned as a required virtue of the abbot in chapter 64; and 'chaste love' is one of the characteristics of the good zeal in chapter 72.

consecrating yourself without impediment to a life of intimate union with God"? *Eo quod facultatem praebeat sine impedimento Dominum obsecrandi.*[59]

It is in terms of protecting the chastity of both body and soul that Blessed Columba explains the need for mortification. Mortification is a *means* and a *guard*. Knowing that, for women, chaste spousal love is at the heart of their vocation, Blessed Columba knows that they will both grasp the need for mortification and be motivated to practice it when such practices are viewed as guardians of chastity. 'A virginal heart,' he writes 'which does not protect itself by the guard of the senses and mortification runs great risks.'[60] In *Christ, The Ideal of the Monk*, Blessed Columba explains the need for mortification in a manner more adapted to men. Men are motivated by a common mission; women are motivated by love of an individual. In the common mission, God 'wills that we should go to Him by walking in the footsteps of His Son, Christ Jesus.'[61] Just as Christ suffered, so must we follow Him. 'Having solidarity with Christ in suffering, we are however condemned to bear it for quite a different reason.... By sin, we have contracted a debt towards God's justice, and, when the offense has been remitted, the debt still remains for us to pay. This is the role of satisfaction. Moreover, the spirit of self-renunciation assures perseverance.'[62]

The detachment and the mortification required of the spouse of Christ are essential as *means*. The *end* of chastity is love: 'Charity, love, is then absolutely essential for that soul who wishes to be admitted to the rank of spouse; it is the very bond of union.'[63] After the chapter on detachment, '*Relictis omnibus*', Blessed Columba dedicates the remaining and longest part of *Sponsa Verbi* to the *end* of chastity: to union, to living *for* the Word, to the fecundity of chastity.

---

59 *Sponsa Verbi*, pp. 27–28.
60 *Ibid.*, p. 29.
61 *Christ, The Ideal of the Monk*, p. 195.
62 *Ibid.*, p. 198.
63 *Sponsa Verbi*, p. 37.

Blessed Columba asks: 'What is it to be united to the Spouse?'[64] 'It is to follow Him everywhere and always, to have the same thoughts, the same interests, to share the same labours, to be associated in the same destiny. One word completely sums up all these duties: fidelity.'[65] He explains fidelity in terms of the Spousal nature of the sister's life:

> This fidelity must be universal; with regard to the Spouse, it must extend to all that relates to His person, His rights, His interests, and His glory; on the part of the soul it should touch all the faculties; ennoble every act for the whole of life. Nothing should escape this fidelity.[66]

After many years of experience in guiding religious sisters, Blessed Columba knew well the ways in which a good sister typically fails in fidelity. The infidelities, even though *seemingly* small, harm union: 'nothing is more certain than that Our Lord will never give Himself intimately to an unfaithful soul.'[67] The examples he lists reveal his intimate knowledge of women religious:

> To admit carelessness in exercises of piety, break the silence without necessity, disobey willingly and without concern the smallest point of the Rule, take no notice of established usages, even small and trivial ones, under pretext of largeness of view, waste time futilely, linger over imprudent thoughts, be knowingly lacking in charity, criticize orders or actions of superiors: all such acts impair fidelity, and enfeeble the life of union.[68]

The final chapter of *Sponsa Verbi*, dedicated to 'union with the Spouse' is, again, quite distinct from a similar chapter in *Christ, The Ideal of the Monk*. In the latter work, the 'life of union with Christ' is considered in chapters dedicated to the Divine Office, to monastic prayer, to the spirit of abandonment,

---

64   *Ibid.*, p. 38.
65   *Ibid.*
66   *Ibid.*
67   *Ibid.*, p. 41.
68   *Ibid.*

to good zeal and to the peace of Christ. All of these are *means* for being united with Christ, especially in being united with His salvific mission. The Divine Office is a sharing in His prayer for souls; our zeal is a participation in His zeal for souls.

In *Sponsa Verbi*, Blessed Columba speaks of but one means of union, namely, the reception of Holy Communion, even though he mentions in passing some other means, such as silence, the Rule, the Holy Scripture, the Church, the Divine Office, and the sacraments.[69] In Holy Communion (which is not mentioned in *Christ, The Ideal of the Monk*), the religious is united not primarily to Christ's *mission*, but to *Him* as a Person. The religious sister longs for union *with Him*; it is *from* that union that she then desires to share in His mission. Blessed Columba emphasizes that

> above all, the Word gives Himself in Eucharistic Communion. This banquet constitutes the union *par excellence*, because in it Christ is at the same time the Spouse, guest, and food. Communion is undoubtedly the means to enable the soul to realize as it should do the state of perfection necessary to be a spouse of the Word.[70]

Blessed Columba as spiritual director helped to guide innumerable religious sisters to the heights of union—only in heaven will we know how much he assisted souls. The tribute offered by a Carmelite nun of Louvain, who had been directed by Blessed Columba, provides fitting testimony to Blessed Columba's service to the spouses of the Word:

> He was venerated as much as loved, and he loved his daughters as much as he respected them, as he venerated in them the spouses of his Divine Master. He wished them to be beautiful for Him, and rejoiced—he often said so—to be able to embellish and enrich them for Him. His words by which they profited, his lights that he shared, his gifts that he distributed open-handedly, from the abundance of

---

69 See *Ibid.*, pp. 52–53.
70 *Ibid.*, p. 53.

his heart, were to adorn his daughters with jewels which would eternally rejoice the Divine Bridegroom, and which the Bridegroom would point out to him throughout eternity, saying to him: 'It is through thee that I have thus adorned them.'[71]

In his preface to the 2022 revised edition of *Christ, The Ideal of the Monk*, Abbot Xavier Perrin, OSB, relates the following:

> I have never forgotten the two sisters encountered on a visit to a poor Passionist convent in France in the 1980s. These two venerable nuns, well into their eighties, were in charge of the cooking, at least on certain days of the week. They had on the kitchen table a worn copy of the present book [*Christ, The Ideal of the Monk*]. "We take turns," they explained with a great smile, "while one is cooking, the other reads out from the book. When we have finished, we begin again from the beginning. We are never bored. It is so beautiful!" Like these two sisters, generations of monks and nuns have fed on the rich teaching of Blessed Columba Marmion.[72]

The less well-known book *Sponsa Verbi* has been a source of inspiration for women in a similar way. More than one religious sister has confided to me that her vocation to the monastery or to the convent was inspired by the reading of *Sponsa Verbi*. As young women, these sisters received abundant light from the reading of *Sponsa Verbi* and were fired with desire to become spouses of the Word. From heaven, Blessed Columba continues his apostolate of guiding the spouses of the Word to the heights of union. We can hear him speak today the words recorded in *Sponsa Verbi*, urging his dearest children:

> Aspire, then, without ceasing, with the help of grace, by a life of humility and humble devotion, to attain the height of that intimate union Our Lord wishes

---

71 Thibaut, *Abbot Columba Marmion: A Master of the Spiritual Life: 1858–1923*, p. 267.
72 Preface to *Christ, The Ideal of the Monk*, p. vii.

to contract with your souls: there is nothing which can please His Sacred Heart more. If you strive to live this life of union, you will realise to the full the sublimity of your vocation, you will attain the supreme goal of the religious life.[73]

Blessed Columba Marmion, pray for us!

---

[73] *Sponsa Verbi*, pp. 91–92.

8

A SPIRITVAL FRIENDSHIP

DOM COLUMBA MARMION AND MOTHER MARIE-JOSEPH VAN AERDEN

MSGR JOSEPH MURPHY

'I THINK THAT OUR LORD AGREES THAT we should help each other.'[1] In late September 1918, during a period of rest on health grounds at the Redemptorist house in Beauplateau, in south-eastern Belgium, Dom Columba Marmion turned to a Carmelite nun, Mother Marie-Joseph van Aerden, twenty-four years his junior, asking her to act as his spiritual guide. By then, Marmion had been Abbot of Maredsous for the previous nine years and was a well-known spiritual director and preacher of retreats. He had achieved universal fame in the Catholic world the previous year, following the publication of his first book, *Christ, The Life of the Soul*. However, sensing the need to give an account of his soul from time to time, and realizing that he could not ask any of his monks to take on the task of directing him, he decided to seek the assistance of Marie-Joseph, since, as he put it, 'You know me inside out' (*'Vous me connaissez à fond'*).[2]

---

1 Marmion to Marie-Joseph van Aerden, 25 September 1918, in Columba Marmion, *Correspondance 1881–1923*, ed. M. Tierney, R.-F. Poswick and N. Dayez (Paris: François-Xavier de Guibert, 2008), p. 938. Many of Marmion's letters to Mother Marie-Joseph are published, without identifying the addressee, in *Union with God according to the Letters of Direction of Dom Marmion*, ed. R. Thibaut (Brooklyn: Angelico Press, 2022); this edition is a reprint of the second impression of the work originally published in 1949 by B. Herder Book Co., St Louis. Unless otherwise indicated, all translations are mine.
2 Marmion to Marie-Joseph van Aerden, 25 September 1918, in Marmion, *Correspondance*, p. 938.

A Spiritual Friendship

She would act as Marmion's spiritual guide for the remaining five years of his life.

Who was Mother Marie-Joseph van Aerden? How did Abbot Columba come to know her? What was the nature of their relationship? What does their evolving friendship tell us about his approach to spiritual direction?

MARIE-JOSEPH VAN AERDEN'S CORRESPONDENCE WITH DOM COLUMBA MARMION

Mother Marie-Joseph, whose baptismal name was Henriette, was born in Liège on 14 June 1882. She had a younger brother, Hubert, who died in 1903 and a younger sister, Camilla, who died at the age of sixteen in 1906. Her father was an army officer, a fact of which she was proud and which, as she admits, shaped her own character.[3]

Marmion came to know the van Aerden family when he was prior of the Abbey of Mont-César (Kaizersberg) in Louvain. According to the first extant letter from Marmion to Henriette, dated 4 October 1900, her aunt had just made religious profession. Henriette too was thinking about entering the convent and Marmion encouraged her in her vocation. She joined the Carmelites in Louvain in December 1902 and persevered in her vocation, eventually becoming novice mistress. Marmion was her spiritual director during his Louvain years. He continued to act in this capacity after he was elected third Abbot of Maredsous in 1909 and would do so until his death in 1923. Henriette, who received the name Marie-Joseph du Cœur de Jésus on becoming a Carmelite, was to prove an ardent disciple of Dom Columba, and she frequently refers in her correspondence to characteristic themes of his spiritual teaching. Their friendship was such that they came to address each other as Paul and Thecla, in reference to the

---

3 Cf. Marie-Joseph van Aerden to Marmion, 7 June 1914. Mother Marie-Joseph's letters to Marmion are preserved in the archives of Maredsous Abbey and are to date unpublished; I thank Abbot Bernard Lorent, OSB for making copies available to me.

apocryphal story of St Paul the Apostle's spiritual influence on the young virgin Thecla.[4]

Henriette van Aerden was eighteen years old when Dom Columba first met her. During his Louvain years, he encountered her frequently in the Carmelite convent, where he acted as spiritual director and confessor. From this period, we have 16 letters from Marmion to Henriette: nine were written prior to her entry into religious life and seven subsequently. We also have 13 letters from Marmion to Henriette's sister Camilla, five to her father and one to her mother. Unfortunately, none of Henriette's letters to Marmion survive from this period.

Following Marmion's election, his correspondence with Mother Marie-Joseph intensified. We have 64 letters from Abbot Marmion to her and 41 from Marie-Joseph to him. The documentary evidence is far from complete; many letters have been lost. While we possess numerous letters from Mother Marie-Joseph to Marmion for the years 1914 and 1918, we have only one letter for the period 1919 to 1923. Hence, any attempt to give an account of their spiritual friendship will necessarily be incomplete. That said, the documents available to us give us an interesting insight into their concerns and confirm the main elements of Marmion's spiritual teaching, expressed in an accessible manner determined by concrete circumstances.

HENRIETTE'S RELIGIOUS VOCATION

Between 1900 and 1902, Dom Columba wrote a number of letters to Henriette van Aerden to encourage her in her religious vocation and to assist her in overcoming certain difficulties she encountered. Nine of these letters survive.

---

[4] It is not certain when Marmion and Mother Marie-Joseph began to call each other Paul and Thecla. From the evidence available, this usage predates his election. In his correspondence Marmion first uses the name "Thecla" in reference to Mother Marie-Joseph in a letter dated 13 February 1910 (cf. Marmion, *Correspondance*, p. 381). Shortly before his election, on 22 September 1909, he writes to her from Mont-César; after the date he adds a reference to the feast of St Thecla, without explicitly applying the name to her (cf. *ibid.*, p. 345). In almost all her surviving letters to Abbot Marmion, Mother Marie-Joseph refers to herself as "Thecla".

A Spiritual Friendship

In his first letter to Henriette,[5] Marmion is convinced that she has a genuine Carmelite vocation and encourages her to be steadfast in her resolve. She wonders whether she should remain in the world, where she could be more useful, and follow the path indicated for her by her parents, so as not to disappoint them or give the impression of being ungrateful. Interpreting these thoughts as temptations and typical of the trials and struggles of a religious vocation, Marmion encourages her to be faithful and trust in the Lord. He invites her to do all things out of pure love for God, uniting herself with the dispositions of the Sacred Heart. Recognizing that she has a somewhat impetuous character, Marmion promises to help her submit to the workings of grace, inviting her to practise subjecting herself to what others ask of her.

In his second letter,[6] where he first refers to Henriette as Marie-Joseph, the name she would receive at the beginning of her religious life, Marmion insists that she should follow the indications of one director alone; this is a constant of his teaching. He advises her on her daily routine and on the frequency of reception of Holy Communion. He again insists that she should act only out of love for God in all that she does. The more it costs us to act in this way, the greater and more meritorious is our love. It was on the cross that Our Lord displayed the greatest love. We find this love not in ourselves but in the Sacred Heart of Jesus, an infinite furnace of love, to which we can unite ourselves every time we receive Holy Communion. The secret, then, is to unite ourselves often with the Sacred Heart and love with Him and through Him. Regarding Henriette's vocation, Marmion is confident that her parents, whom he has recently met, will eventually agree to allow her to enter the convent.

A few months later, after receiving three letters from Henriette, Marmion writes to express satisfaction that she feels

---

[5] Cf. Marmion to Henriette van Aerden, 4 October 1900, in Marmion, *Correspondance*, p. 103.
[6] Cf. Marmion to Henriette van Aerden, 21 November 1900, in *ibid.*, pp. 103–104.

inspired to unite herself to Christ as Bride and to give herself without holding anything back.[7] He advises her not to be discouraged by her inconstancy: the Lord is happy with her efforts to be pleasing to Him. She is once again tempted to stay in the world to assist with the education of her sister; Marmion believes this to be a temptation coming directly from the devil. He reminds her that decisions should be taken only after discerning carefully in prayer whether the inspirations are coming from God or His enemy. Marmion exhorts her to pray frequently; if she remains faithful, God will arrange everything for the best and remove the obstacles, though they may appear insurmountable. He concludes by giving her instructions on what she should tell him in future about her spiritual progress; in this regard, he mentions the importance of frequent union with God during the day, purity of intention and the practice of inner mortification in order to counteract her natural vivacity.

In his letter of 25 July 1901, Marmion encourages Henriette to continue praying with confidence; in so doing, nothing will prevent her from following her vocation. When things seem hopeless from a human point of view, God likes to show his wisdom and love which thwart all the plans of men. However, we must do all that depends on us; when we can do no more, Our Lord will intervene. Marmion does not hesitate to advise Henriette to accept a place at a superior school run by religious sisters, rather than the one her parents desire for her, since it will be easier for her to leave later in order to pursue her religious vocation.[8]

Marmion's advice to Henriette proves effective. Some months later,[9] he is pleased that she has succeeded in remaining united to God; this, ultimately, is what counts. He then gives advice for her spiritual life on the lines of what he had said previously regarding purity of intention, reception of Holy Communion,

---

7   Cf. Marmion to Henriette van Aerden, 6 March 1901, in *ibid.*, pp. 108–109.
8   Cf. Marmion to Henriette van Aerden, 25 July 1901, in *ibid.*, pp. 111–112.
9   Cf. Marmion to Henriette van Aerden, 13 November 1901, in *ibid.*, pp. 115–116.

avoidance of relationships that could turn her away from her goal, spiritual reading, and submission of nature to grace.

In his letter of 17 December 1901, Marmion desires Henriette to persevere and make progress in love. If we give ourselves up completely to Jesus, in a spirit of self-abandonment, He will look after the details of our lives. Marmion explains that giving oneself to Jesus entails giving oneself to others out of love for Him; in reality, it means giving oneself to Him in the person of our neighbour. This teaching is theologically grounded in the Incarnation of Christ: 'Just as God became incarnate in the Sacred Humanity of Jesus Christ, He became incarnate in a way in our neighbour, and just as one can go to God only through the Sacred Humanity, so too we can unite ourselves to Christ only by accepting Him united as He is to our neighbour.'[10]

In a previous letter, which has not survived, Henriette had asked Marmion for advice on dealing with children who behave badly in her class and exercise a negative influence on others. Marmion explains that when the Lord entrusts someone with souls, suffering is inevitable, especially when one witnesses evil that cannot be eliminated. He gives her some practical advice and advises her to rely on prayer.

The same teaching about the trials that souls whom God wishes to unite to Himself must face and about the consequent need for complete self-surrender and trust is found in a letter dated 14 March 1902.[11] The more a soul has experienced these trials the more it will soar once it is definitively engaged in God's service. Marmion is convinced that Henriette is called to become a Carmelite and that God will not forsake her in the pursuit of her vocation. In this context, he recommends her to practise self-abandonment and, in this regard, suggests she calmly read the ninth book of the *Treatise on the Love of God*. To those he directed, Marmion

---

10 Marmion to Henriette van Aerden, 17 December 1901, in *ibid*, pp. 118–119.
11 Cf. Marmion to Henriette van Aerden, 14 March 1902, in *ibid.*, pp. 130–131.

frequently recommends the writings of St Francis de Sales, whom he regarded as a kindred spirit. Some years earlier, he had given similar advice on self-abandonment in the face of trials to Jeanne de Brouwer, reassuring her that she would find in the teachings of St Francis de Sales an account of the dispositions needed to face times of trial.[12]

Marmion also senses that Henriette still places too much confidence in her own activity and does not place herself sufficiently in the Lord's hands. In this context, he paraphrases two New Testament texts to which he frequently refers in order to emphasize our dependence on Christ: 'I am the vine, you are the branches. As the branches cannot bear fruit if they do not abide in the vine, you will not be able to do anything good, unless you abide in me, for without me you can do nothing' (cf. Jn 15:4) and 'God gave us his Son Jesus to be our wisdom, our righteousness, our sanctification and our redemption' (cf. 1 Cor. 1:30). All our efforts are to no avail unless Jesus Christ acts in us and helps us.

Sometime later, Marmion writes to assure Henriette that he continues to pray for her.[13] Once again, in the face of various trials, he encourages her: 'The best vocations are those that have been tested.' Both he and the prioress of the Carmelite convent are convinced about her vocation and hope that she will enter soon. If she continues to be faithful, God will arrange everything: 'In this regard you must have great faith, perfect trust in Him, and then try, by being very faithful, not to place any obstacle in the way of His plans for you.' He hopes to obtain her father's permission soon and encourages her in the practice of spiritual communion.

Shortly afterwards, Marmion asked and obtained her father's permission for her to enter the convent.[14] Subse-

---

[12] Cf. Marmion to Jeanne de Brouwer, 13 January 1895, in *ibid.*, p. 67. Jeanne entered the Benedictine convent of Maredret the following year, received the religious name Hildegarde and was prioress from 1901 to 1930.
[13] Cf. Marmion to Henriette van Aerden, 18 May 1902, in *ibid.*, pp. 137–138.
[14] Cf. Marmion to Mr van Aerden, 15 June 1902, in *ibid.*, pp. 140–141; Marmion to Mr van Aerden, 19 August 1902, in ibid., pp. 144–145.

quently, he writes to tell her that the moment of sacrifice has arrived and that in becoming the bride of the Crucified One, Jesus associates her with his sufferings.[15] Since she desires close union with Jesus, she, like Him, will have to endure the world's mockery and incomprehension. Marmion invites her to be courageous: these are the signs that Our Lord wishes to unite her closely to Himself and associate her with the works He carries out for the glory of His Father. Marmion promises to help her become a good and holy Carmelite and assures her that he will pray for her and take responsibility for her soul before God. In return, he asks her to pray that he may belong completely to the Lord and aim to do nothing other than what is in accordance with the Lord's will.

Marmion was at Erdington Priory in England when Henriette entered the convent in December 1902. From there he writes to encourage her to give herself up to the wisdom and love of the Lord, completely, unhesitatingly, and unconditionally.[16] This is not as easy as it may seem. Marmion believes that very few of Christ's brides love Him for Himself and that the majority love themselves more than they love Jesus. Much depends on the Carmelite's generosity during her novitiate. She must not start bargaining with the Lord or hold things back for herself. Jesus will ask sacrifices of those who give themselves up completely to Him, but He will also be generous in giving the graces and helps necessary to carry the cross. To have doubts about this is to have doubts about Christ's love and fidelity; nothing could hurt Him more.

At the beginning of her religious life, Henriette received the religious name of Marie-Joseph du Coeur de Jésus. Marmion explains that this name was given to her in honour of a saintly Carmelite whom he had had the great grace of

---

15   Cf. Marmion to Henriette van Aerden, 31 August 1902, in *ibid.*, pp. 145.
16   Cf. Marmion to Marie-Joseph van Aerden, 2 December 1902, in *ibid.*, pp. 151–152.

knowing before her death three years earlier. She had made a vow to abandon herself unreservedly to all that her Divine Bridegroom willed and to seek no joy other than in Him. Marmion affirms that her fidelity to this generous abandonment led her to the heights of holiness.

EARLY YEARS OF RELIGIOUS LIFE (1902–1909)

Marmion continued to correspond with Marie-Joseph following her entry into religious life. Seven letters survive from the years 1902–1909. In the first, dated 23 November 1903, referring to the teaching of St Teresa of Avila, he reminds her that the all-powerful grace of Christ can completely rid us of all our weaknesses and bad inclinations, and bring us to a high degree of union with Him, provided we remain faithful to giving ourselves up every day to His divine action in prayer.[17] In this letter, Marmion is frank with her. While he recognizes that she is capable of becoming a saint, there are two obstacles preventing her from making progress: her tendency to see the faults of others, without noticing her own, and her lack of habitual recollection during the day. To overcome these obstacles he recommends prayer, with a particular request for true charity in her heart, since external acts are but the manifestation of what lies in the depths of the heart.

Two letters survive from the year 1906. In the first, he recommends detachment from all created things, even the most trivial, in order to give herself unreservedly to Jesus.[18] The second, a much longer letter, was written by way of a spiritual gift to Marie-Joseph as she prepared to make her religious profession.[19] It sets out a demanding programme outlining the journey she must undertake in order to reach spiritual perfection in line with the Carmelite tradition. Without any

---

[17] Cf. Marmion to Marie-Joseph van Aerden, 23 November 1903, in *ibid.*, pp. 174–175.
[18] Cf. Marmion to Marie-Joseph van Aerden, 26 November 1906, in *ibid.*, pp. 252–253.
[19] Cf. Marmion to Marie-Joseph van Aerden, 6 December 1906, in *ibid.*, pp. 254–256.

merit on her part, the Lord Jesus has given her many gifts and calls her to a high degree of union with Him, inviting her to share His pains and sufferings for the glory of the Father and the salvation of souls.

Marmion foresees that Marie-Joseph will suffer and will need much courage, faith and trust. He warns her that there are deserts to be crossed, that she will have to pass through darkness, overcome obstacles, face moments when she will feel powerless and forsaken. However, if she remains faithful and abandoned to Jesus, He will always guide her by the hand: 'Even though I walk through the shadow of death, I fear nothing for you are with me' (cf. Ps. 22:4).

Marmion encourages her to give herself unreservedly and fearlessly to Christ, who will come to her every day in the Eucharist in order to transform her into Himself. Christ's Eucharistic life should be her model. In the Eucharist, Christ is the victim sacrificed for the glory of his Father and given over as food to His brethren, even to those who receive Him with coldness and ingratitude, and to those who offend Him. Marie-Joseph is to be a victim sacrificed to the glory of the Holy Trinity in prayer, the Divine Office, and mortification. She is also to be a victim of charity sacrificed to souls by expiation and to her sisters by patience, goodness, and indulgence. Marmion concludes with a stirring invitation: 'Be a great soul who forgets herself to think of the interest of Jesus and of souls. Do not be stayed by the trifles which occupy the thoughts and the life of so many consecrated souls. Let us help one another to arrive at this sublime ideal which I desire for myself as I do for you.'[20]

Marie-Joseph took Marmion's words to heart and made rapid progress. In a letter addressed to her on 4 March 1907, Marmion extols the beauty and greatness of the Carmelite vocation to be Christ's bride.[21] To respond adequately to this

---

20 Marmion to Marie-Joseph van Aerden, 6 December 1906, in *ibid.*, pp. 255–256; for the English translation, see Marmion, *Union with God*, p. 91.
21 Cf. Marmion to Marie-Joseph van Aerden, 4 March 1907, in *ibid.*, pp. 263–264.

vocation the bride must fulfil her role with perfect fidelity and great perfection. Marmion prays that Marie-Joseph may be worthy of her magnificent vocation. She must never give in to the promptings of her own nature but place every fibre of her being in the hands of the Bridegroom, so that nothing may stir in her except at His command and for love of Him. Referring to the teachings of St John of the Cross, Marmion invites her to look upon each member of her community in a spirit of faith as sent by Jesus to test and form her. For this reason, she should not be annoyed by those who upset her.

In October 1908, Marmion addressed a brief letter to Marie-Joseph from the Abbey of Maria Laach to express his contentment for an action of hers.[22] He invites her to show great humility and sweetness, and to see Jesus in everyone. Marmion's Christocentric focus is once again evident. He states that he is greatly consoled that he and St Marie-Joseph are one in Christ. Jesus is to be sought in all things. We are to live for the Father in Jesus, with Him, and through Him. Marie-Joseph is invited once again to do all things with great love, not in her own name, but in the name of Jesus.

Just before he was elected Abbot of Maredsous, Marmion addressed a letter to Marie-Joseph on the feast of St Thecla.[23] Since he was aware that he could be elected, he speaks of their possible future separation. He assures her that he will continue to be her father and offer her daily through Jesus to the Father in the celebration of the Mass. In characteristic fashion, he invites her to live for Jesus and to be filled more and more with the spirit of Jesus the Bridegroom.

MARIE-JOSEPH'S SPIRITUAL PROGRESS

Following Dom Columba's transfer to the Abbey of Maredsous as its third abbot, his correspondence with Marie-Joseph intensified. For the years 1910–1923, 64 items of correspondence

---

[22] Cf. Marmion to Marie-Joseph van Aerden, 21 October 1908, in *ibid.*, p. 306.
[23] Cf. Marmion to Marie-Joseph van Aerden, 22 September 1909, in *ibid.*, pp. 344–345.

A Spiritual Friendship

from Marmion to Marie-Joseph survive, as well as 41 from Marie-Joseph to Marmion. Her first surviving letter, written on 17 January 1910, testifies to her spiritual progress under Marmion's direction.[24] She believes herself called to give herself up completely in order to be 'possessed' by God. She sees her previous sufferings as a preparation for a new life, in which Jesus lives in her for the glory of his Father; this is the 'moral extension of the Incarnation' about which she had sometimes spoken to Marmion. She is not simply united with Jesus but one with him, so that when she prays the Divine Office, Jesus is praying through her. She strives to do all things for Him, but in a hidden way, without drawing attention to herself.

In two subsequent letters, Abbot Columba encourages her spiritual progress. In the first,[25] he speaks of the necessity of spiritual direction and reminds her that since all souls are different one should not try to imitate another in a servile way. It is important to preserve one's freedom of spirit and God's freedom of action in the soul. God is calling Marie-Joseph to close union, and she must follow Him, who asks her for great poverty and bareness of spirit; this is the Carmelite spirit. Marmion reassures her that the Holy Spirit is guiding him in what he writes to her, and she can be certain that he is pointing out the correct path for her. 'The more that God unites you to Himself, the more your only life will be Jesus Christ, and the greater will be your poverty and suffering, at the times when God withdraws. The soul sacrificed to God in the bareness of pure faith, hope, and perfect union does more for the Church in one hour than others in their entire lives.'[26]

---

24 Unlike Marmion's letters to Marie-Joseph, her letters to him have not previously been published.
25 Cf. Marmion to Marie-Joseph van Aerden, 29 January 1910, in Marmion, *Correspondance*, pp. 376–377.
26 In his letters of spiritual direction, Marmion frequently invokes this principle, derived from the writings of the Benedictine author Louis of Blois (1506–1566), to emphasize the spiritual fruitfulness of the contemplative

A few weeks later, Marmion wrote a second letter to Marie-Joseph, the first in which he refers to her explicitly as Thecla.[27] He encourages her spiritual journey, confirming that Jesus is the 'way' and that he (Marmion) is guiding her to where Jesus abides 'in the bosom of the Father' (*'in sinu Patris'*). There is no danger of illusion for those whom the Lord leads to this goal along this path. She should avoid curiosity about particular mysteries, but seek only to know God, in pure faith, through Jesus Christ. If God wishes to show her something in particular, she should remain very humble, in the awareness that such communications are much less useful to the soul than the infused knowledge of faith in which God communicates Himself immediately to the soul, filling it with divinity and love. In this context, Marmion quotes a text from the prophet Hosea: *'Sponsabo te mihi in fide'*, 'I will betroth you in faith' (Hs. 2:20, Vulgate). These, he says, are the words of the Divine Bridegroom, who speaks the truth for He is 'Truth' (cf. Jn 14:6).

Over the next few years, Abbot Columba continued to correspond with Marie-Joseph, giving her news about himself and sharing some of his difficulties and trials with her. Their friendship continued to deepen. He regularly emphasizes the importance of basing one's entire spiritual life on Christ, the Way who leads to the 'bosom of the Father'. He gives advice on dealing with the jealousy of another sister.[28] He reminds her that nothing glorifies God like the recognition of our own weakness and powerlessness without Jesus, and our consequent need to place our trust in Him; this is why

---

life. It is to be found in chapter 1 of Louis de Blois's *Book of Spiritual Instruction*, the English translation of his *Institutio Spiritualis*, published in London in 1901. In a letter dated 19 January 1905 to his niece, Dame Caecilia Joyce, who entered the convent of Maredret in 1902, Marmion mentions that he is currently reading the *Book of Spiritual Instruction*, which he describes as 'a very beautiful book': 'It is true Benedictine asceticism, simple, yet profound'; cf. Marmion, *Correspondance*, p. 213.

27 Cf. Marmion to Marie-Joseph van Aerden, 13 February 1910, in Marmion, *Correspondance*, pp. 381–382.
28 Cf. Marmion to Marie-Joseph van Aerden, 22 April 1911, in *ibid.*, p. 453.

A Spiritual Friendship

poverty and dryness are necessary elements of the spiritual life.[29] Since we are poor, Jesus is our 'supplement': God has sent Him to be our wisdom, our justice, our sanctification, and our redemption (cf. 1 Cor. 1:30).[30] Jesus comes to our aid in our weakness. Using an interesting image, Marmion says that through Jesus we can be, as St Paul says, the aroma of Christ to God (cf. 2 Cor. 2:15), somewhat like Jacob who presents himself to his father Isaac in Esau's clothes and thus with Esau's smell in order to receive his blessing (cf. Gen. 27:27). In short, Christ is truly the source of our life and in Him we are one.[31] It is His life in us that should be the source of all our activity. His life was a human life expressing the divine life in human form. The more our activity derives from this divine source, the more it is pleasing to the Father.

Acutely aware of the sufferings caused by the difficulties of convent life, Marmion assures Marie-Joseph that he has prayed much for her. He tells her that the perfection of obedience is to accept all the circumstances of the situation in which God has placed us. This includes loving those who do us wrong, as Jesus did. With regard to one particular sister, Marmion advises Marie-Joseph to be very kind, pray much and say little.[32]

At the end of 1913, Marmion assures Marie-Joseph that he continually prays that she may correspond perfectly to God's designs. While she needs to be aware of the depths of her lowliness in order to reach final union, she must see this lowliness in God. Jesus is all-powerful. He wishes to sanctify us, and He is capable of doing so.[33]

---

29 Cf. Marmion to Marie-Joseph van Aerden, 27 June 1911, in *ibid.*, pp. 465–466.
30 Cf. Marmion to Marie-Joseph van Aerden, 28 September 1911, in *ibid.*, pp. 478–479.
31 Cf. Marmion to Marie-Joseph van Aerden, 22 January 1912, in *ibid.*, pp. 504–505.
32 Cf. Marmion to Marie-Joseph van Aerden, 10 September 1913, in *ibid.*, pp. 627–628.
33 Cf. Marmion to Marie-Joseph van Aerden, 18 December 1913, in *ibid.*, pp. 648–649.

A DISPUTE ABOUT FORMATION

In 1914, Marie-Joseph was novice mistress. She enjoyed the full confidence of the prioress, Mother Amélie, who like her was a close friend and spiritual daughter of Abbot Columba.[34] Marie-Joseph's approach to formation took its cue from Abbot Columba's teachings. Writing to another Carmelite novice mistress in 1917, Marmion advised her to lead her novices to God through Jesus Christ, for He is the only Way.[35] Marie-Joseph had always applied this method.

Like Marmion, she had an extraordinary love of the Sacred Scriptures: 'I would not be able to say what a treasure the book of the Sacred Scriptures is to me and how the good God opens it to me and inscribes it in the innermost part of my soul and in my memory, to draw from it and present me with what is most flavoursome and most appropriate to my needs.'[36] She fully supported Cardinal Mercier's insistence that all the faithful should read the New Testament and that female religious, like their male counterparts, should read the entire Bible.[37] To help her novices visualize the physical setting of the various episodes of the life of Christ, she obtained a large volume of photographs and maps of the Holy Land from Abbot Marmion, which she put to good use.[38] Unusually for the time, she devoted considerable energy to the study of the Hebrew language in order to read the Old Testament in the original.[39]

---

34 Mother Amélie de l'Immaculée Conception was prioress on three separate occasions: from 1906 to 1909, from 1912 to 1915 and from 1918 to 1924. 35 letters from Marmion to Mother Amélie survive, the first of which dates from January 1902; these letters are particularly numerous in the years 1907, 1908, 1912 and 1914.
35 Cf. Marmion to Mother Gabrielle Cambon, 20 February 1917, in Marmion, *Correspondance*, p. 840; cf. Marmion, *Union with God*, p. 258.
36 Marie-Joseph van Aerden to Marmion, 2 March 1914.
37 Cf. Marie-Joseph van Aerden to Marmion, 2 March 1914.
38 Cf. Marie-Joseph van Aerden to Marmion, 7 April 1914.
39 She first refers to her efforts to learn Hebrew in a letter to Abbot Marmion at the end of December 1916. Her confessor, Dom Bruno Destrée encourages her in this; cf. Marie-Joseph van Aerden to Marmion, 7 February 1917. Marmion, too, is supportive of her efforts: cf. Marmion to Marie-Joseph van Aerden, 4 April 1917, in Marmion, *Correspondance*, p. 848.

In her letter of 2 March 1914, Marie-Joseph tells Marmion that the Holy Bible is the only manual she consults for the novitiate, finding in it all she needs. Together with her novice, Maria Pia, she meditates every evening on the Gospel of the day. She encourages her novice to find solitude 'in the bosom of the Father' and learn how to draw power and grace from the mysteries of Christ's life as they unfold in the course of the liturgical year. She believes that when we contemplate Christ Jesus *'in sinu Patris'* we come to possess not just a power deriving from Him but Christ in his entirety.

The following week, the canonical visitation of the Louvain convent took place. Marie-Joseph wrote two letters to Abbot Marmion, giving him an account of what happened.[40] Since the Provincial declared publicly that the prioress should see to it that the novice is formed just as the others were, Marie-Joseph suspected that her approach had been reported to him and called into question. She tells Marmion that she does indeed have a special method as far as the interior life of the novice is concerned, which she has no intention of abandoning. She is convinced that she cannot be reproached for the content of her teaching: 'Can Thecla speak differently to St Paul?'[41] However, she admits that the means she employs could be criticized. In particular, she does not use the traditional manuals of the Venerable John of Jesus and Mary (1564–1615), general of the Discalced Carmelites from 1611 to 1614, then in general use for the formation of novices. She is of the view that, while these represent a precious family heritage, they are less effective for formation when compared with Marmion's approach: 'Just as you showed me the Way, Jesus, I have shown it to the novice and she makes progress.'

In her letter of 16 March 1918 to Marmion, she writes the divine Name in Hebrew characters; later, in a letter dated 31 August 1918, she refers to the Messiah in Hebrew.
40 The first was begun on 10 March 1914 and completed on 12 March; the second is dated 15 March 1914.
41 Marie-Joseph van Aerden to Marmion, 15 March 1914.

Marie-Joseph explains that the Bible is her only manual and that she interprets the Rule, the Constitutions, and the community observances in the light of Scripture. She admits that this is an innovation, but it is also a simplification. The Gospel and St Paul are far more effective for the formation of a true Carmelite than any books, because they form the true Christian woman. Her special method, she says, gives knowledge of Christ Jesus. 'He himself is the Religious of the Father and to see Him so occupied with the honour of His Father, to hear the Father say that His delights are in Him, I believe this soul desires to be united with Him, to place all her being in His hands, to be the true religious, the bride.'[42] Where there is hope that there can be union with Christ in order to live for the Father, it becomes possible to pronounce the vows, which are the necessary means to bring about this union.

The young novice mistress seeks reassurance from Abbot Marmion. May she continue on this path? Can her innovation be bad, given that it would introduce the Sacred Books more and more in the convent, as well as the simple faith of the early Christians, which, it seems, should flourish anew in our days?

Marmion replied on 17 March. Having prayed about the matter, he reassures her that her conscience can be at peace and that she should continue doing what she has been doing, without being displeasing to God or disobedient to her superiors. There is fundamentally only one religious life, which is Christianity or, put in another way, the life of Christ in us. A religious simply wishes the life of Christ to flourish fully in himself or herself. Religious life can be summarized with reference to two texts: 'If you wish to be perfect, sell what you have and come, follow me' (Mt. 19:21) and 'Behold, we have left all things and we have followed you' (Mt. 19:27). Hence, all religious life involves giving up all things in order to follow Jesus Christ.[43] Formation of young religious on these lines

---

42 Marie-Joseph van Aerden to Marmion, 15 March 1914.
43 Cf. Marmion to Marie-Joseph van Aerden, 17 March 1914, in Marmion, *Correspondance*, p. 678. The plan of Marmion's book on the monastic vocation, *Christ, The Ideal of the Monk*, is inspired by these verses.

is essential. Marmion says that he formed the Carmelites of Louvain in this way for ten years to the satisfaction of all and that no one had understood and assimilated his teachings, which are not his but Christ's, like Marie-Joseph. This teaching is perfectly in line with Carmelite spirituality, as is clear from the teachings of St Teresa of Avila.

Marmion goes on to affirm that apart from what is essential, which is common to all the Orders, there is also something specific to each one. While the *'reliquimus omnia'* ('we have left all things') is the same for all religious Orders, the manner of following Christ can differ. In the case of the ancient Orders, like the Benedictines and the Carmelites, almost everything is contained in Sacred Scripture and in the formation that the usages and customs of the Order give to its subjects. In Marie-Joseph's case, all is contained in the ceremonial and constitutions of the Order. He advises her, as novice mistress, to acquire a profound knowledge of the spirit and doctrine of St Teresa, which will, without noticing or suspecting it, influence her way of understanding holiness and reading the Scriptures. What counts is that she should see things in the way St Teresa saw them, which she already does. She should insist that the interior life of her charges be in accordance with the usages and customs of her Order. She can continue as before; the sisters who denounced her are not in a position to judge the interior formation she imparts.

THE CASE OF JEANNE VAN ROOSBROECK

Towards the end of 1916, Marie-Joseph wrote to Abbot Marmion regarding a wealthy unmarried benefactress, Jeanne Van Roosbroeck, who desired to enter religious life.[44] Jeanne was in regular contact with the monks of Mont-César. Dom Bruno Destrée, confessor of the Louvain convent, was also her confessor. Prior to the outbreak of the First World War, she had tried to enter the Benedictine convent of Maredret but was refused. Subsequently, another monk of Mont-César,

---

44   Cf. Marie-Joseph van Aerden to Marmion, end of December 1916.

Dom Eugène Vandeur, attempted, without success, to interest her in a foundation project of his.[45] Meanwhile, a close friend of Marmion and Marie-Joseph, Canon Armand Thiéry (1866–1955), had restored an ancient abbey near the church of St Gertrude in Louvain, which he hoped to use for some religious purpose, possibly a new foundation of Benedictine nuns. He had spoken to Jeanne of his plans, but she indicated that she would take no decision without first having spoken to Abbot Marmion and Dom Bruno.

Jeanne subsequently met Abbot Marmion and was pleased with her meeting.[46] It seems that Marmion was initially in favour of Jeanne's entering a Benedictine novitiate, possibly with a view to becoming involved at a later date in the projected Louvain foundation. Marie-Joseph suggested that she do her novitiate at Tyburn convent in London. Marmion was a close friend of Mother Pierre-Adèle Garnier, the foundress of the Adorers of the Sacred Heart of Jesus of Montmartre, and regularly visited their convent at Tyburn. Under his influence, this institute adopted the Rule of St Benedict in 1914.

In the end, Jeanne entered the Benedictine convent of La Paix Notre-Dame in Liège.[47] At first, all seemed to go well. Marmion assured Marie-Joseph that he was praying that all would proceed smoothly. He did not intend to become closely involved with the new Louvain foundation, believing it best that the foundation should be assisted by Mont-César.[48] In December 1917, Marmion wrote positively to Marie-Joseph about Jeanne's progress: 'Jeanne is progressing admirably. She

---

45 Dom Eugène Vandeur (1875–1967) was a monk of Maredsous and succeeded Dom Marmion as prior of Mont-César in 1909, remaining there until 1925. He was a well-known lecturer and spiritual writer. He founded a community of Benedictine nuns who settled first in Wépion, near Namur, in 1922 and later in Ermeton-sur-Biert, near Maredsous, in 1936. From 1925 to his death, he resided in Maredsous.
46 Cf. Marie-Joseph van Aerden to Marmion, 15 February 1917.
47 Cf. Marmion to Marie-Joseph van Aerden, 3 May 1917, in Marmion, *Correspondance*, p. 851; Marmion to Marie-Joseph van Aerden, 9 May 1917, in *ibid.*, p. 855.
48 Cf. Marmion to Marie-Joseph van Aerden, 9 May 1917, in *ibid.*, p. 855.

A Spiritual Friendship

has great admiration for the Benedictine life and her Superiors; she is highly esteemed. The novice mistress has told me that it is astonishing the efforts she has made to be a good little novice without plans and completely given over to obedience.'[49]

However, Jeanne did not persevere. On 1 March 1918, Marmion informed Marie-Joseph that he had seen Jeanne in Liège but 'they were rather hesitant about her' and she was in great need of prayers.[50] On 9 March, Jeanne left the convent. A few days later, Marie-Joseph wrote to Marmion to express her indignation that Jeanne had been dismissed.[51] Marie-Joseph, who had a somewhat impetuous character, was initially inclined to blame the Liège community, especially the novice mistress, Dame Émilie Jacmin, for Jeanne's dismissal, and wrote a strongly worded letter to the Abbess, Dame Placide Delhaes.

Marmion first refers to Jeanne's departure in a letter addressed to Marie-Joseph on 17 March. In his view, Jeanne is too old and set in her ways to change; 'the little branch, when it is young bends easily; when it is old it breaks.'[52] Marmion's letter seems to have provoked a short-lived misunderstanding between them.[53] Concerning Jeanne's vocation, he goes to the heart of the problem in characteristic fashion: 'I am convinced that Jeanne's departure was according to the Divine Will. She is very good, she seeks God sincerely, but that absolute and unconditional gift of self that the Benedictine profession presupposes, was, I think, beyond her grace. The preoccupation with her work remained unconsciously in the depth of her heart.'[54]

---

49 Marmion to Marie-Joseph van Aerden, 4 December 1917, in *ibid.*, p. 890.
50 Marmion to Marie-Joseph van Aerden, 1 March 1918, in *ibid.*, p. 900.
51 Cf. Marie-Joseph van Aerden to Marmion, 13 March 1918.
52 Marmion to Marie-Joseph van Aerden, 17 March 1918, in Marmion, *Correspondance*, p. 904.
53 Cf. Marmion to Marie-Joseph van Aerden, 29 March 1918, in *ibid.*, pp. 905–906; Marmion to Marie-Joseph van Aerden, 1 April 1918, in *ibid.*, pp. 906–907.
54 Marmion to Marie-Joseph van Aerden, 1 April 1918, in *ibid.*, p. 906.

Marie-Joseph was satisfied with Marmion's guidance in the matter and told him that her confessor, Dom Bruno Destrée, believed Jeanne to be more suitable to the various good works she had undertaken in Louvain than to religious life.[55] However, Jeanne was still attracted to the Benedictine life. She thought of reapplying to the Liège community and remained interested in the proposed foundation at St Gertrude. In this regard, Marie-Joseph told Marmion that Canon Thiéry and Dom Bruno held differing views as to Jeanne's religious vocation and informed him that Jeanne would send him a report, in the hope that he could advise her.[56]

After prayer and reflection, Abbot Columba sent Jeanne a long and carefully worded reply,[57] in which, characteristically, he considers the matter from a theological point of view, with a profound reflection on the meaning of Benedictine profession. He affirms that while she and her superiors had acted in good faith, she had encountered insurmountable difficulties in pursuing her vocation in the Benedictine Order because she did not fully appreciate the need to give herself fully to the Lord, without imposing conditions and without setting her heart on a particular project. According to Marmion, Jeanne places her desire to promote a major liturgical initiative on the same level as the essential aim of the Benedictine life; indeed, she seems to subordinate everything to her project. She therefore appears incapable of giving herself up absolutely and blindly to God's guidance. Marmion is therefore of the view that for the moment she should occupy herself with her work in Louvain and avoid thinking about returning to Liège. After the war, he says, Liège will make a new foundation in Louvain and she will be able to enter, provided she gives herself up humbly and absolutely. Meanwhile, she should

---

55 Cf. Marie-Joseph van Aerden to Marmion, 4 April 1918.
56 Cf. Marie-Joseph van Aerden to Marmion, 28 April 1918. On the subject of Jeanne Van Roosbroeck, Marie-Joseph wrote again to Marmion on 3 May 1918.
57 Cf. Marmion to Jeanne van Roosbroeck, 8 May 1918, in Marmion, *Correspondance*, pp. 916–920.

avoid recrimination and remove all bitterness from her soul. Jeanne was not happy about Marmion's reply, but he believed that since he had said what he thought, he did not intend to engage in further discussion on the matter.[58] In the end, Jeanne never joined a religious community.

On 29 April 1919, the Benedictine convent of Liège made a new foundation in the ancient abbey of St Gertrude, sending five nuns. The prioress of the new community was Dame Charlotte Rensonnet. The nuns ran a house of studies and a student residence. During the Second World War, the convent was heavily damaged. Following the 1968 linguistic division of the Catholic University of Louvain, the Benedictines decided to leave the site, which was subsequently converted into residential property.

MARMION'S SPIRITUAL GUIDE

As their spiritual friendship deepened, Abbot Marmion continued to encourage Marie-Joseph and assure her of his prayers. In his letters, he regularly gives her spiritual advice and makes suggestions as to how she can best discharge her responsibilities as novice mistress. Marie-Joseph suffers from time to time from health problems, such as haemorrhages and chronic fatigue. She complains that she is not always understood by other members of the community and that some are jealous of her. In this regard, Marmion shows considerable understanding and compassion.[59] He reassures her that he finds nothing in her writings other than the pure teaching of Jesus as He preached it and as St Paul presented it.[60] To help her overcome a scruple, he advises her not to become too dependent on caffeine, which she sometimes takes to overcome her tiredness, although its use is legitimate.[61]

---

58 Cf. Marmion to Marie-Joseph van Aerden, 3 June 1918, in *ibid.*, p. 924.
59 Cf. Marmion to Marie-Joseph van Aerden, 5 January 1918, in Marmion, *ibid.*, pp. 894–895.
60 Cf. Marmion to Marie-Joseph van Aerden, 24 June 1916, in *ibid.*, pp. 806–807; Marmion to Marie-Joseph van Aerden, 22 August 1916, in *ibid.*, pp. 810–811.
61 Cf. Marmion to Marie-Joseph van Aerden, 29 July 1914, in *ibid.*, pp. 707–708.

BELOVED OF GOD AND MEN

Marmion also tells her more and more about his own experiences. In his letters, he speaks of his relationship with Christ, to whom he confides all his worries and concerns,[62] his difficulties and infidelities,[63] his health problems,[64] and his disappointments and trials.[65] Marmion has a sensitive character: he is hurt by the criticisms of his fellow monks, arising from his frequent absences and his manner of government.[66] He tells her that he has a great desire to live in habitual adoration before the Word, submitting himself entirely to Christ in union with His Sacred Humanity.[67] The prayer of pure faith, without consolation but in truth, attracts him.[68] Our Lord has detached him from everything and has given him a great attraction for the truth and simplicity of the faith. Marmion is guided by the sure path of faith and has led Marie-Joseph along this path.[69]

In a letter dated 4 April 1917, Abbot Marmion writes:

> I have the feeling that Our Lord desires you not only to be my daughter, but also, in Him, my sister, my confidant, my guide. You know me so well. Our Lord gives you the light to say exactly what is suitable for me and what others would not wish to say to me. I

---

62 Cf. Marmion to Marie-Joseph van Aerden, 29 July 1914, in *ibid.*, pp. 707–708.
63 Cf. Marmion to Marie-Joseph van Aerden, 15 March 1914, in *ibid.*, pp. 675–676.
64 Cf. Marmion to Marie-Joseph van Aerden, 9 October 1916, in *ibid.*, pp. 815–816; Marmion to Marie-Joseph van Aerden, 4 September 1918, in *ibid.*, 931–932; Marmion to Marie-Joseph van Aerden, 25 September 1918, in *ibid.*, pp. 938–939; Marmion to Marie-Joseph van Aerden, 9 May 1919, in *ibid.*, p. 982; Marmion to Marie-Joseph van Aerden, 8 January 1923, in *ibid.*, p. 1262.
65 Cf. Marmion to Marie-Joseph van Aerden, 1 June 1916, in *ibid.*, p. 801.
66 Cf. Marmion to Marie-Joseph van Aerden, 14 October 1917, in *ibid.*, pp. 877–878; Marmion to Marie-Joseph van Aerden, 6 November 1920, in *ibid.*, p. 1110.
67 Cf. Marmion to Marie-Joseph van Aerden, 9 October 1916, in *ibid.*, pp. 815–816.
68 Cf. Marmion to Marie-Joseph van Aerden, 20 November 1916, in *ibid.*, p. 819.
69 Cf. Marmion to Marie-Joseph van Aerden, April 1917, in *ibid.*, pp. 845–846.

A Spiritual Friendship

> therefore give you all the rights of a sister and I ask you, out of love for Jesus, in all simplicity to be my consolation and my help here below, as I have tried to be for you, and which I shall not cease to be until Our Lord unites us in heaven.[70]

Marmion is happy to have someone to whom he can express everything without fear of being misunderstood.[71] The publication of his first volume, *Christ, The Life of the Soul*, is imminent; to him it is a great consolation that the work will help people to know and love Jesus. He confesses that many of the thoughts it contains are due not only to himself but also to Marie-Joseph: 'Often some thought, some light, half understood by me, was in your heart in a developed state and came to complete fruition when I recognized through you all that it contained.'[72] Marmion believes that the Lord has given him Marie-Joseph in order to communicate His will and keep him in His love, complete him and prevent his impetuous character from hindering God's action.

From the beginning of 1918, Marie-Joseph addresses Abbot Marmion not only as 'Father' but also as 'Brother', in keeping with his request that she be his sister.[73] She informs him of all the good his book is doing, recognizing in it something of the joy and hope she experienced when she received its teaching from him.[74] She recognizes that Marmion's doctrine is not his own; it is in reality what Jesus taught in the name of His Father (cf. Jn 7:16). It is the teaching on which St Paul and St John commented, which the Church prepares for souls and distributes to them. Marmion is indeed blessed to be numbered among those who sow and harvest!

---

70 Marmion to Marie-Joseph van Aerden, 4 April 1917, in *ibid.*, p. 847.
71 Cf. Marmion to Marie-Joseph van Aerden, 9 June 1917, in *ibid.*, pp. 859–860.
72 Marmion to Marie-Joseph van Aerden, 9 June 1917, in *ibid.*, p. 860.
73 According to the documentary evidence available, Marie-Joseph first addresses Marmion as "Brother" in a letter addressed to him on 28 February 1918.
74 Cf. Marie-Joseph van Aerden to Marmion, 21 March 1918.

Towards the end of his sojourn in Beauplateau, Abbot Marmion repeated his request that Marie-Joseph be his spiritual guide.[75] He tells her that the Lord has united him closely to Himself in simple faith. He has the impression that Jesus wishes to lead him in this way. He does not have any perceptible consolations, nor does he want them. He does have insights into revealed truths and is particularly drawn to compunction. While he has carefully read St John of the Cross, he is not attracted by his teaching. Marmion is drawn to find all things in and through Jesus. Jesus is the way that the Father gives us; it is through him we should go. Marmion cannot pray in the void; he is paralysed if he has to leave aside the words, images, and comparisons that Jesus uses in his teaching. Instead, Marmion likes to unite himself to Christ's own prayer, which parallels his threefold beatific, infused, and acquired human knowledge. In this same letter, Marmion quotes two texts, one from St Bernard and the other from St Albert the Great, on which he has reflected during these days. He concludes by telling Marie-Joseph that he has begun work on the fourth volume, which is for priests. He says that he wishes to write it with her and sends her the plan, asking her for some thoughts.

Marie-Joseph sends a long letter in reply.[76] She admits to knowing Marmion's soul possibly even better than her own. They have similar spiritual attractions and tastes. While she agrees that the Lord has united Marmion to Himself by simple faith, she says that he should consider faith not only as a theological virtue but also as a fruit of the Holy Spirit. By faith, understood as a theological virtue, we submit to God, by way of admiration and adoration. We do not require proofs or perceptible joys or felt devotion. Our joy is simply to believe.

---

75 Cf. Marmion to Marie-Joseph van Aerden, 25 September 1918, in Marmion, *Correspondance*, pp. 938–939.
76 Her letter is dated 31 August 1918, while Marmion's is dated 25 September 1918. At least one of these dates is erroneous. While it is difficult to be sure, it seems more likely that Marmion's letter is incorrectly dated; it may have been written on 25 August, not 25 September.

A Spiritual Friendship

That said, faith is also a fruit of the Holy Spirit, which is to be tasted and enjoyed. Marie-Joseph believes that Marmion does not sufficiently enjoy this fruit. He should not simply say that he does not want perceptible consolations. Instead, he should let God be the Master; if God wishes to instruct us in a perceptible and gentle way, we should let Him do so! She believes there is humility in this: 'Let us suck the juice of His fruit and thank Him in terms of love'. Marmion should not be afraid to become more childlike in the expression of his love; his soul needs love: delicate, tender, and ardent love. We should, she says, let our hearts escape from the stranglehold and overflow towards God: 'Let us become inebriated like the Bride of the Canticle, and shed tears for not honouring the Beloved, and sing when He gives Himself up to our embrace.' She advises him to read the Canticle of Canticles, which will do him good. It is not enough to believe; we must above all love. Quoting Angela of Foligno: 'When one knows in the light one loves in the fire', she concludes: 'This is the response that the Lord is waiting for, since this light is meant to set the heart ablaze.'

Marie-Joseph also comments on Marmion's attraction for compunction, the importance of adoration, his views on the teaching of St John of the Cross and his manner of praying in union with Christ. She suggests that he should also pray as a priest in union with Christ the Priest. While she likes the plan of his proposed book on the priesthood, she believes that he should make space to speak of priestly functions other than the celebration of the Mass, since these are also important. Finally, she thanks him for the texts from St Bernard and St Albert, which she intends to use for her own meditation.

Addressing Marie-Joseph as 'My dear Sister in the Lord', Marmion replies to say that he has read her letter in the presence of Our Lord. Her advice corresponds perfectly to the needs of his soul and sheds much light on the points on which he consulted her.[77] When he says that he does not desire

---

[77] The letter in question is dated 2 September, but does not indicate the year. The editors of the volume of Marmion's correspondence believe that

consolations, he is referring to perceptible ones. He knows that the sweetness (*'suavité'*) of love is a precious grace. He regards what she says about faith as a fruit of the Holy Spirit as a precious insight. He also appreciates what she says about sharing in the priesthood of Christ. While Christ was already beginning to draw Marmion in this direction, Marie-Joseph's words clarify matters further and confirm him in this approach.

In later years, we find Marmion thanking Marie-Joseph for her proposals for a retreat he was due to preach in Maredsous from 14 to 21 September 1919.[78] Unfortunately, we do not have the letter containing her ideas. Marmion simply says that the outline she gave him pleases him very much. He adds that he prefers to receive no more than indications with some references, so that he remains free to follow the inspirations of the Holy Spirit.

For the subsequent period, the Maredsous archives contain only one letter on spiritual matters from Marie-Joseph to Abbot Marmion.[79] In it, she thanks him for his confidence in her, which she attributes to their spiritual union in the Heart of Christ. She speaks about the new confessor of the community, Fr Hyacinthe van Parys, OP, whom she appreciates for his detachment, about her health and about rumours of a plan to make a foundation, in which she has no part, despite its having been incorrectly attributed to her. Previously, Marmion had informed her that he had received an invitation to preach a retreat to a community of Poor Clare sisters in Ireland.[80] She encourages him to go and preach what he had always

---

it was written probably in 1920, but the content indicates that it is more likely a response to Marie-Joseph's letter of 31 August 1918, and hence it must date from 1918. For the text, see Marmion, *Correspondance*, p. 1099.

78 Cf. Marmion to Marie-Joseph van Aerden, 16 August 1919, in Marmion, *Correspondance*, p. 1008; Marmion to Marie-Joseph van Aerden, 20 August 1919, in *ibid.*, p. 1010.

79 Cf. Marie-Joseph van Aerden to Marmion, 22 September 1921.

80 Marmion preached a retreat to the Poor Clare sisters in College Road, Cork, from 2 to 15 November 1921 and subsequently wrote a number of letters to them: cf. *The English Letters of Abbot Marmion* (Dublin: Helicon, 1962), pp. 208–213.

preached to the Carmelites, adding some elements that have completed his teaching in recent years: trust, abandonment, and the heart to heart with Jesus. For some time, Marie-Joseph has been encouraging greater devotion to the Sacred Heart of Jesus. Accordingly, she proposes that Marmion should either open or close the retreat by enthroning the Sacred Heart or renewing the enthronement if it has already been done. She says this will please Jesus, who will bless Marmion's mission, not only to the sisters, but wherever he goes. She recognizes how good a friend Jesus is to them and looks forward to rejoicing with Abbot Columba when they see each other again.

For the years 1920–1923, ten items of correspondence from Marmion to Marie-Joseph are preserved. They refer, in the main, to Marmion's concerns, his health and various events in his life. Some deal with spiritual topics, such as the meaning of suffering, their union in Christ, and the necessity of trust in God and abandonment to the divine will. He sends her a copy of *Christ, The Ideal of the Monk*, which, he says, many people regard as his best. She will undoubtedly be familiar with its contents: 'You know it by heart, but you will be content to reread it.'[81]

CONCLUSION

Though incomplete, the correspondence between Blessed Columba Marmion, third Abbot of Maredsous, and Mother Marie-Joseph van Aerden, novice mistress of the Carmelite convent in Louvain, provides a fascinating insight into the personalities of both. It illustrates the development of their friendship and the increasing reliance of Marmion on the observations and advice of the young Carmelite sister.

These letters also show how Marmion excelled as a spiritual director. He constantly prayed for those he directed and asked for their prayers in return. He insisted that a person could have only one spiritual director, so as to avoid confusion and conflicting advice. He was capable of listening carefully,

---

81 Marmion to Marie-Joseph van Aerden, 16 September 1922, in Marmion, *Correspondance*, pp. 1233–1234.

he showed compassion and understanding, but he was never overly indulgent. He was honest in pointing out faults and weaknesses and would give a kindly word of advice in order to correct behaviour, encourage appropriate spiritual attitudes, and make progress. He was reassuring when people suffered from scruples or had doubts about the correctness or otherwise of their actions. Drawing on theological and spiritual principles, he offered clear directions to those who consulted him.

Not surprisingly, we find in his letters many references to the central elements of his resolutely Christocentric teaching. Christ is all things for us, and He is the Way leading us to the Father. Our spiritual attitude towards God should be characterized, on the one hand, by a spirit of adoration, respect for the divine majesty, humility and compunction, and, on the other, by childlike trust and confidence in God, and abandonment to His will. He had a high regard for the religious vocation and insisted on a complete, unreserved, and unconditional gift of self to God as the condition for perseverance and a fulfilled and joyful religious life. While it requires abandoning all things, the rewards are great: God will never be outdone in generosity.

Marmion's spiritual relationship with Marie-Joseph was unique. While he had many spiritual daughters who maintained a regular correspondence with him, Marie-Joseph was in many respects a soul-mate. He had accompanied her vocation from the outset and regarded her as the person who had best integrated his teaching. He encouraged her in forming her young charges in an innovative way, drawing on the resources of Sacred Scripture reread in the light of the Carmelite tradition and her own experience of the religious life.

Abbot Columba and Mother Marie-Joseph understood each other very well; she admitted that she knew his soul probably better than her own. While Marie-Joseph had learned much from Marmion, especially during her formative years, she also taught him much, helping him to integrate his more doctrinal approach with a greater openness to the affective dimension of the spiritual life. She advised him to read the Canticle of Canticles; he did so, together with St Bernard's commentary, while resting in Beauplateau during the summer of 1918. The fruits of his reading are to be seen in the talks he gave to the nuns of Maredret following his return. Later published in his posthumous work *Sponsa Verbi*, they testify to his ability to interweave sublime doctrinal principles with a more immediate appeal to the affectivity of his listeners.

The friendship of Abbot Columba Marmion and Mother Marie-Joseph van Aerden recalls other close spiritual relationships: Francis and Clare of Assisi, Francis de Sales and Jeanne de Chantal, Vincent de Paul and Louise de Marillac, etc. These intimate friendships, lived out unambiguously and in constant reference to Christ, demonstrate in different ways how men and women, including those in religious life, can learn from each other and be mutually enriched through sharing their complementary spiritual gifts.

9
BLESSED COLVMBA MARMION AND THE SPIRITVAL DIRECTION OF PRIESTS

RAYMOND LEO CARDINAL BURKE

INTRODUCTION

SPIRITUAL DIRECTION ASSISTS US IN knowing who we are as sons and daughters of God the Father in God the Son Incarnate through the inhabitation of the Holy Spirit in our souls, so that we can be, in daily life, true to our identity and thus find abiding happiness now imperfectly in this life and then perfectly in the life to come. While spiritual direction is important for every Christian, it is pre-eminently important for ordained priests who have the care of souls, daily providing spiritual counsel and nourishment, in various forms, to the portion of God's flock entrusted to their care. If an ordained priest does not regularly ponder, through spiritual direction, his identity in Christ the High Priest, God the Son Incarnate, he will fail to renew the gift of his entire being to Christ Who acts through him for the glory of God the Father and for the salvation of souls. The spiritual theology of Blessed Columba Marmion, especially as it is expressed in his books, *Christ, The Life of the Soul*[1] and *Christ, The Ideal of the Priest*[2],

[1] Marmion, Columba, *Le Christ Vie de l'âme* in Columba Marmion, *Œuvres Spirituelles* (Maredsous, Belgique: P. Lethielleux-Maredsous, 1998) [= *Vie*]. English translation: Columba Marmion, *Christ, The Life of the Soul*, tr. Alan Bancroft (Bethesda, MD: Zaccheus Press, 2005).

[2] Marmion, Columba, *Le Christ idéal du prêtre* (Belgique: Les Éditions de Maredsous, 1952) [= *Prêtre*]. English translation: Columba Marmion, *Christ, The Ideal of the Priest*, tr. Matthew Dillon (San Francisco: Ignatius Press, 2005).

provides exceptional spiritual guidance for priests. The present essay is intended to be an introduction to spiritual direction for priests, according to these writings of Blessed Columba.

THE GRACE OF SUPERNATURAL ADOPTION

The ordained priest's identity in Christ the High Priest has its origin in his adoption as a true son by God the Father in Christ, His Only-Begotten Son. Faith in God is not some idea, as in the case of someone who has come to believe that God exists simply by way of reason, but is, rather, a personal relationship with God Who has chosen the priest as His own dear son through the sacrament of baptism. Faith is the union of the Divine Heart with human hearts. It is daily communion with God the Father in God the Son through God the Holy Spirit poured forth into the hearts of the faithful from the glorious pierced Heart of God the Son Incarnate.

Dom Columba Marmion reflects on the great mystery of God's love, the great mystery of God's choice of us as sons and daughters, when He had no need to adopt us:

> And see how God, not in order to add to His plenitude but to enrich other beings by it, will extend, so to speak, His Paternity. This Divine life, so transcendent that only God has the right to live it, this eternal life communicated by the Father to the only Son, and, by them, to the Spirit common to them—this life, God decrees creatures shall be called to share. By a transport of love which has its source in the fullness of the Being and the Goodness that is God, this life will overflow from the heart of Divinity to reach and beatify—by elevating them above their nature—beings drawn from nothingness. God will ennoble these purely created beings and make them hear the sweet name of "children." By nature, God has only one Son. By love, He will have a multitude of them, without number. This is *the grace of supernatural adoption*.[3]

---

3   *Vie*, p. 41; *Christ, The Life of the Soul*, p. 7.

Supernatural adoption is an act of fatherly love, the love of God the Father who wants to share fully His life with man. The foundation of the priest's relationship with Christ is his identity as an adopted son of God.

God the Father accomplishes His great act of love for us by the Redemptive Incarnation of God the Son. Having inherited Original Sin from our first parents, together with its effects, above all, the capital vice of pride and rebellion before God Who is the font of all being, we are alienated from God Who alone can re-establish in us the filial love for which He created man from the beginning: 'So God created man in his own image, in the image of God he created him; male and female he created them' (Gen. 1:27). Dom Marmion writes:

> Realized in Adam from the dawn of creation, then cut across by the sin of the head of humankind who drew the whole of his race with him into his disgrace, this Decree of love would be restored through a marvellous devising of justice and mercy, of wisdom and goodness. See how the only Son (who lives in the eternal heart's-embrace of the Father) unites Himself to a human nature within the sphere of time; but in so close a way that this nature, while being perfect in itself, belongs entirely to the Divine Person to whom it is united. The Divine life, communicated in its fullness to this humanity, makes it the Son of God's own humanity: this is the admirable work of *the Incarnation*. It is to say of this man, called Jesus Christ, that He is God's own Son.
>
> But this Son who, by nature, is the only Son of the eternal Father—"only-begotten" Son of God [Jn 1:18; 3:16]—appears here below simply so as to become the firstborn of all those who would receive Him, after having been ransomed by Him: "the firstborn among many brethren" [Rom. 8, 29]. Only-begotten of the Father in the eternal splendours, only Son by right, He is constituted the head of a multitude of brethren, to whom, by His work of redemption, He will restore the grace of divine life.
>
> And this, in such a way that the same divine life which flows from the Father into the Son, which

streams from the Son into the humanity of Jesus, will circulate, through Christ, into all those who are willing to accept Him. It will draw them up to the beatifying heart of the Father, where Christ has gone before us [Jn 20:17; 14:2] after having paid—by His blood, for us here below—the price of such a gift.[4]

From the moment of the reception of baptism, the divine grace of Christ, the grace of the Holy Spirit, is at work in our souls, in our hearts, so that we develop ever more fully to maturity in Christ.

Divine grace is living, it penetrates our very being. Indeed, Our Lord deigns to call us friends. He makes clear the total purity and selflessness of His love for us. He lays down His life for us and, at the same time, gives us the grace so to lay down our lives for love of Him.

That grace has been at work in us from the day of our baptism. For the ordained priest, it reaches its highest expression on the day when he presents himself for ordination to the Holy Priesthood. On that day, he gives his whole being to Christ, so that Christ can act in him for the glory of God the Father and the salvation of souls.

THE OFFERING OF FITTING HOMAGE TO THE HOLY TRINITY

Spiritual direction for the priest begins by reflecting upon the foundation of his divine vocation in his supernatural adoption by God the Father. Such reflection leads to the consideration of his call to full maturity as an adopted son of God the Father in God the Son Incarnate through the outpouring of the Holy Spirit into his soul. In specific, it leads him to consider his growth in Christ the High Priest of whom he has become a brother by ordination to the holy priesthood.

The priestly call to act in the person of the Christ, the Anointed of the Lord, Head and Shepherd of God the Father's flock in every time and place, is most profoundly understood

---

4 Ibid., p. 42; *Christ, The Life of the Soul*, pp. 7–8.

in the context of supernatural adoption as Dom Marmion sets it forth for us. Regarding the holy priesthood, Dom Marmion speaks thus to priests:

> St Paul has revealed to us that the absolute dependence of all creatures on the sovereignty of God imposes on man the obligation to give glory to the divine majesty. *Ex Ipso et per Ipsum et in Ipso sunt omnia: Ipsi gloria in saecula. Amen* (Rom. 11:36). All glory to the Holy Trinity.
>
> God renders to Himself a praise that is perfect and infinite. All the canticles of the angels and of the whole universe can add nothing to it.
>
> However, God requires of His creatures that they should associate themselves with this glorification which is a part of His intimate life. According to the divine plan, the glory which man must render to the Lord is outside the scope of natural religion; it ascends to the Holy Trinity through the priesthood of Christ, the official mediator between heaven and earth.
>
> This is the splendid prerogative of the priesthood of Christ and His priests: to offer to the Holy Trinity in the name of man and of the universe a homage of praise agreeable to God. It is the privilege of this priesthood to ensure the return of creation in its entirety to the Master of all things. With all the respect of a lively faith let us begin by fixing our eyes on the mystery of this glorification in the bosom of the Trinity; it has existed before all ages like God Himself; and will last for ever, *sicut erat in principio et nunc et semper*. It is the perfect model of all praise, human or angelic. We are called to unite ourselves to it on earth and in heaven. This is our sublime destiny.[5]

Because God is Truth, Beauty, and Goodness in themselves and thus the source of all truth, all beauty, and all goodness, He is glorified in Himself: One and Three. As Dom Marmion states: 'God could have refrained from creation; He could have remained without us in the ineffable and blessed society

---

5 *Prêtre*, p. 13; *Christ, The Ideal of the Priest*, p. 21

of light and of love of the Divine Persons.'[6]

Dom Marmion illuminates the Mystery of the Holy Trinity in terms of the glory due to God, One and Three:

> The Father engenders the Son: from all eternity He communicates to Him that supreme gift: the life and the perfections of the divinity; He communicates to Him all that He is Himself excepting that which is "proper" to Him: His paternity.
>
> Being His perfect substantial image, the Word is "the splendour of the glory of the Father", *Splendor gloriae et figura substantiae eius*" (Heb. 1:3). Born of the focus of all light, His brilliance is reflected back like an unbroken canticle towards Him from Whom He comes. "All things are Thine and Thine are Mine" (Jn 17:10).
>
> Thus, by the natural impulse of His filiation, the Son reciprocates to the Father all that He has from Him.
>
> The Holy Spirit, Who is charity, has His exclusive source of origin in the love of the Father and the Son. This union of infinite love between the three Persons effects the eternal communication of life in the bosom of the Trinity. Such is the glory which God renders to Himself in the sacred intimacy of His eternal life.[7]

Nothing is more pertinent to our self-understanding, to our self-identification, than the intimate life of the Trinity, for we have been created in the image of God, Three and One, and have been restored to our relationship with God, Three and One, by God the Son sent by God the Father to win for us the life of God the Holy Spirit.

The glorious pierced Heart of Jesus, seated in glory at the right hand of God the Father, is the inexhaustible and enduring source of divine grace for our hearts. From the Heart of Jesus, God the Father never ceases, with superabundance, to pour into our hearts the grace of the Holy Spirit—the love which God the Father and God the Son share always. Thus, the life of the Holy Family of Jesus, Mary, and Joseph is

---

6 Ibid., p. 14; *Christ, The Ideal of the Priest*, p. 22.
7 Ibid.

intimately and essentially connected to the life of the Holy Trinity, for God the Son, Second Person of the Most Holy Trinity, is truly the Son of Mary, Spouse of the Holy Spirit, whose virginal spouse is Saint Joseph, the virginal father of Jesus. God, Three in One, wishes that God the Son be the most important member of each human family.

How then are we to understand the High Priesthood of God the Son Incarnate and the holy priesthood which shares in it? As Dom Marmion points out, the Letter to the Hebrews provides the definition of the priesthood: 'For every high priest chosen from among men is appointed to act on behalf of men in relation to God, to offer gifts and sacrifices for sins' (Heb. 5:1). Dom Columba goes on to explain the High Priesthood of Our Lord Jesus Christ:

> From what source does Christ hold His priesthood? St Paul gives us the answer. The priesthood, he tells us, is of such grandeur that no one, not even Christ in His humanity, has been able to assume for Himself this dignity. *Nec quisquam sumit sibi honorem sed qui vocatur a Deo—sic et Christus non semetipsum clarificavit, ut pontifex fieret.* Then he continues: "The Father Himself has established His Son as eternal priest; He has said to Him: *Filius meus es tu, ego hodie genui te—Tu es sacerdos in aeternum* (Heb. 5:4–6).
>
> Thus the priesthood is a gift bestowed on the humanity of Jesus by the Father. As soon as the Word was made flesh the eternal Father looked on His Son with infinite complacency. He acknowledged Him as the one mediator between heaven and earth, a pontiff for ever.
>
> As Man-God Christ was to have the privilege of uniting in Himself the whole of humanity to purify it, to sanctify it and to bring it back to the bosom of the divinity. By this He was to render to the Lord a perfect glory in time and in eternity.
>
> He did not need to be consecrated by an external anointing like other priests. The soul of Jesus Christ was not stamped with the ineffaceable priestly character as was ours on the day of our ordination. Why? We touch here on the very heart of the mystery. By

virtue of the hypostatic union the Word enters into and takes possession of the soul and the body of Jesus; He consecrates them. When the Son of God became flesh He took complete possession of this humanity. The moment of the priestly consecration of Christ was the moment of His Incarnation; at that moment Christ was marked for ever as the one eternal mediator between man and God. "He was anointed with the oil of gladness," says St Paul (Heb. 1:9), for the Word Himself was this anointing of infinite sanctity. Jesus is the priest par excellence. "For it was fitting that we should have such a high priest, holy, innocent, undefiled and made higher than the heavens" (Heb. 7:26). Until the end of time the priests of this earth will receive no power which is not part of His; He is the one source of the whole priesthood which glorifies God in the manner conceived by Him.[8]

The soul of the ordained priest has received, in addition to the indelible character of baptism and the indelible character of confirmation, the indelible character of the holy priesthood.

Christ is the Incarnation of Divine Love for the glory of God and the salvation of men. So, too, the sacramental character of the holy priesthood is Christ's pastoral charity. By the grace of ordination, the ordained priest, no matter what may be his limitations and flaws, brings the love of the Divine Shepherd, His pastoral charity, to men. Even as the seal on Christ by God the Father, by His divine nature from His eternal generation, is anointing for the glory of God and the salvation of souls, so, too, the seal on the ordained priest is for the glory of God and the salvation of souls, most of all, through the gift of the entirety of his life to Christ for Christ's pastoral charity—here one notes the particular theological fittingness of the perfect continence of the clergy—, the gift which finds its highest expression in the offering of the Eucharistic Sacrifice.

---

8   Ibid., pp. 15–16; *Christ, The Ideal of the Priest*, pp. 23–24.

PRIEST AND VICTIM

Dom Marmion then illustrates the unique prerogative of the Priesthood of Christ, namely to be both Priest and Victim. Referring to the distinction of priest and victim in the sacrifices of the Old Testament, he declares:

> In the sacrifice offered by Jesus it is not so. By an astonishing and admirable prerogative of His priesthood, on Calvary as on our altars, His sacrifice is divine by virtue both of the dignity of the pontiff and the excellence of the victim which is immolated. Priest and victim are united in the one person, and this sacrifice constitutes the perfect homage which gives glory to God, makes the Lord propitious to men, and obtains for them the grace of eternal life.
>
> The *consummatum est* pronounced by the dying Christ was at once the last sigh of love of the Victim who has made full expiation, and the solemn attestation of the Pontiff completing the supreme act of His priesthood.[9]

Christ as Sovereign Priest saw the Father, knew the Father. Dom Marmion explains: 'The full depth of the divine perfections were open to His sight: the absolute sanctity of the Father, His sovereign justice, His infinite goodness.'[10] It was His vision of the Father, His knowledge of the Father, which inspired in Him as Sovereign Priest the virtue of religion of which sacrifice is the highest expression.

As Victim, Christ also was inspired by His knowledge of the Father and of the mission for which His Father had sent Him into the world. Dom Columba writes:

> What was the fundamental attitude of Jesus the Victim? It was likewise adoration, but here it finds its expression in the acceptance of destruction and death. Jesus knew that He was destined to the Cross for the remission of the sins of the world; before the divine justice He felt Himself burdened with the crushing

---

9   *Ibid.*, p. 17; *Christ, The Ideal of the Priest*, pp. 24–25.
10 *Ibid.*

weight of all the sins of the world. He gave His full consent to this role of Victim. He had not, however, contrition like a penitent who mourns for his own personal faults. But on many occasions He experienced a sadness unto death at seeing Himself overwhelmed by the burden of so much iniquity. Did He not say in the Garden of Olives: "My soul is sorrowful even unto death." We can see that the attitude of the victim is in perfect conformity with that of the priest.

We must not consider the eternal designs from our short-sighted human point of view; let us envisage them as God has conceived them and revealed them to us. Let us not enquire what the Lord in His absolute power could have accomplished but see rather what He willed to do. He could have pardoned sin without requiring an expiation proportioned to the greatness of the offence, but, in His wisdom, He decreed the salvation of the world by the death of Christ. "Without the shedding of the blood of Jesus Christ there is no remission of sin for us": *Sine sanguinis effusione non fit remissio* (Heb. 9:22).

So, coming into the world, the Son of God assumed "a sacrificial body" suited for enduring suffering and death. He was truly a member of the human race, like us, and it is in the name of His brethren that He is to offer Himself as victim to reconcile them with their Father in heaven. Tertullian has given us this penetrating thought: "No one is so supremely a Father as God, no goodness can approach His goodness": *Tam Pater nemo, tam Pius nemo* [De poenitentia, 8; PL 1, 1353]. We may also say: "No one is so supremely a brother as Jesus": *Nemo ita frater ac ille*. According to St Paul, in the eternal predestination, Christ is the "first born among many brethren" (Rom. 8:29) and again, "He is not ashamed to call them brethren" (Heb. 2:11). What did Christ Himself say to Mary Magdalen after His resurrection? "Go to My brethren and say to them: I ascend to My Father and your Father" (Jn 20:17). And what a brother Jesus was! He was a God who willed to share our infirmities, to experience our sorrows and our pains. By personal experience He learned to sympathize with our troubles. "Our high priest is not incapable of having compassion on our infirmities, having willed to experience them all like us, excepting sin" (Heb. 4:15).[11]

The Incarnation is essentially redemptive. Christ the Priest at His virginal conception in the womb of the Virgin Mary is Christ the Victim Who alone can restore man to the fullness of communion with God the Father.

While the Incarnation achieved its fullness in the Passion, Death, Resurrection, and Ascension of Christ, His entire life—the hidden life at Nazareth and His public ministry—is an expression of His identity as Priest and Victim. Dom Columba Marmion comments:

> The whole life of Jesus was that of a supreme pontiff dedicated to the glory of the Father and to the salvation of man. This priesthood attained its climax at the Last Supper and on Calvary. But the whole existence of the Saviour is stamped with the priestly character. The first movement of His most sacred soul at the time of the Incarnation was a sovereign act of religion. The evangelists have not revealed to us the secret of this priestly oblation of the Saviour; St Paul, whose role it was to make known to us the mysteries of God and of His Christ, had knowledge of it: "Wherefore when He cometh into the world," writes the apostle, "Christ said, 'sacrifice and oblation Thou wouldst not: but a body Thou has fitted to Me. Holocaust nor sacrifice for sin did not please Thee. Then said I: Here I am—for it is written of Me in the head of the Book—I come to do Thy will, O God'" (Heb. 10:5–7). In recognition of the supreme dominion of the Father, Christ offered Himself to Him without reserve. This ineffable offering was His reply to the unparalleled grace of the hypostatic union; it was a priestly act, the precursor of the redemptive sacrifice and of all the acts of the heavenly priesthood. We cannot insist too strongly on this text which gives us a glimpse of the interior priestly life of Jesus.[12]

---

11   *Ibid.*, pp. 17–18; *Christ, The Ideal of the Priest*, pp. 25–26.
12   *Ibid.*, p. 19; *Christ, The Ideal of the Priest*, pp. 26–27.

So, it is that the entire life of Christ, consummated in the Passion, Death, Resurrection, and Ascension is a constant contemplation of both the glory of God and 'the immense injury done to God by sin and the inadequacy of the victims offered until then.'[13]

In the words of Dom Marmion, '[Christ] understood that God, in giving Him His human nature, had consecrated it so that it might be offered as a victim and that He was Himself the priest of this sacrifice.'[14] We see a beautiful, early reflection of the self-consciousness of Christ, Priest and Victim, in the Mystery of the Finding of the Child Jesus in the Temple. In the exchange with His Virgin Mother and in His obedience to His Virgin Mother and Virginal Father Saint Joseph, Christ expresses His total abandonment to the will of the Father. Regarding the life of Christ, Dom Marmion declares: 'His will to glorify the Father, to satisfy divine justice, and to offer Himself for our salvation... remains fixed for ever in the centre of His heart.'[15] Dom Marmion concludes: 'At His death Christ represented the whole of mankind, and in the unique sacrifice of the Cross which He accepted freely and the first movement of which dates from the Incarnation, He saved and sanctified us all.'[16]

THE EUCHARISTIC SACRIFICE AND THE SACRIFICE ON CALVARY

The self-oblation of Christ, Priest and Victim, has its supreme act in the Last Supper and on Calvary. In the words of Dom Marmion, 'There, while He presents His sacrifice to the Father, He reveals Himself to us in all the majesty and power of His supreme pontificate.'[17] At the Last Supper Christ anticipated sacramentally the offering of His Body and Blood on Calvary for the salvation of men. Dom Columba Marmion thus teaches his brothers in the holy priesthood:

---

13 *Ibid.*
14 *Ibid.*
15 *Ibid.*, p. 20; *Christ, The Ideal of the Priest*, p. 28.
16 *Ibid.*, p. 21; *Christ, The Ideal of the Priest*, p. 29.
17 *Ibid.*

> The words pronounced by Him over the bread and wine leave no room for doubt as to the meaning which He attached to this gesture. Beyond all doubt it was "His own body which was to be offered up" and "His own blood. The blood of the New Testament—which shall be shed unto the remission of sins". This oblation was made to the Father. The Council of Trent asserts it: "At the Last Supper, declaring Himself to be a priest established for ever according to the order of Melchizedek, He offered to the Father His body and blood under the appearance of bread and wine" (Sess. 22, c. 1). On our altars, as at the Last Supper, Christ is priest and victim: it is still He who gives Himself as food; but in the Mass, Christ makes use of the ministry of His priests; at the Last Supper He employed no minister. As sovereign priest by His own immediate authority, He instituted three supernatural prodigies which He bequeathed to His Church: the sacrifice of the Mass, the sacrament of the Eucharist, intimately united to the Mass, and our priesthood, derived from His own and destined to perpetuate until the end of time His gesture of power and mercy.[18]

Even as the offering of Himself to the glory of the Father and for the salvation of men was always at the centre of Christ's Heart, both human and divine, so, in the offering of the Holy Mass, is sacramentally gathered all the glory to be given to God the Father by His priests in Christ the High Priest and all the saving grace reaching innumerable souls through the consecrated heart, voice, and hands of the ordained priest.

Referring to the thanksgiving essential to the Passover and to the Last Supper as the institution of the Holy Eucharist and the holy priesthood, Dom Marmion reflects upon the thanksgiving offered by Christ at the Last Supper to God the Father 'not only for His past bounties toward the chosen people, but also for those of the New Testament.'[19] In

---

18 Ibid., pp. 21–22; *Christ, The Ideal of the Priest*, pp. 29–30.
19 Ibid., p. 22; *Christ, The Ideal of the Priest*, p. 30

instituting the Holy Eucharist and the holy priesthood at the Last Supper, Christ offered thanks to the Father for these heavenly gifts. Dom Marmion concludes: 'This incomparable act of gratitude accomplished by the Saviour in His own name and in that of all His members gave to the Father immeasurable glory.'[20]

The unbloody Sacrifice of the Mass makes present sacramentally the bloody Sacrifice of Calvary. In accord with the eternal will of the Father, God the Son Incarnate has accomplished our redemption 'by the most noble of all acts of religion: sacrifice.'[21] Dom Marmion helps us to ponder the sublime nature of the Sacrifice of Calvary:

> This sacrifice was pre-eminently propitiatory. By virtue of the infinite dignity of His divine person and the immensity of His human love, Jesus presented to the Father an act of homage more pleasing than the iniquities of the world had been displeasing. In the eyes of God, the value of the immolation of His Son exceeded beyond all measure His aversion for our wrongdoing. According to the bold expression of St Paul, Jesus has "snatched from the justice of the Father the decree which condemned us": *Chirographum decreti quod est contarium nobis*; "He has destroyed it, fastening it to the Cross": *affigens illud Cruci* (Col. 2:14). The attitude of God towards us has been transformed: we were "children of wrath": *filii irae* (Eph. 2:3) but now the Lord has become for us "rich in mercy": *dives in misericordia* (Eph. 2:3–4).
>
> This is what Jesus, our brother, has done for us. And if we understood the greatness of this love, how readily we would unite ourselves to this sacrifice, saying, like the Apostle: "He hath loved me, and delivered Himself up for me" (Gal. 2:20). He does not say: *Dilexit nos* but *Dilexit me*: it was "for me". All this concerns me personally.
>
> We must appreciate clearly that what God asked of Jesus, and what gave the sacrifice all its value, was

---

20   *Ibid.*
21   *Ibid.*; CIP, p. 31.

> not the mere shedding of His blood in itself, but the shedding of it animated by the spirit of love and of obedience.[22]

We must not overlook the word 'obedience' because Christ Himself insists that His sacrifice was offered in obedience to the Father.

In the Garden of Gethsemane, undergoing His agony, Our Lord asked that, if it were possible, the chalice of His Passion and Death be taken away. Regarding the obedience which is inseparably united to the love of Christ, Dom Marmion teaches us:

> In the Garden of Olives, during His agony, three times Jesus asked that the chalice be removed from Him. And in the face of the inexorable silence of heaven, freely, by an act of supreme submission and in an impulse of love the Saviour conforms His human will to the will of the Father: "Not My will, but Thy will be done" (Lk 22:42). St Paul can say of Jesus: "He made Himself obedient unto death, even unto the death of the Cross" (Phil 2:8). Isaiah had foretold this free acceptance of His suffering by the Saviour: "He was offered because it was His own will," *quia ipse voluit* (Is. 53:7). And so, whatever may be the number and the enormity of the sins of the world, the reparation offered by our divine Master will always be superabundant. The words of the Apostle, throbbing with admiration at the mystery, express it admirably: "Where sin abounded grace did more abound" (Rom. 5:20).[23]

The words of Saint Paul's Letter to the Philippians are appropriately the refrain of the Sacred Liturgy during the holiest days of the Church Year, the Sacred Triduum: "*Christus factus est pro nobis obediens usque ad mortem, mortem autem crucis*' (Phil. 2:8).

22　Ibid., pp. 23–24; *Christ, The Ideal of the Priest*, pp. 31–32.
23　Ibid., p. 24; *Christ, The Ideal of the Priest*, p. 32.

THE ETERNAL HIGH PRIESTHOOD OF CHRIST

In conclusion, the High Priesthood of Our Lord Jesus Christ is eternal and therefore the offering of the Holy Sacrifice of the Mass on earth finds its consummation in the Heavenly Liturgy. Dom Marmion reminds us: 'Jesus is the true pontiff who, after having been immolated and after shedding His blood, entered on the glorious day of His Ascension into the true tabernacle in the highest seat of heaven: *Introivit semel in sancta*. "He entered there for ever and once for all" (Heb. 9:12).'

Dom Marmion continues his reflection:

> When the high priest penetrated into the sanctuary, he did not gain access for the people who accompanied him, but Christ, our Pontiff, leads us after Him into heaven. Never forget this marvellous doctrine of our faith: we cannot enter except through Him. No man, no creature can attain the eternal tabernacles, can enjoy the beatific vision except after and by the power of Jesus: this is the triumphant reward of His sacrifice.
>
> All the elect contemplate God, but whence comes this light by which they see the divinity? The Apocalypse of St John gives us the answer again and again: In the Heavenly Jerusalem it is the Lamb who will be the light: *Lucerna eius est Agnus* (Rev. 21:23). All the inhabitants of the holy city will realize always that it is only the graces springing from the sacrifice of Jesus which have gained for them access to the Father and given them the power to praise Him. They will chant without ceasing: "You have redeemed us by Your blood from every tribe and every nation and You have made of us the kingdom of God."
>
> As man, the Saviour has certainly the right to penetrate into the secret of the divinity, for His humanity is the humanity of the Word Itself. But Christ is also "pontiff", *Pontem faciens*, mediator, head of the mystical body: by these titles and by virtue of His Passion, He introduces us with Himself into the bosom of the Father.
>
> Thus, we are justified in deducing from the Scriptures that a majestic liturgy is celebrated in Heaven. Christ offers Himself in all His splendour and this

glorious oblation is, as it were, the completion, the consummation of the redemption.

In this celestial liturgy we shall be united to Jesus and to each other. We shall be the trophy of His glory. We shall take part in the adoration, the love, and the thanksgiving which He and all His members send up to the supreme majesty of the Holy Trinity. The word-pictures of Revelation give us a glimpse of the realities. The Epistle to the Ephesians proclaims it: "at the end of time in His kingdom the Father will accomplish His design: to bring all things to Himself, uniting them all under one chief": *recapitulare omnia in Christo*. This is certainly the sense intended by St Paul. The expression of the Vulgate *Instaurare omnia in Christo* (Eph. 1:10) has not the same vigour.

Everything shall be "subject to Jesus Christ", says St Paul again. *Oportet illum regnare* (1 Cor. 15:25) and the Son Himself with all His elect will do homage to Him who has made all things subject to Him so that God may be "all in all": *Cum autem subiecta fuerint illi omnia, tunc et ipse Filius subiectus erit ei qui subiecit sibi omnia, ut sit Deus omnia in omnibus* (1 Cor. 15:28).

For all eternity it shall be our joy to realize that our beatitude comes to us from Jesus, that His priesthood is the source of all graces which we shall have received during our sorrowful earthly pilgrimage. Is it not to Him that we owe our divine adoption, our priesthood, and the look of pardon, of tenderness and of love from Him whom at the Mass we call *Clementissime Pater*?[24]

Reflection on the Eternal High Priesthood of Christ, in which the ordained priest, by sacred ordination, participates, always extends beyond the ordinary circumstances of this life to their extraordinary destiny which is the Wedding Feast of the Lamb. Indeed, eternal life must be the form of daily life.

The Eternal High Priesthood of Our Lord Jesus Christ is His by His divine nature. Ordained priests participate in it by virtue of the sacramental consecration which imparts the

---

24 *Ibid.*, pp. 27-28; *Christ, The Ideal of the Priest*, pp. 34-36.

indelible character of the holy priesthood upon their souls. Dom Marmion counsels us:

> As we await the vision and the full clarity of the city of God let it be our joy to repeat: O Jesus, for Your elect You are everything! for us also be everything while we march on in the spirit of faith towards the eternal Jerusalem; "so that they who live may not now live to themselves but unto Him Who died and rose again for them": *Ut et qui vivunt iam non sibi vivunt, sed ei qui pro ipsis mortuus est et resurrexit* (2 Cor. 5:15).[25]

Meditating on Christ the Eternal High Priest and the sacramental participation in His priestly office, the priest is immediately conscious of the holiness which must mark the life of every priest. The soul which bears the indelible character of the holy priesthood must reflect that character in attitude, in word, and in action.

CHRIST THE HIGH PRIEST: MODEL AND SOURCE OF PRIESTLY HOLINESS

Dom Columba Marmion reminds priests that God the Father Himself provides for them the model and source of priestly holiness:

> The heavenly Father has Himself undertaken the task of establishing for us, ministers of Christ, our ideal of sanctity. He has predestined us to become like, not to some creature, not to an angel, but to His Son, Whom the Incarnation has consecrated priest in His human nature. St Paul reveals to us this thought of the Father when he says: *Praedestinavit nos conformes fieri imagines Filii sui* (Rom. 8:29). God provides for us a divine model of perfection. He wishes to see reproduced in us the characteristics of His incarnate Son and by that very fact to see our soul resplendent with the reflection of His sanctity.
>
> If it is true that the grandeur of every human life depends on the ideal which it pursues, to what heights

---

25 Ibid., p. 28; *Christ, The Ideal of the Priest*, p. 36.

must the sincere desire to makes ourselves like to Jesus Christ elevate the whole existence of us priests? With the Word the Father is well pleased; and thus our assimilation with Christ is for us an abundant source of benedictions and graces.[26]

The sanctifying grace conferred with priestly ordination is the source of a priest's lifetime pursuit of an ever-greater conformity to the holiness of Christ the High Priest.

Even as God the Son, the Word is the perfect expression of the grandeur—the Being: the Truth, Goodness, and Beauty—of God the Father, so God the Father has sent His Son into the world to lead the ordained priest into holiness of life. Dom Marmion teaches priests:

> The Father has given us this Son as a model and as the source of all sanctity. "In Him are hid all the treasures of wisdom and knowledge" (Col. 2:3). An eternity of contemplation would not suffice to exhaust the depths of this mystery and to thank God for this benefit.[27]

Dom Marmion then immediately corrects a tendency among priests to seek holiness of life not according to the divine plan but according to their own spiritual constructs.

In reflecting upon the holiness of life to which priests are called, the ordained priest must ponder first the fact that it is a supernatural work. It is a work of divine grace with which he cooperates. Dom Marmion reminds priests of the supernatural character of holiness:

> It is the realization in time of the eternal designs of the Father. God, in His goodness, has destined man to find His beatitude in the vision of the divinity face to face, a vision which is natural to God alone. Revelation, the Incarnation, the Redemption, the Church, faith, the sacraments, grace, and sanctity, all belong to the munificence of his plan of which Christ and our

---

26 *Ibid.*, p. 29; *Christ, The Ideal of the Priest*, p. 37.
27 *Ibid.*, p. 30; *Christ, The Ideal of the Priest*, p. 38.

adoption in Him form the centre. This communication is absolutely gratuitous; it exceeds the needs and the requirements of all created nature, whether angelic or human: that is why it is *super*natural. We have here a glorious ensemble, a world of graces to which is connected the whole activity of the man destined to celestial beatitude. For nature, left to its own devices, has not the capacity to tend efficaciously toward its supernatural end.[28]

In pursuing holiness of life, the priest must keep his eyes fixed upon the supernatural, fixed upon the Mystery of Faith, the Mystery of the Redemptive Incarnation at work in his personal life.

Dom Marmion comments upon the result when the ordained priest does not seek holiness of life in the supernatural:

> One meets, even among priests, persons who are marking time in the spiritual life in spite of a more or less exact fidelity to their religious exercises: all their application does not succeed in making them live the interior life of Christ. They make an effort without knowing exactly towards what ideal they should direct that effort; they are in doubt as to the best manner of going towards God. In contrast to this we have St Paul who said: "I therefore so run, not as at an uncertainty: I so fight, not as one beating the air" (1 Cor. 9:26). It is of utmost importance for us and for those whom we direct to have a clear idea of the sanctity to which we aspire so that we may not "beat the air".[29]

And where do we find examples of seeking sanctity of life in the supernatural? Dom Marmion goes on to explain:

> When we study the Acts of the Apostles and the history of the early Christians to whom St Paul addresses his epistles, we can see that they were truly abounding in the gifts of the Holy Spirit. These Christians found the inspiration of their life in Jesus Christ, in the grace

---

28   Ibid.
29   Ibid.

of their baptism, in the expectation of the heavenly kingdom, in the doctrine of the divine plan as the apostles taught it to them. I do not blame those who, for their sanctification, have recourse to such means of supererogation as may appeal to them, because they feel the need of the stimulation which they afford: it is better to walk on crutches than not to move at all. But I should like to reassert most emphatically for your benefit the immense riches which we possess in Jesus Christ. Men are too much inclined to want to substitute their ideas for those of God, to want to attain perfection according to their own short-sighted point of view. St Paul draws attention to this tendency in his day: "Beware lest any man cheat you by philosophy and vain deceit; according to the traditions of men, according to the traditions of the world, and not according to Christ" (Col. 2:8).[30]

We are witnesses today, within the Church, of a spirituality of slogans which have no reference to Christ or to the constant teaching and practice of the Catholic faith. Priests are told that they need to leave the sacristy in order to be close to the flock for whom they were ordained. They are told that attention to what the Church has always taught and practiced is a manifestation of psychological rigidity or an ideological attachment to the past. The truth is that the priest who is not first attentive to the sacristy, to the service of Our Lord in the Sacred Liturgy, and to sacred doctrine and discipline cannot respond to the deepest need of those for whom He was ordained: the need to know, love, and serve Christ.

The Christian participates in the sanctity of Christ by sanctifying grace. In the words of Blessed Columba:

> This grace is, as it were, a reflection of the divine light which enters into the soul, establishes it in a state of justice, and makes it resemble the Son-by-nature. This initial sanctification, which is destined to increase, is given at the moment of baptism. When by their good

---

[30] Ibid., p. 31; *Christ, The Ideal of the Priest*, p. 39.

actions, the sons of adoption imitate the virtues of Christ, they contribute to the perfecting in themselves of the life of Christ.

At the Last Supper, after having washed the feet of His disciples, Jesus pronounced these solemn words: *Exemplum enim dedi vobis ut quemadmodum ego feci vobis, ita vos faciatis.* "For I have given you an example that as I have done to you, so you do also" (Jn 13:15). Whether it be a matter of religion, of humility, of patience, indulgence, or charity, all the virtues of Christ must be the inspiration of our virtues: they are the model, especially for His priests. If the essence of our priestly perfection consists in acting always as adoptive sons of the Father and as ministers of Christ, we must, like Him, the Son of God and the supreme Pontiff, constantly relate all our activity to the love and the glory of the Father in imitation of the virtues of which He provides the model.

This resemblance to Christ will appear especially in the ever-increasing domination of charity over all our conduct. Love will orient every deliberate action towards our supernatural end; its rays will extend to the whole of our life, and by virtue of its ever-widening sphere of dominion, it will take firmer root in our hearts, and control them in all things. In this manner the kingdom of God becomes more and more firmly established in the Christian soul. Is this soul therefore confirmed in grace? No; it remains exposed to temptation and to sin; but God, Christ, and their rule become the sole motive power of its actions. The Lord is in full possession of this soul, *Dominus regit me*: "The Lord leads me" (Ps 22:1), for, in all truth, by reason of the absolute supremacy of charity, it only lives through Him, by Him and for Him. From this moment the saying of the Apostle begins to be fully realized in this member of Christ: "And I live now, not I, but Christ liveth in me" (Gal. 2:20). It is then that the soul attains sanctity. Certainly, there are many degrees of sanctity. Generosity in self-sacrifice, heroism in the practice of the virtues, can assume many forms, and are capable of almost infinite development. We must not be too quick to believe we have attained it. Here, as elsewhere, time must play its part. The fidelity required of true servants of God is generally of long duration and there are many trials to increase its strength and its merit. The gifts of contemplative prayer have also their special influence on the elevation of the faithful and on the perseverance of the elect.[31]

In all things and at all times, the grace of the Holy Spirit is at work in our souls, not to eliminate temptations and trials but to have our cooperation in confronting temptations and trials in fidelity to our identity in Christ, in fidelity to our dignity as adopted sons in the Only-Begotten Son and as ministers of Christ, as priests in Christ the High Priest.

THE SINCERE DESIRE FOR PRIESTLY PERFECTION

In this context, Dom Marmion addresses a particular word to priests:

> In practice, for you, priests, apart altogether from the mystery of predestination and of grace, it is essential to develop a very sincere desire for priestly perfection. You cannot remain indifferent to the divine invitation. If my words do not find in you a profound desire to respond to the greatness of your vocation, they will be of no effect. I do not say to you: "Aspire straightaway to the highest sanctity." But I do recommend you strongly—for it is of utmost importance—to try to walk in the way of sanctity which God has chosen for you. He alone knows your weakness: *ipse cognovit figmentum nostrum* (Ps 102:14, and, in His wisdom, He has measured exactly what you are capable of, and what is the power of the graces destined to support your progress. It is from this desire of sanctity that all true spiritual life proceeds: by it the soul prepares itself to receive the gift from on high; in its acknowledgement of its powerlessness and in its expectation of the help of grace, it lays itself open to the influence of the Lord, and increases its capacity for the divine. The

---

31 *Ibid.*, pp. 35–36; *Christ, The Ideal of the Priest*, pp. 43–44.

pursuit of sanctity is like an interior flame, a sacred fire which we bear within us. At times this fire seems to be only a spark, but, believe me, it can be revived and become bright again. If we wish the Father, when He looks at us, to be able to say, as He said of Jesus: "This is my beloved Son," let all our efforts and all our aspirations tend towards the establishment of the reign of charity in our hearts.[32]

The priestly heart is conformed to the Divine Heart in its pastoral charity. Growth in holiness in the life of the priest will manifest itself principally in a greater attention to the worthy offering of the sacraments and other sacred rites, and in the constant desire to bring all souls to Christ.

In the Sermon on the Mount, Christ expressed the holiness of life to which we are called: 'Be ye perfect as your heavenly Father is perfect.'[33] Dom Marmion asks:

> Why must our perfection and our sanctity reproduce the divine sanctity, so infinitely removed from our human weakness? Are we given the power to know the mystery of this divine life? The answer to this double question is contained in these words: We must resemble the heavenly Father because we are His children by adoption. And to know the perfection of this Father, it suffices to turn to Jesus Christ. St John tells us, "No one has ever seen God"; *Deum nemo vidit umquam* (Jn 1:18). Must we, then, despair of ever knowing Him? No, because the disciple adds immediately the glorious truth: "His only Son, Who is in the bosom of the Father, He hath declared Him." St Paul, inspired by this same revelation, declares: "God inhabits light inaccessible," *Deus lucem inhabitat inaccessabilem* (1 Tim. 6:16), but "He Who by His word commanded the light to shine out of the darkness hath shined in our hearts ... by the resplendent brilliance of the faith of Jesus Christ" (2 Cor. 4:16). The liturgy of Christmas repeats it to us each year: "Knowing God visibly, let us be transported by

---

32 *Ibid.*, p. 36; *Christ, The Ideal of the Priest*, pp. 44–45.
33 Mt. 5:48.

Him unto the love of things invisible." Christ is God adapted to our capacity, in human form. After the Last Supper, Philip said to Jesus: "Lord, show us the Father," *Domine ostende nobis Patrem* (Jn 14:8). And Our Lord replied in solemn words which contain, as it were, the key to the mystery: "Philip, he that seeth Me seeth the Father also" (Jn 14:9). Everything in Jesus Christ is therefore a revelation of God. Saint Augustine proclaims it: *Factum verbi verbum nobis est* [*Tractatus in Joannem* 24, PL 35, 1593].[34]

What is said of the faithful, in general, in this regard, finds a special realization in the ordained priest. 'To a much greater extent than [the faithful] can, he contemplates Jesus Christ in reading the Scriptures, in following the course of the liturgical year and in celebrating the sacrifice of the Mass.'[35]

Christ alone is the source of all holiness by virtue of the Mystery of the Redemptive Incarnation. It is, therefore, foolishness to lack attention to Christ while pretending to develop our own way to holiness of life. Dom Marmion teaches us:

> If the Word—Who by His simple and infinite activity expresses all that the Father is—has revealed the secrets of the divine life in human language, and by examples adapted to our weak intelligence, it is not the height of folly on the part of men to be inattentive to His message, and to think of becoming holy in their own way without making Jesus Christ the object of their aspirations, of their confidence, and of their life?[36]

We simply cannot imitate the way of Christ unless He grant us the grace so to do. Christ 'impresses upon the soul His own resemblance.'[37]

---

34 'The deed of the Word is for us a word.' *Prêtre*, pp. 37–38; *Christ, The Ideal of the Priest*, pp. 45–46.
35 Ibid., p. 38; *Christ, The Ideal of the Priest*, p. 46.
36 Ibid., p. 39; *Christ, The Ideal of the Priest*, p. 48.
37 Ibid., p. 40; *Christ, The Ideal of the Priest*, p. 49.

Blessed Columba Marmion and the Spiritual Direction of Priests

In the very troubled and troubling times in which we live in the Church and in the world, priests can easily suffer a profound discouragement, especially if they have been inattentive to their fundamental relationship with Christ as their brother in the Eternal High Priesthood. Dom Marmion instructs his brother priests:

> In Jesus Christ, everything radiates life: His words, His actions, the different phases of His life. All the mysteries of His life on earth, those of His childhood, as well as those of His death, possess an ever efficacious power of sanctification. In Him the past is not effaced: "Christ dieth no more: death shall no more have dominion over Him" (Rom. 6:9). "Jesus Christ yesterday and today and the same for ever" (Heb. 13:8). He never ceases to pour into our souls His supernatural life.
>
> But too often our inattention or lack of faith paralyses the effect of His action on our souls. For us, to live is to possess sanctifying grace, and by our attention inspired by faith and love, to make our thoughts, our affections and all our activity emanate from Christ. If anyone should say to you: "To aspire to such elevation of soul is beyond my capacity, I must give up the idea," you should reply firmly: "Yes, it is impossible for you if you must rely on your natural strength and without allowing the necessary length of time." But so powerful is the action of Christ, so sanctifying the influence of a Mass well celebrated, of Holy Communion, of the atmosphere of prayer and of noble generosity in which the priestly life is normally lived, that you must fill your heart with unlimited confidence. If you show even a little fidelity to Him, Christ, by His grace, will raise you up.
>
> Even if your life as a priest appears mediocre in the eyes of some—the world often judges thus—you may be sure that, in the eyes of God, it is great and agreeable because the Father sees in it the image of

the life of His Son. "For you are dead: and your life is hid in Christ with God" (Col. 3:3).[38]

Our priestly souls are indelibly marked with the grace of holy orders. Christ, Head and Shepherd of the Father's flock, is ever at work in us. It only remains for us to cooperate with His grace. He will accomplish the rest.

It is helpful for priests to recall frequently the words of Saint Paul, at the end of his apostolic ministry, to the Bishop Saint Timothy:

> I charge you in the presence of God and of Christ Jesus who is to judge the living and the dead, and by his appearing and his kingdom: preach the word, be urgent in season and out of season, convince, rebuke, and exhort, be unfailing in patience and in teaching. For the time is coming when people will not endure sound teaching, but having itching ears they will accumulate for themselves teachers to suit their own likings, and will turn away from listening to the truth and wander into myths. As for you, always be steady, endure suffering, do the work of an evangelist, fulfil your ministry.
>
> For I am already on the point of being sacrificed; the time of my departure has come. I have fought the good fight, I have finished the race, I have kept the faith. Henceforth there is laid up for me the crown of righteousness, which the Lord, the righteous judge, will award to me on that Day, and not only to me but also to all who have loved his appearing. (2 Tim. 4:1–8)

How actual for today is Saint Paul's admonition to Saint Timothy! The ordained priest has received the grace to heed the admonition so that, at the end of his days, he may be able to say with Saint Paul: 'I have fought the good fight, I have finished the race, I have kept the faith.' May priests never fail in confidence in the crown of righteousness which Our Lord reserves for his faithful 'fellow laborers in the truth' (3 Jn 1:8).

---

38 *Ibid.*, pp. 43–44; *Christ, The Ideal of the Priest*, pp. 52–53.

CONCLUSION: THE BLESSED VIRGIN MARY, MOTHER OF THE ETERNAL HIGH PRIEST AND OF PRIESTS

There are many more riches of spiritual direction for priests which flow from these fundamental considerations of the spiritual doctrine of Blessed Columba Marmion. It is my hope that these fundamental considerations will inspire in priests the desire to plumb the depths of Blessed Columba's spiritual writings, especially as they illuminate the sacramental character of the holy priesthood.

I conclude with Blessed Columba's reflection upon the Blessed Virgin Mary, Mother of the Eternal Priest Jesus Christ and Mother of priests. Dom Marmion introduces us to the treatment of our relationship with the Virgin Mother of God in his spiritual doctrine:

> Mary is Queen and Mother of all Christians. She is in a special manner Queen and Mother of priests. Because of their resemblance to her divine Son, Our Lady sees Jesus in each one of them. She loves them, not only as members of the mystical body, but on account of the priestly character imprinted on their souls, and for the sacred mysteries which they celebrate *in persona Christi*.
>
> No one has understood as well as she the role of the priest in the Church. The priest carries on the work of her Son by the ministry of the Word, by the administration of the sacraments, and especially by perpetuating the divine immolation under the veil of the sacred species. It is the desire of Mary to come to the aid of each of us on all occasions: to support our weakness, to elevate our souls. At the altar and all during life it is supremely useful to invoke frequently the powerful intercession of our heavenly mother. She knows the greatness of our dignity and how much we stand in need of heavenly grace.
>
> Exempt from sin, she does not know within herself human misery. Yet, of all His creatures, Mary has been, in a certain sense, the object of the greatest mercies of God. The divine goodness has operated in her regard, not to pardon, but to preserve her from all

BELOVED OF GOD AND MEN

stain. We cannot doubt that Mary, for her part, will be full of commiseration for us: *Salve Regina, Mater misericordiae.*[39]

Our relationship with the Virgin Mary is one of filial devotion. What do we mean by devotion? Dom Marmion helps us with the following description of Christian devotion:

> In its primary sense the term "devotion" means the gift, total or partial, of oneself and one's activities to a person or to a work. For us priests it is to God and His cause that we dedicate ourselves and all the resources of our activity. But if God, in His goodness, loves and overwhelms with honour one of His creatures, our devotion to the supreme Majesty makes it incumbent on us to imitate His attitude and render to this privileged creature the homage of our profound veneration.[40]

The first and fundamental aspect of our devotion to the Blessed Virgin Mary is imitation of the divine devotion to her. So that our devotion may be as full and perfect as possible, we must consider how God the Father shows His devotion to her.

The first foundation of our devotion to the Blessed Virgin Mary is God's predestination of her to be the Mother of His Only-Begotten Son at the Redemptive Incarnation. Included in her predestination is the Immaculate Conception and the Virginal Conception and Birth, her Assumption and Coronation as Queen of Heaven and Earth. Dom Marmion comments:

> The divine maternity of Our Lady is the reason for her singular prerogatives. It is to this dignity that she owes her Immaculate Conception, her preservation from all sin, her sanctification. Her sanctification is like the rising dawn: *velut aurora consurgens*, developed from the childhood of Mary until the day when, having been assumed into heaven, she was crowned in glory and power on the right hand of Jesus.

---

39 *Ibid.*, p. 312; *Christ, The Ideal of the Priest*, p. 331.
40 *Ibid.*, p. 315; *Christ, The Ideal of the Priest*, p. 334.

> You can see that devotion to the Blessed Virgin Mary is not an accidental matter; it belongs to the very essence of Christianity. One would cease to be a true disciple of Christ if one did not give His mother the respectful homage which the Incarnation imposes on us. The Church recognizes her incomparable excellence by a form of veneration superior to that offered to all other saints: the veneration of *hyperdulia*.[41]

A sound and vital interior life always has reference to the Mother of God and her truly unique participation, cooperation, in the Redemptive Incarnation.

Dom Marmion also places the devotion to the Blessed Virgin Mary on the solid foundation of her Motherhood of the Church. As adopted sons in the Only-Begotten Son we share in His love of His Virgin Mother. He explains:

> Firm as is this first basis for our devotion to her, we have another powerful motive for honouring Our Lady: she is our mother. By the veneration which we offer her as sons are we not still more like Jesus Who loved and venerated His mother?
>
> We are the children of God, not merely in name but in truth (1 Jn 3:1); so also we are truly the children of the Virgin Mary. This is not a mere figure or metaphor, but the teaching of our faith.
>
> What is the foundation for this happy certainty that we are the children of the Queen of heaven? First of all it is founded on the dogma of our incorporation with Christ as members of His body. Is not a woman a mother when she is the source of life for others—when she communicates to another the life which she enjoys herself. Now, in the supernatural order, whence comes to us this divine life which is destined not to end with death like our corporal life, but to bloom into glory in eternity? Eve gave us life according to nature and to sin; but life and grace have come down to us through Mary. Mary is the new Eve associated by her predestination to the new Adam. How efficacious her cooperation has been for

---

41   CIP, p. 315. English translation: CIPEng, p. 334.

the work of redemption! At the time of the Annunciation, as we have already said, God willed to make the coming of His Son subject in a certain way to her consent. Henceforth the Virgin was to be the privileged creature who communicated to all the gift of God, supernatural life; she accepted her motherhood in all the fullness of the divine intentions. Now, it was in the designs of God that she should be mother not only of Christ but of all His members....

However, it was at the foot of the Cross in the grief of her compassion that Mary was finally declared mother of the human race. Had she not at this moment reached the culmination of her life here on earth? She had accomplished to the full the *fiat* of the Incarnation and fulfilled the role which had been ordained for her by the sovereign Wisdom. A partner in the immolation of her Son, she was, as it were, transfused into Him by love and had with Him the one will of submission to the Father, the one intention to suffer and to carry out the eternal designs. By virtue of this moral union and in complete subordination to the one true Mediator, Mary was a co-redeemer. In this way she engendered us to supernatural life, and became in a true sense our mother.

Jesus willed that we should hear these great truths from His own lips. Let us go in spirit to Calvary. From the height of the Cross where He is in His agony, Jesus utters those sublime words, the full profound truth of which has been only gradually revealed in the Church. The last words spoken by a son at the hour of death are sacred to the heart of a mother. Mary loved Jesus more than any other creature ever loved Him. As a mother and as a mother endowed with all the gifts of grace, she cherished her Son with all the intensity of her affection. Now, what were the last words of Jesus to His mother? Mary was standing close to Him at the foot of the Cross; her eyes were fixed on the countenance of Her Son and she treasured every word that He spoke: "Father, forgive them" (Lk. 23:240. "This day you will be with me in paradise" (Lk. 23:43). Then Jesus lowered His eyes towards her and His well-beloved disciple. What is He going to say? In a voice which is failing, He pronounces these words: "Woman, behold thy son" (Jn 19:26). These last words of Jesus are for Mary a testament of incomprehensible value.

We may see in St John all the faithful souls to whom Mary became a mother, but we must not forget the fact that he had been ordained priest the evening before. On this account, he represents especially all priests. We like to think that at the hour of His death, at that moment of supreme solemnity, Jesus turned to us; in the person of the apostle whom He loved, He entrusted us to His mother....

As we are assimilated to Christ by our baptism and still more by our ordination, let us confirm this grace by filling our hearts with respect, with confidence and with devotion in regard to Our Lady; let us strive to have for her the most perfect filial dispositions. We have the perfect model in the dispositions of Jesus towards His mother.

What a consolation to reflect that by our veneration and love for Mary we are gradually perfecting our resemblance to the Saviour![42]

The spiritual reality which Dom Marmion describes has been confirmed by the many approved apparitions of the Virgin Mother of God to Christ's faithful, her children, over the centuries and in the various parts of the household of God.

Dom Marmion provides a final exhortation to priests:

> In closing I would like to make this final point. Before drawing His last breath, Jesus entrusted His mother to St John. In this moment of unique solemnity He gave His disciple a legacy which was supremely precious. And what was the reaction of the apostle, the priest to whom Jesus confided the care of His mother? As a son, "he took her for his own": *Accepit eam in sua* (Jn 19:27).
>
> Let us also take Mary for our own, as a son full of affection receives his mother; let us dwell with her,

---

42 *Ibid.*, pp. 315-318; *Christ, The Ideal of the Priest*, pp. 334-337.

that is to say, let us associate her in our works, in our troubles, in our joys.

Does not she desire, more than anyone else, to help each one of us to become a holy priest and to reproduce in himself the virtues of Jesus?[43]

Following the spiritual teaching of Blessed Columba Marmion, may priests confide themselves and the souls in their priestly care to the Immaculate Heart of the Blessed Virgin Mary, and to the Most Sacred Heart of Jesus, the Eternal High Priest.

---

43 *Ibid.*, p. 326; *Christ, The Ideal of the Priest*, p. 345.

APPENDIX

YEAR SERVICE/CORRESPONDENT

1881 Chaplain to the Convent of the Nuns of the Sacred Heart, Mount Anville (Ireland).[1]

1882 *1 September:* Nominated chaplain to the Redemptoristine Convent, Drumcondra, Dublin (Ireland).[2]

1883 Continued service as chaplain to the Redemptoristine Convent.

1884 Continued service as chaplain to the Redemptoristine Convent.
18–19 August: Assisting Sister M. Clare, a Redemptoristine novice, on her death bed.[3]
20 August: Letter to an Irish Sister.[4] (one of only three known letters from that year).

1885 Continued service as chaplain to the Redemptoristine Convent.
29 April, 27 November: Letters to Sister Alphonsus Waddock. She was a woman from Dublin, whose baptismal name was Katie, who entered the Convent of the Sisters of Mercy at Dunmore East, where Mother Columba, Blessed Columba's sister, was the superior. Blessed Columba was acquainted with the Waddock Family. These two are the only known letters of the year 1885.[5]

1886 *26 June:* Conclusion of his service as chaplain to the Redemptoristine Convent.[6]
1–4 November: Visit with his blood Sisters of Mercy at Clonakilty and Waterford.[7]

1887 *24 June, 11 September:* Letters to Mother Gabriel Gill, OP (1837–1905), a Dominican Sister, born at Dublin on 22 June 1937, who became Prioress of the Novitiate Convent of Beaumont at Dublin. She made her profession at the Monastery of Sion Hill at Dublin on 18 August 1854. She was the foundress of

---

1   See Thibaut, *Abbot Columba Marmion: A Master of the Spiritual Life: 1858–1923*, p. 31.
2   Marmion, *Correspondance 1881–1923*, "*Chronologie des Lettres et de la vie du Bienheureux Columba Marmion,*" p. 1320.
3   *Ibid.*, p. 1320.
4   *Ibid.*, p. 1319.
5   *Ibid.*, "Index: Waddock, Alphonsus," p. 1316.
6   *Ibid.*, "*Chronologie des Lettres et de la vie du Bienheureux Columba Marmion,*" p. 1319.
7   *Ibid.*, p. 1321.

numerous convents in New Zealand. From New Zealand, she left to found a new convent in Australia in 1899. These are only two of three known letters of the year 1887.[8]

1891 *17 October:* Letter to Mother Peter (his sister Rosie) (only one of two known letters of that year).[9]

1894 *12 and 16 September; 2 October; 27 November; 5 and 15 December:* Letters to Jeanne de Brouwer (1853–1930), born at Bruges (Belgium). She entered the Abbey of St Scholastica at Maredret in 1896, and received the name of Dame Hildegarde.[10]

1895 Retreat given to nuns.[11]

13 January, 25 February, 19 March, 12 April, 21 May: Letters to Jeanne de Brouwer (only known letters of that year).[12]

1896 *2 July:* Letter to Sister Alphonsus Waddock.[13]

1898 *30 November–8 December:* First retreat given to the Benedictine Nuns of the Abbey of Saint Scholastica at Maredret.[14]

1899 *12 February:* Nominated ordinary Confessor and spiritual director at Carmel at Louvain. On confession day, he would give a conference to the nuns.[15]

20 February, 10 April: Letters to Mother Marie-Jeanne of the Cross, Prioress of the Carmel at Louvain.[16]

June: Letter to Dame Cécile de Hemptinne (1870–1948), whose baptismal name was Agnes, the blood sister of Dom Hildebrand de Hemptinne. After completing her novitiate at the Abbey of Saint Cecilia at Solesmes (France), she made her profession in 1890. In 1893, she became the foundress of the Abbey of Saint Scholastica at Maredret, of which she became the first Abbess (1900–1948). She had important correspondence with Blessed Columba; 76 letters have been preserved.[17]

---

8   Ibid., "Index: "Gill, Gabriel," p. 1292.
9   Ibid., p. 1321.
10   Ibid., "Index: de Brouwer, Jeanne," p. 1280.
11   See Thibaut, *Abbot Columba Marmion: A Master of the Spiritual Life: 1858–1923*, pp. 107–108. See footnote 3: "We have not been able to discover who these nuns were."
12   Marmion, *Correspondance 1881–1923*, "*Chronologie des Lettres et de la vie du Bienheureux Columba Marmion*," p. 1322.
13   Ibid.
14   Ibid.
15   Ibid. See Thibaut, *Abbot Columba Marmion: A Master of the Spiritual Life: 1858–1923*, p. 133.
16   Marmion, *Correspondance 1881–1923*, "Index: Marie-Jeanne de la Croix," p. 1300.
17   Ibid., "Index: de Hemptinne, Cécile," p. 1280.

Appendix

July: Letter to Jeanne de Brouwer.[18]

30 October: Letter to Mother Marie of Jesus, a Carmelite nun at Louvain. Blessed Columba often called her by her baptismal name of Céline.[19]

1900 Ordinary Confessor and spiritual director at Carmel at Louvain. On confession day, he would give a conference to the nuns.[20]

8 September: Attends the abbatial blessing of Dame Cécile de Hemptinne as first Abbess of the Abbey of Saint Scholastica at Maredret.[21]

1901 Ordinary Confessor and spiritual director at Carmel at Louvain. On confession day, he would give a conference to the nuns.[22]

1 February: Letter to Dame Scholastica Casier (1872–1948), a nun of the Abbey at Maredret, who had a brother at Maredsous (Dom Hubert). She made profession on 10 February 1894.[23]

8 February: Letter to Dame Cécile de Hemptinne.[24]

25 June, 17 September, 8 October: Letters to Jeanne de Brouwer.[25]

30 November–8 December: Preached retreat for the nuns at the Abbey at Maredret.[26]

1902 *January:* Letter to Mother Amélie of the Immaculate Conception, a Carmelite nun of Louvain, who was one of the closest spiritual daughters of Blessed Columba. She was Prioress at the Carmel during the following years: 1906–1909; 1912–1915; 1918–1924.[27]

2, 19 and 30 January; 8, 11 and 28 February; 5 and 10 March; 1, 4, and 28 April; 10 August; 1 and 28 October; 16 December: Letters to Dame Cécile de Hemptinne.[28]

---

18   *Ibid.*, p. 1323.
19   *Ibid.*, "Index: Marie de Jésus," p. 1299.
20   See Thibaut, *Abbot Columba Marmion: A Master of the Spiritual Life: 1858–1923*, p. 133.
21   Marmion, *Correspondance 1881–1923*, "Chronologie des Lettres et de la vie du Bienheureux Columba Marmion," p. 1323.
22   See Thibaut, *Abbot Columba Marmion: A Master of the Spiritual Life: 1858–1923*, p. 133.
23   Marmion, *Correspondance 1881–1923*, "Index: Casier, Dame Scholastique," p. 1274.
24   *Ibid.*, "*Chronologie des Lettres et de la vie du Bienheureux Columba Marmion*," p. 1323.
25   *Ibid.*
26   *Ibid.*
27   *Ibid.*, "Index: Amélie de l'Immaculée Conception," p. 1267.
28   *Ibid.*, "*Chronologie des Lettres et de la vie du Bienheureux Columba Marmion*," p. 1324.

13–21 September: Preached retreat for the Benedictine nuns of Douai at Reading (Great Britain).[29]

19 November: Letter to Dame Caecilia Joyce (1881–1956), his niece, who was a nun at the Abbey of Saint Scholastica at Maredret. She began the novitiate in 1902 and made her first profession on 5 October 1903. She translated and copied long extracts from the correspondence she had received from her uncle. The originals seem to have disappeared.[30]

2 December: Letter to Mother Marie-Joseph van Aerden, a Carmelite nun at Louvain. She entered Carmel in December 1902, on the advice of Blessed Columba. He kept up a long correspondence with her until the eve of his death. He confided many of his spiritual experiences to her. In his letters, he often called her 'Thecle' or 'Thecla,' and signed himself 'Paul,' an allusion to the *Acts of Paul and Tecla*.[31]

1903 Ordinary Confessor at Carmel at Louvain. On confession day, he would give a conference to the nuns.[32]

1 January, 23 February, 9 April, 17 May, 4 August, 4 December: Letters to Dame Cécile de Hemptinne.[33]

16 February, 10 April: Letters to Dame Caecilia Joyce.[34]

1–3 July: Visit to the Benedictine nuns at Douai, Reading.[35]

23 November: Letter to Mother Marie-Joseph van Aerden.[36]

1904 Ordinary Confessor at Carmel at Louvain. On confession day, he would give a conference to the nuns.[37]

20 January, 28 February, 3 April, 7 June: Letters to Dame Cécile de Hemptinne.[38]

1 February: Letter to Dame Scholastica Casier.[39]

3 February: Letter to Dame Caecilia Joyce.[40]

---

29 *Ibid.*
30 *Ibid.*, "Index: Joyce, Caecilia," p. 1295.
31 *Ibid.*, "Index: van Aerden, Henriette," p. 1313.
32 See Thibaut, *Abbot Columba Marmion: A Master of the Spiritual Life: 1858–1923*, p. 133.
33 Marmion, *Correspondance 1881–1923*; "Chronologie des Lettres et de la vie du Bienheureux Columba Marmion," pp. 1324–1325.
34 *Ibid.*, p. 1324.
35 *Ibid.*, p. 1325.
36 *Ibid.*
37 See Thibaut, *Abbot Columba Marmion: A Master of the Spiritual Life: 1858–1923*, p. 133.
38 Marmion, *Correspondance 1881–1923*, "Chronologie des Lettres et de la vie du Bienheureux Columba Marmion," p. 1325.
39 *Ibid.*
40 *Ibid.*

Appendix

24 July: Letter to the Carmelites of Louvain.[41]

26 July–3 August: Preached retreat for the Benedictines at Douai, Reading.[42]

1905 Ordinary Confessor at Carmel at Louvain. On confession day, he would give a conference to the nuns.[43]

Unknown date: Letter to Dame Mechtilde de Volder (1869–1958), a nun of Saint Scholastica Abbey in Maredret, who made her profession in 1893.[44] 'She transcribed many of Dom Marmion's lectures as they were being given. Her transcription was later used by Dom Raymond Thibaut for the edition of Dom Marmion's lecture collections.'[45]

19 January, 16 August: Letters to Dame Caecilia Joyce.[46]

12 May, 14 July: Letters to Dame Cécile de Hemptinne.[47]

12 July: Letter to Mother Marie–Élise of Jesus, the Superior General of the *Filles du Cœur de Jésus* (Daughters of the Heart of Jesus).[48]

1–8 December: Preached retreat for the nuns at the Abbey at Maredret.[49]

1906 *23 March, 9 September:* Letters to Mother Amélie of the Immaculate Conception.[50]

2 and 6 April: Letters to Mother Mary Stanislaus Liefmans (1854–1938). She was a Canoness of Saint Augustine, who entered the English Convent in Bruges on 16 July 1874, where she made profession on 25 January 1876. From 1889 to 1898 she was Prioress of Hayward's Heath (Great Britain). Subsequently, she twice served as Prioress of the English Convent of Bruges (1901–1911 and 1917–1919).[51]

19 April; 1 May; 5 October; 5 and 29 November: Letters to Mother Mary Berchmans Durrant (1864–1949), who served as Prioress of the Convent of the Canonesses of Saint Augustine at Hayward's

---

41 *Ibid.*
42 *Ibid.*
43 See Thibaut, *Abbot Columba Marmion: A Master of the Spiritual Life: 1858–1923*, p. 133.
44 Marmion, *Correspondance 1881–1923*, "Chronologie des Lettres et de la vie du Bienheureux Columba Marmion," p. 1326.
45 *Ibid.*, "Index: de Volder, Dame Mechtilde," p. 1285.
46 *Ibid.*, "Chronologie des Lettres et de la vie du Bienheureux Marmion," p. 1326.
47 *Ibid.*
48 *Ibid.*, "Index: Marie-Élise de Jésus," p. 1299.
49 *Ibid.*, "Chronologie des Lettres et de la vie du Bienheureux Columba Marmion," p. 1326.
50 *Ibid.*, pp. 1326–1327.
51 *Ibid.*, "Index: Liefmans, Mary Stanislaus," p. 1298.

Heath from 1905–1919. On 7 May 1919, she was appointed Prioress of the English Convent at Bruges and remained there until 14 September 1922, at which time she returned to Hayward's Heath. 'She had a very close relationship with Dom Marmion, whom she frequently invited to preach to her community.'[52]

30 August, 13 November: Letter to the Carmelites of Louvain.[53]

1–9 September: Preached retreat for the Canonesses at Hayward's Heath.[54]

17 September; 14, 17, 20, and 26 November; 7 December: Letters to Dame Cécile de Hemptinne.[55]

26 November, 6 December: Letters to Mother Marie-Joseph van Aerden.[56]

1907 Ordinary Confessor at Carmel at Louvain. On confession day, he would give a conference to the nuns.[57]

1 and 10 January; March (one undated letter); 19 and 26 April; 5 June; 9 September; 11 and 19 December: Letters to Mother Mary-Berchmans Durrant.[58]

16, 22, and 27 January; 9 March; 21 November: Letters to Dame Cécile de Hemptinne.[59]

4 March: Letter to Mother Marie-Joseph van Aerden.[60]

7 March and 20 November: Letters to Dame Caecilia Joyce.[61]

15 June: Letter to Dame Mechtilde de Volder.[62]

22 July; 21 August; 7, 20, 25, and 30 September; 2 October; 7, 10, and 16 December: Letters to Mother Amélie of the Immaculate Conception.[63]

16–25 August: Preached retreat at the English Convent at Bruges.[64]

3–12 September: Preached retreat at Hayward's Heath.[65]

---

52 Ibid., "Index: Durrant, Mary-Berchmans," p. 1287.
53 Ibid., "*Chronologie des Lettres et de la vie du Bienheureux Columba Marmion,*" p. 1327.
54 Ibid.
55 Ibid.
56 Ibid.
57 See Thibaut, *Abbot Columba Marmion: A Master of the Spiritual Life: 1858–1923,* p. 133.
58 Marmion, *Correspondance 1881–1923,* "*Chronologie des Lettres et de la vie du Bienheureux Columba Marmion,*" pp. 1327–1328.
59 Ibid.
60 Ibid., p. 1327.
61 Ibid., pp. 1327–1328.
62 Ibid., p. 1327.
63 Ibid., p. 1328.
64 Ibid.
65 Ibid.

Appendix

1908 Ordinary Confessor at Carmel at Louvain. On confession day, he would give a conference to the nuns.[66]

8 January, 28 April, 26 May, 8 July, and 15 November: Letters to Mother Mary-Berchmans Durrant.[67]

24 March; 22 June; 30 August; 28 October; 1 and 26 November; 2, 18, and 21 December: Letters to Mother Pierre Adèle Garnier (1838–1924), foundress of the Adorers of the Sacred Heart of Jesus at Montmarte (France) in 1897. 'In 1901... the community was expelled from France and found refuge at the Tyburn convent in London [Great Britain]. Mother Pierre Adèle lived there for the rest of her life. Under the influence of Dom Marmion, who became her spiritual director in 1908, Mother Garnier and the community decided to adopt the Rule of Saint Benedict. The community was incorporated into the Benedictine Confederation in 1914. Mother Pierre Adèle died in the odor of sanctity, and her cause of beatification has been introduced.'[68]

3 April; 4 May; 3 and 17 September; 10 October; 1 November: Letters to Mother Amélie of the Immaculate Conception.[69]

27 April; 8 and 12 September: Letters to the Carmelite Nuns at Louvain.[70]

11 July: Letter to Mother Marie-Christine, a religious of the English Convent at Bruges.[71]

August: Preached retreat for the Canonesses of Saint Augustine at Jupille.[72]

3–12 September: Preached retreat at Hayward's Heath.[73]

8 October: Letter to Jeanne de Brouwer (Dame Hildegarde).[74]

21 October: Letter to Mother Marie-Joseph van Aerden.[75]

21 October: Letter to Dame Cécile de Hemptinne.[76]

26 November: Letter to Dame Lucie de Montpellier (1871–1951), a nun at the Abbey of Saint Scholastica at Maredret, professed

---

66 See Thibaut, *Abbot Columba Marmion: A Master of the Spiritual Life: 1858–1923*, p. 133.
67 Marmion, *Correspondance 1881–1923*, "Chronologie des Lettres et de la vie du Bienheureux Columba Marmion," pp. 1328–1329.
68 *Ibid.*, "Index: Garnier, Pierre Adèle," p. 1291.
69 *Ibid.*, "Chronologie des Lettres et de la vie du Bienheureux Columba Marmion," pp. 1328–1329.
70 *Ibid.*
71 *Ibid.*, "Index: Marie-Christine," p. 1299.
72 *Ibid.*, "Chronologie des Lettres et de la vie du Bienheureux Columba Marmion," p. 1329.
73 *Ibid.*
74 *Ibid.*
75 *Ibid.*
76 *Ibid.*

in 1898. She was the blood sister of Dom Frédéric and Dom Marc de Montpellier.[77]

1909 Ordinary Confessor at Carmel at Louvain. On confession day, he would give a conference to the nuns.[78]

Weekly ascetical conference to the Benedictine nuns at Maredret.[79]

16 and 23 January; 5 and 20 March; 11 and 26 May; 6 June; 14 July; 13 and 31 August; 6, 20, 28 and, 30 September; 12 and 13 October: Letters to Mother Pierre Adèle Garnier.[80]

23 January; 19 and 23 March; 24 April; 28 July: Letters to the Carmelites at Louvain.[81]

26 January, 20 November: Letters to Dame Cécile de Hemptinne.[82]

7 March, 2 August, 7 September, 12 December: Letters to Mother Mary-Berchmans Durrant.[83]

16 March: Letter to Dame Caecilia Heywood (1852–1931), the Abbess of the Benedictine Abbey at Stanbrook, Allow End, Worcester (Great Britain).[84]

17 March: Letter to Mother Marie-Gabriel, a Carmelite at Louvain.[85]

19 April, 4 July, 2 September, 11 October: Letters to Mother Marie-Jeanne of the Cross.[86]

28 July–2 August: Preached retreat for the Benedictine nuns of Douai, Reading.[87]

4 August: Letter to Mother Amélie of the Immaculate Conception.[88]

1 September: Visit to the Ursulines of Toldonk at Wespelaer (Belgium).[89]

---

77 Ibid., "Index: de Montpellier, Lucie," p. 1283.
78 See Thibaut, *Abbot Columba Marmion: A Master of the Spiritual Life: 1858–1923*, p. 133.
79 See *Ibid.*, p. 178.
80 Marmion, *Correspondance 1881–1923*, "Chronologie des Lettres et de la vie du Bienheureux Columba Marmion," pp. 1329–1330.
81 Ibid.
82 Ibid., p. 1329, 1331.
83 Ibid., pp. 1329–1331.
84 Ibid., "Index: "Heywood, Caelia ou Cécile," p. 1294.
85 Ibid., "Index: "Marie-Gabriel," p. 1299.
86 Ibid., "Chronologie des Lettres et de la vie du Bienheureux Columba Marmion," p. 1330.
87 Ibid.
88 Ibid.
89 Ibid.

Appendix

22 September: Letter to Mother Marie-Joseph van Aerden.[90]

28 September, 27 October, 14 December: Letters to Mother Mary Stanislaus Liefmans.[91]

16 October, 10 November: Letters to Mother Emmanuelle Skerrett, the biological mother of Dom Columba Skerrett. She had been married an Irishman, who worked first in Norwich (England), then in Brussels (Belgium). After her husband's death, she became a nun in Binche (Belgium), with the *Servantes du Sacrement*.[92]

20 November: Letter to Dame Cécile de Hemptinne.[93]

1910 Weekly ascetical conference to the Benedictine nuns at Maredret.[94]

8 January; 14 February; 25 March; 14 June; 28 Jun;, 19 July; 25 October; 16 November; 15 and 21 December: Letters to Mother Pierre Adèle Garnier.[95]

29 January, 13 February, 2 September, 8 November: Letters to Mother Marie-Joseph van Aerden.[96]

26 March, 25 May, 29 June, 7 September: Letters to Dame Caecilia Heywood.[97]

20 April; 11 August; 12, 13, and 26 September; 9 and 20 November: Letters to Dame Cécile de Hemptinne.[98]

16 June, 19 November: Letters to Mother Mary-Berchmans Durrant.[99]

5–13 August: Preached retreat for the Benedictine Nuns at Stanbrook.[100]

14 October, 19 November: Letters to the Carmelites at Louvain.[101]

1911 Weekly ascetical conference to the Benedictine nuns at Maredret.[102]

---

90 Ibid.
91 Ibid., pp. 1330–1331.
92 Ibid., "Index: "Skerrett, Emmanuelle," p. 1310.
93 Ibid., *"Chronologie des Lettres et de la vie du Bienheureux Columba Marmion,"* p. 1331.
94 See Thibaut, *Abbot Columba Marmion: A Master of the Spiritual Life: 1858–1923*, p. 178.
95 Marmion, *Correspondance 1881–1923*, pp. 1331–1333.
96 Ibid.
97 Ibid., pp. 1332–1333.
98 Ibid.
99 Ibid.
100 Ibid., pp. 1332.
101 Ibid., p. 1333.
102 See Thibaut, *Abbot Columba Marmion: A Master of the Spiritual Life: 1858–1923*, p. 178.

3 January: Letter to Dame Caecilia Heywood.[103]

12 January: Letter to Mother Emmanuelle Skerrett.[104]

6 February: Letter to Mother Louise Vandenhende (1882–1952), a lady who entered the convent of the Adorers of the Sacred Heart of Jesus of Montmarte at Ganshoren (Belgium) in 1909. She succeeded Mother Agnes Andrade as prioress in December 1910 and remained in office until August 1921. She then became novice mistress at Bierghes for six months.[105]

14 February: Letter to Mother Agnès Andrade (1876–1926), foundress, with Mother Pierre Adèle Garnier, of the Adorers of the Sacred Heart of Jesus at Montmarte (France) in 1897. In 1901, she left Paris for London. From 1909 until 1910, she served as Prioress of the foundation of Tyburn at Ganshoren. Her being recalled to London in December 1910 was largely due to Blessed Columba. From 1914–1922 she served as Prioress and Mistress of Novices at Tyburn. In 1924, after the death of Mother Pierre Adèle Garnier, she was elected as Superior General.[106]

22 April, 27 June, 28 September: Letters to Mother Marie-Joseph van Aerden.[107]

20 May: Letter to Dame Cécile de Hemptinne.[108]

27 June: Letter to Mother Marie-Christine.[109]

7 July: Letter to Mother Amélie of the Immaculate Conception.[110]

6 December: Letter to Mother Mary-Berchmans Durrant.[111]

6 December: Letter to Mother Mary Michael Bonnaud (1876–1969). Born in Calcutta, India, Mary Michael returned to England with her parents as a young child. Her mother, Mary O'Brien, was Irish. Mary Michael entered the English Convent in Bruges in 1903, but moved to the Priory Convent in Hayward's Heath in 1908. She spent the rest of her life there. During the last year of his life (1922), Blessed Columba

---

103 Marmion, *Correspondance 1881–1923*, "*Chronologie des Lettres et de la vie du Bienheureux Columba Marmion*," p. 1333.
104 *Ibid.*
105 *Ibid.*, "Index: "Vandenhende, Louise," p. 1314. There seems to be a mistake in the text, as it is unlikely that she entered in 1909 and become prioress in 1910.
106 *Ibid.*, "Index: "Andrade, Agnès," p. 1268.
107 *Ibid.*, "*Chronologie des Lettres et de la vie du Bienheureux Columba Marmion*," pp. 1333–1334.
108 *Ibid.*, p. 1334.
109 *Ibid.*
110 *Ibid.*
111 *Ibid.*, p. 1335.

Appendix

was actively involved in settling the difficult estate of Mary Michael's sister, Louline Bonnaid.[112]

19 December: Letter to Mother Pierre Adèle Garnier.[113]

1912 Weekly ascetical conference to the Benedictine nuns at Maredret.[114]

22 January: Letter to Mother Marie-Joseph van Aerden.[115]

6 February; 13 March; 3 May; 5 and 15 August; 31 October; 10 November: Letters to Mother Pierre Adèle Garnier.[116]

6 February, 22 September, 5 December: Letters to Mother Mary Berchmans Durrant.[117]

8 February, 27 February, 14 August, 17 September, 22 September, 14 October: Letters to Mother Amélie of the Immaculate Conception.[118]

1, 5, and 13 March, 2 May, 18 July, 1 August: Letters to Dame Cécile de Hemptinne.[119]

29 March: Letter to Mother Mary Michael Bonnaud.[120]

21 July: Letter to the Carmelites at Louvain.[121]

26 August–7 September: Preached retreats to the nuns at Hayward's Heath and the Diocesan Clergy of Westminster.[122]

29 December: Letter to Dame Scholastique Joyce (1886–?), Blessed Columba's niece.[123]

1913 Weekly ascetical conference to the Benedictine nuns at Maredret.[124]

7 January, 6 May, 6 June: Letters to the Carmelites at Louvain.[125]

---

112   Ibid., "Index: "Bonnaud, Mary Michael," p. 1271–1272.
113   Ibid., "*Chronologie des Lettres et de la vie du Bienheureux Columba Marmion*," p. 1335.
114   See Thibaut, *Abbot Columba Marmion: A Master of the Spiritual fe: 1858–1923*, p. 178.
115   Columba Marmion, *Correspondance 1881–1923*, "Chronologie des Lettres et de la vie du Bienheureux Columba Marmion," p. 1335.
116   Ibid., pp. 1336–1337.
117   Ibid.
118   Ibid.
119   Ibid., p. 1336.
120   Ibid.
121   Ibid.
122   Ibid., p. 1337.
123   Ibid., "Index: Joyce, Scholastique," p. 1296.
124   See Thibaut, *Abbot Columba Marmion: A Master of the Spiritual Life: 1858–1923*, p. 178.
125   Marmion, *Correspondance 1881–1923*, "Chronologie des Lettres et de la vie du Bienheureux Columba Marmion," pp. 1337, 1339.

7 January, 16 February, 15 September, 8 December, 30 December: Letters to Mother Mary-Berchmans Durrant.[126]

29 January: Letter to Mother Amélie of the Immaculate Conception.[127]

29 January; 21 February; 6 April; 14 May; 5 and 23 August; 12, 27, and 30 September; 4 and 6 October; 19 and 21 November; 18 December: Letters to Mother Pierre Adèle Garnier.[128]

6 March; 19 and 31 May; 21 August: Letters to Dame Cécile de Hemptinne.[129]

27 March, 1 April: Letters to Mother Agnès Andrade.[130]

1 July, 11 September: Letters to Mother Emmanuelle Skerrett.[131]

25–31 August: Preached retreat at the Abbey of La Paix Notre Dame at Liège.[132]

6 September, 8 December: Letters to Mother Mary Michael Bonnaud.[133]

10 September, 18 December: Letters to Mother Marie-Joseph van Aerden.[134]

16–28 October: Preached retreat for the Adorers of the Sacred Heart at Tyburn, London.[135]

21 November: Letter to Mother Louise Vandenhende.[136]

26 December: Letter to Dame Marie Constance (1852–1937), a Benedictine nun of the Abbey of La Paix Notre Dame. She served as Prioress from 1892 until 1936.[137]

1914 Weekly ascetical conference to the Benedictine nuns at Maredret.[138]

6 January, 14 March, 23 September, 15 December: Letters to Mother Mary-Berchmans Durrant.[139]

---

126 *Ibid.*, pp. 1337–1338, 1340.
127 *Ibid.*, p. 1338.
128 *Ibid.*, pp. 1338–1340.
129 *Ibid.*, pp. 1338–1339.
130 *Ibid.*, p. 1338.
131 *Ibid.*, pp. 1339–1340.
132 *Ibid.*, p. 1340.
133 *Ibid.*
134 *Ibid.*
135 *Ibid.*
136 *Ibid.*
137 *Ibid.*, "Index: Constance, Dame Marie," p. 1277.
138 See Thibaut, *Abbot Columba Marmion: A Master of the Spiritual Life: 1858–1923*, p. 178.
139 Marmion, *Correspondance 1881–1923*, "Chronologie des Lettres et de la vie du Bienheureux Columba Marmion," pp. 1341, 1343.

Appendix

6 and 29 January; 20 March; 1 April; 4 and 11 May; 17 June: Letters to Mother Pierre Adèle Garnier.[140]

8 and 13 January; 24 June: Letters to Dame Cécile de Hemptinne.[141]

11 January; 6 March; 14 and 19 June: Letters to Mother Amélie of the Immaculate Conception.[142]

24 January, 29 February: Letter to Mother Marie of Jesus.[143]

1–9 February: Preached retreat at the Benedictine Abbey of Saint Scholastica at Maredret.[144]

4 March: Letter to Mother Louise Vandenhende.[145]

15 and 17 March; 20 July: Letters to Mother Marie-Joseph van Aerden.[146]

14 April: Letter to Mother Mary Michael Bonnaud.[147]

16 June: Letter to Mother Mary Margaret, a Canoness of Saint Augustine, whom Blessed Columba came to know at Hayward's Heath, and who was then called to the English Convent at Bruges to take up the office of Mistress of Novices.[148]

1915 Weekly ascetical conference to the Benedictine nuns at Maredret.[149]

2 March, 28 June: Letters to Mother Mary-Berchmans Durrant.[150]

5–21 March: Visit at Hayward's Heath and London.[151]

2 April: Letter to Mother Pierre Adèle Garnier.[152]

3, 7, 17 May: Letters to Mother Hildegarde Clayton (1874–1932), a religious at Tyburn, London.[153]

10 June: Letter to Dame Cécile de Hemptinne.[154]

---

140   Ibid., pp. 1341–1342.
141   Ibid.
142   Ibid.
143   Ibid., p. 1341.
144   Ibid., p. 1341.
145   Ibid.
146   Ibid., pp. 1341–1342.
147   Ibid., p. 1342.
148   Ibid., "Index: Mary Margaret," p.1300.
149   See Thibaut, *Abbot Columba Marmion: A Master of the Spiritual Life: 1858–1923*, p. 178.
150   Marmion, *Correspondance 1881–1923*, "Chronologie des Lettres et de la vie du Bienheureux Columba Marmion," pp. 1343–1344.
151   Ibid., p. 1343.
152   Ibid., p. 1344.
153   Ibid., "Index: Clayton, Hildegarde," p. 1275.
154   Ibid., "Chronologie des Lettres et de la vie du Bienheureux Columba Marmion," p. 1344.

16 June: Letter to the Carmelites at Louvain.[155]

19–25 August: Stay at the Benedictine Abbey at Ventnor,[156] Isle of Wight (Great Britain).

30 August–8 September: Preached retreat for the Sisters of the Assumption, Kensington, London (Great Britain).[157]

4 and 8 September: Letters to Dame Patricia Murphy (1887–1961), a Benedictine nun at the Monastery of Saint Cecilia at Ryde on the Isle of Wright, where Blessed Columba stayed several times in 1915 and 1916. She was born in Melbourne (Australia), but came to England at an early age. In a letter dated 8 September 1915, Blessed Columba spoke of the 'holy friendship' that bound them together. For her 33rd birthday (1920), she received from Blessed Columba a 9-volume Latin Bible dedicated by him.[158]

3 November: Letter to Mother Mary Stanislaus White, Prioress of the Redemptoristinnes at Drumcondra where Blessed Columba served as chaplain from 1882 until 1886.[159]

1916 Weekly ascetical conference to the Benedictine nuns at Maredret.[160]

1, 22, and 31 January: Letters to Mother Pierre Adèle Garnier.[161]

5 January (2 letters): Letters to Dame Patricia Murphy.[162]

23 January: Letter to Mother Mary Stanislaus White.[163]

27 February: Letter to Mother Benventura Costello, a Dominican nun who made profession on 27 April 1905 at the Convent of Sion Hill at Dublin (Ireland). She was a directee of Blessed Columba.[164]

23 March–17 April: Convalescence at the Benedictine Abbey of Ventnor.[165]

20 May; 1 and 24 June; 22 August; 9 October; 18 December: Letters to Mother Marie-Joseph van Aerden.[166]

---

155 *Ibid.*
156 *Ibid.*
157 *Ibid.*
158 *Ibid.*, "Index: Murphy, Patricia," p. 1303.
159 *Ibid.*, "Index: White, Mary Stanislaus," p. 1317.
160 See Thibaut, *Abbot Columba Marmion: A Master of the Spiritual Life: 1858–1923*, p. 178.
161 Marmion, *Correspondance 1881–1923*, "Chronologie des Lettres et de la vie du Bienheureux Columba Marmion," p. 1345.
162 *Ibid.*
163 *Ibid.*
164 *Ibid.*, "Index: Costello, Benventura," p. 1278.
165 *Ibid.*, "*Chronologie des Lettres et de la vie du Bienheureux Columba Marmion*," p. 1346.
166 *Ibid.*, pp. 1346–1347.

Appendix

8 October, 2 November: Letters to Mother Marie of Jesus.[167]

14 and 20 November; 1, 12, and 27 December: Letters to Mother Marguerite-Marie de Richoufftz (of the Sacred Heart) (1870–1956). She entered the Carmelite Monastery of Saint Joseph at Virton (Belgium). A gifted musician, she entered Carmel at the age of 25. She served as Prioress from 1915–1938.[168]

Spiritual Director of the Carmelite nuns at the Carmel of Saint-Joseph at Virton.[169]

7 December: Letter to Mother Emmanuelle Skerrett.[170]

13–18 December: Preached retreat for the Benedictine nuns at Maredret.[171]

30 December: Letter to Mother Joseph-Marie.[172]

1917 Weekly ascetical conference to the Benedictine nuns at Maredret.[173]

Spiritual Director of the Carmelite nuns at the Carmel of Saint-Joseph at Virton.[174]

11 February, 20 February, 14 March, 18 August: Letters to Mother Marguerite-Marie de Richoufftz.[175]

20 February; 14 and 20 March: Letters to Mother Gabrielle Cambon (of the Sacred Heart) (1882–1947), a Carmelite nun at Virton. She entered in 1900, and served as Mistress of Novices in 1917. She served as Sub-Prioress from 1920–1938 and as Prioress 1938–1947.[176]

4, 22, (and one undated) April; 3 and 9 May; 9 June; 10 and 31 July; 1, 14, 25 October; 4 and 17 December: Letters to Mother Marie-Joseph van Aerden.[177]

12 April, 20 July, 12 December: Letters to Mother Emmanuelle Skerrett.[178]

---

167 Ibid., p. 1346.
168 Ibid., "Index: de Richoufftz, Marguerite-Marie," p. 1284.
169 Ibid.
170 Ibid., "*Chronologie des Lettres et de la vie du Bienheureux Columba Marmion,*" p. 1347.
171 Ibid.
172 Ibid.
173 See Thibaut, *Abbot Columba Marmion: A Master of the Spiritual Life: 1858–1923,* p. 178.
174 Marmion, *Correspondance 1881–1923,* "Index: de Richoufftz, Marguerite-Marie," p. 1284.
175 Ibid., "*Chronologie des Lettres et de la vie du Bienheureux Columba Marmion,*" pp. 1347–1348.
176 Ibid., "Index: Cambon, Gabrielle," p. 1273.
177 Ibid., pp. 1347–1349.
178 Ibid., pp. 1348–1349.

10 May: Letter to Dame Winfrida Kraemer (?–1930), a Benedictine nun at Oosterhout (the Netherlands). Blessed Columba stayed with the Kraemer Family in La Hayde (the Netherlands) in April–May 1916, during his journey from Ireland and England to Maredsous. Liete, a daughter of the house, became a Benedictine nun, under the name Dame Winfrida. Blessed Columba sometimes called her 'my dear niece.' Her sister Wally and her brother Jean Kraemer were friends of Blessed Columba, who was very grateful for the welcome he had received in this family in 1916.[179]

1 July: Letter to Dame Cécile de Hemptinne.[180]

1–8 September: Preached retreat for the Benedictine nuns at La Paix Notre-Dame.[181]

8 September: Letter to Dame Marie Constance.[182]

23 September–1 October: Preached retreat for the Dominicans at Louvain,[183] probably for the Dominican Sisters at the Priory Terbank, a former house of the Augustinian Canonesses, which served as a Dominican Convent from 1858–1971.

1918 Weekly ascetical conference to the Benedictine nuns at Maredret.[184]

Spiritual Director of the Carmelite nuns at the Carmel of Saint-Joseph at Virton.[185]

3, 5 and 23 January; 1,17, and 29 March; 1 and 9 April; 3 (and one undated) June; 22 July; 4 and 25 September: Letters to Mother Marie-Joseph van Aerden.[186]

9 January: Letter to Mother Emmanuel Skerrett.[187]

22 and 26 April; 2 May; 4 August; 1 September: Letters to Dame Cécile de Hemptinne.[188]

Undated letter of May; undated letter of July: Letters to Mother Amélie of the Immaculate Conception.[189]

---

179   Ibid., "Index: Kraemer, Winfrida," p. 1296.
180   Ibid., "*Chronologie des Lettres et de la vie du Bienheureux Columba Marmion,*" p. 1348.
181   Ibid.
182   Ibid.
183   Ibid.
184   See Thibaut, *Abbot Columba Marmion: A Master of the Spiritual Life: 1858–1923,* p. 178.
185   Marmion, *Correspondance 1881–1923,* "Index: de Richoufftz, Marguerite-Marie," p. 1284.
186   Ibid., "*Chronologie des Lettres et de la vie du Bienheureux Columba Marmion,*" pp. 1349–1350.
187   Ibid., p. 1350.
188   Ibid., p.1349–1350.
189   Ibid., p. 1350.

Appendix

1 May, 7 December: Letters to Dame Winfrida Kraemer.[190]
31 August: Letter to Dame Caecilia Joyce.[191]
15 October: Letter to Mother Marie-Ange Brasseur. She was a Belgian lady who wanted to become a nun, but hesitated about her vocation. In 1918, she entered the 'Home Sainte Elisabeth,' and quickly became its superior. Desiring the Benedictine life, she spent three months (March 23–June 1919) at La Paix Notre Dame Abbey, and completed a novitiate of Benedictine nuns at the Abbey of Saint Nicholas at Verneuil (Belgium), with a view to joining the Wepion community (Belgium). She entered the Benedictine nuns Hurtebise Monastery at Saint-Hubert (Luxembourg), where she became Superior, before leaving the religious life permanently.[192]
16 October: Letter to Mother Marie of Jesus.[193]

1919 Weekly ascetical conference to the Benedictine nuns at Maredret.[194]
Spiritual Director of the Carmelite nuns at the Carmel of Saint-Joseph at Virton.[195]
Undated; 2 February, 9 May, 16 August, 20 August, 5 December, 30 December: Letters to Mother Marie-Joseph van Aerden.[196]
Undated: Letter to Mother Amélie of the Immaculate Conception.[197]
19 January, 1 February, 19 November: Letters to Dame Cécile de Hemptinne.[198]
25 January, 9 February, 15 February: Letters to Mother Marie-Ange Brasseur.[199]
14 February, 9 June, 11 July, 29 July, 16 December: Letters to Dame Raphaël Vauvrecy (1857–1930). She made profession for the Saint-Louis-du-Temple Abbey at Paris (France) in 1889. She was elected 10th Prioress in 1899, a position which she held until her resignation in 1929.[200]

---

190 *Ibid.*
191 *Ibid.*
192 *Ibid.*, "Index: Brasseur, Marie-Ange," p. 1272.
193 *Ibid.*, "*Chronologie des Lettres et de la vie du Bienheureux Columba Marmion*," p. 1350.
194 See Thibaut, *Abbot Columba Marmion: A Master of the Spiritual Life: 1858–1923*, p. 178.
195 Marmion, *Correspondance 1881–1923*, "Index: de Richouffz, Marguerite-Marie," p. 1284.
196 *Ibid.*, pp. 1351–1354.
197 *Ibid.*, p. 1351.
198 *Ibid.*, pp. 1351, 1353.
199 *Ibid.*, p. 1351.
200 *Ibid.*, "Index: Vauvrecy, Raphael," p. 1315.

6–17 March: Time spent in England, at Bournemouth, Tyburn, Hayward's Heath.[201]

9 March; (Undated) May: Letters to Mother Mary Michael Bonnaud.[202]

30 April and 3 May: Visit to the Carmel at Delgany (Ireland).[203]

6 June: Letter to Mother Marguerite-Marie de Richoufftz.[204]

12 June, 3 July, 21 September, 2 October, 27 December: Letters to Mother Emmanuelle Skerrett.[205]

14 June: Letter to Dame Bénédicte Bayart (1862–1964). She was one of the foundresses of the community of Benedictine nuns established by Dom Eugene Vandeur, a monk of Maredsous. In 1922, she professed her vows in the community first established in Brussels, and was one of the foundresses of La Marlagne in Wepion (1922), which later moved to Ermeton-sur-Biert (Belgium).[206]

16 June: Letter to Dame Placide Delhaes (1842–1929), the fifteenth Abbess of the Abbey Paix Notre-Dame and foundress of Saint Getrude in Louvain. She made profession in 1865 and was elected Abbess in 1907.[207]

17 June: Letter to Mother Brigid Burke, an Irish Sister belonging to the Congregation for Christian Education.[208]

16 July: Letter to Mother Mary Berchmans Durrant.[209]

22 August: Letter to Mother Agnès of Jesus and Mary, Prioress at the Carmel of Dijon (France) in 1919.[210]

14 September: Letter to an unknown Religious.[211]

21 September: Letter to Mother Angèle Diktus, a Canoness of Saint Augustine at Jupille.[212]

13 December: Letter to Dame Winfrida Kraemer.[213]

---

201 Ibid., "*Chronologie des Lettres et de la vie du Bienheureux Columba Marmion*," p. 1351.
202 Ibid., pp. 1351–1352.
203 Ibid., "Index: Gavin, Xavier," p. 1291.
204 Ibid., p. 1352.
205 Ibid., pp. 1352–1354.
206 Ibid., "Index: Bayart, Bénédicte," pp. 1269–1270.
207 Ibid., "Index: Delhaes, Placide," p. 1282.
208 Ibid., "Index: Burke, Brigid," p. 1273.
209 Ibid., "*Chronologie des Lettres et de la vie du Bienheureux Columba Marmion*," p. 1352.
210 Ibid., "Index: Agnès de Jésus et Marie," p. 1267.
211 Ibid., p. 1353.
212 Ibid., "Index: Diktus, Angèle," p. 1286.
213 Ibid., "*Chronologie des Lettres et de la vie du Bienheureux Columba Marmion*," p. 1354.

Appendix

21 December: Letter to Mother Pierre Adèle Garnier.[214]

23 December: Letter to Dame Maura Ostyn (1868–1940), the Abbess of the Irish Ladies of Ypres, Benedictines, which was established first in Macmine Castle (1916–1920) and then in Kylemore (both in Ireland).[215]

1920 Weekly ascetical conference to the Benedictine nuns at Maredret.[216]

Spiritual Director of the Carmelite nuns at the Carmel of Saint-Joseph at Virton.[217]

1 January, 25 June: Letters to Mother Marguerite-Marie de Richoufftz.[218]

20 February, 21 September: Letters to Mother Emmanuelle Skerrett.[219]

24 March: Letter to Mother Peter Marmion.[220]

2 April: Letter to Mother Pierre Adèle Garnier.[221]

29 April: Letter to Dame Raphaël Vauvrecy.[222]

21 June, 8 September: Letters to Mother Mary Berchmans Durrant.[223]

24 June: Letter to Dame Patricia Murphy.[224]

18 July: Letter to Dame Cécile de Hemptinne.[225]

2 and 8 (two letters) September; 6 November: Letters to Mother Marie-Joseph van Aerden.[226]

6 October: Letter to Dame Winfrida Kraemer.[227]

29 November: Letter to Mother Marie-Ange Brasseur.[228]

20 December: Letter to Mother Gabrielle Cambon.[229]

---

214 *Ibid.*
215 *Ibid.*, "Index: Ostyn, Maura," p. 1305.
216 See Thibaut, *Abbot Columba Marmion: A Master of the Spiritual Life: 1858–1923*, p. 178.
217 Marmion, *Correspondance 1881–1923*, "Chronologie des Lettres et de la vie du Bienheureux Columba Marmion," p. 1284.
218 *Ibid.*, pp. 1354–1355.
219 *Ibid.*, pp. 1354, 1356.
220 *Ibid.*, p. 1354.
221 *Ibid.*
222 *Ibid.*, p. 1355.
223 *Ibid.*
224 *Ibid.*
225 *Ibid.*
226 *Ibid.*, p. 1355–1356.
227 *Ibid.*, p. 1356.
228 *Ibid.*
229 *Ibid.*

1921 Weekly ascetical conference to the Benedictine nuns at Maredret.[230]

Spiritual Director of the Carmelite nuns at the Carmel of Saint-Joseph at Virton.[231]

1 January, 23 March: Letters to Mother Mary Michael Bonnaud.[232]

10 January: Letter to Dame Maura Ostyn.[233]

March: Preached at the English Convent at Bruges for the renewal of vows.[234]

14 March, 13 July, 19 November: Letters to Mother Marguerite-Marie de Richoufftz.[235]

6 April: Letter to Dame Cécile de Hemptinne.[236]

30 May: Letter to Mother Mary Berchmans Durrant.[237]

2 June: Letter to Mother Gabrielle Cambon.[238]

10 and 26 June, 1 November: Letters to Dame Winfrida Kraemer.[239]

(Undated) August: Letter to Mother Marie-Joseph van Aerden.[240]

20–29 August: Preached retreat for the Canonesses of Saint Augustine at Jupille.[241]

2–15 November: Preached retreat for the Poor Clares of Cork (Ireland).[242]

1 December: Letter to an unknown Religious.[243]

17 December: Letter to the Poor Clares in Cork.[244]

24 December: Letter to Dame Raphaël Vauvrecy.[245]

---

230   See Thibaut, *Abbot Columba Marmion: A Master of the Spiritual Life: 1858–1923*, p. 178.
231   Marmion, *Correspondance 1881–1923*, "Index: de Richoufftz, Marguerite-Marie," p. 1284.
232   *Ibid.*, p. 1356.
233   *Ibid.*
234   *Ibid.*
235   *Ibid.*, pp. 1356–1358.
236   *Ibid.*, p. 1357.
237   *Ibid.*
238   *Ibid.*
239   *Ibid.*, pp. 1357–1358.
240   *Ibid.*, p. 1357.
241   *Ibid.*
242   *Ibid.*, p. 1358.
243   *Ibid.*
244   *Ibid.*
245   *Ibid.*

Appendix

1922 Weekly ascetical conference to the Benedictine nuns at Maredret. [246]

Spiritual Director of the Carmelite nuns at the Carmel of Saint-Joseph at Virton.[247]

2 January, 18 August: Letters to Mother Emmanuelle Skerrett.[248]

3 January, (undated) May, 24 September: Letters to Dame Winfrida Kraemer.[249]

21 January: Letter to Dame Candida Prüm (1888–1968), a nun of the Abbey of Saint Scholastica at Maredret. She made profession in 1912.[250]

7 February: Letter to the Superior of the Visitation of Troyes (France).[251]

24 February; 6, 24, and 27 June; 20 July; 27 and 30 August; 30 September; 17, 20, and 29 October; 16 November; 6 December: Letters to Mother Mary Michael Bonnaud.[252]

6 March: Letter to Mother Pierre Adèle Garnier.[253]

9 March, 1 June, 19 July, 16 September, 24 December: Letters to Mother Marie-Joseph van Aerden.[254]

12 March, 12 July, (undated) September: Letters to Mother Agnès Power (1895–1960), a member of the Poor Clare Colletines at Cork. She entered in 1915 and made her solemn profession on 22 August 1921. Blessed Columba met her when he gave retreat to the community 1–6 October 1921. In 1955, she was one of the foundresses of a Poor Clare monastery at Ennis (Ireland), where she died on 8 April 1960.[255]

28 March, 11 April, 27 November, 29 December (two letters): Letters to Mother Peter Marmion.[256]

31 March; 15 and 27 April; 19 May: Letters to Mother Emmanuelle Hamelin (1900–1972). In 1922, she entered Mont-Vierge (Ancilla Domini) in Wepion, a monastery founded

---

246 See Thibaut, *Abbot Columba Marmion: A Master of the Spiritual Life: 1858–1923*, p. 178.
247 Marmion, *Correspondance 1881–1923*, p. 1284.
248 *Ibid.*, pp. 1358–1359.
249 *Ibid.*, pp. 1358–1360.
250 *Ibid.*, "Index: Prüm, Candida," p.1306.
251 *Ibid.*, "*Chronologie des Lettres et de la vie du Bienheureux Columba Marmion,*" p. 1358.
252 *Ibid.*, pp. 1358–1360.
253 *Ibid.*, p. 1358.
254 *Ibid.*, pp. 1358–1361
255 *Ibid.*, "Index: Power, Agnès," p. 1306.
256 *Ibid.*, "*Chronologie des Lettres et de la vie du Bienheureux Columba Marmion,*" pp. 1358–1361.

by Dom Eugene Vandeur. She made temporary profession on 11 July1923, was appointed prioress eight days later, and made perpetual profession on 6 August 1925. She served as prioress until 1935, when she was relieved of her duties following serious financial problems. Secularized, she then lived in France, Morocco and finally Rome, where she died on 26 February 1972.[257]

(Undated) April: Letter to Dame Marie-Cécile Smeets (1878–1969). Initially a Canoness of Saint-Augustin in Jupille, she later entered the Abbey of Saint Scholastica in Maredret. She was professed on 11 April 1915.[258]

5 April: Letter to Mother Marie of Jesus.[259]

27 April, 28 September, 21 November: Letter to Dame Mary Fidelis Tidmarsh (1897–1984). She entered Hayward's Heath as an Augustinian Canoness in 1918 and was sent to the English Convent at Bruges in 1919. Originally from Richhill near Lisnagry (Ireland) she attended Hayward's Heath School from 1911 to 1916. She met Blessed Columba at the English Convent in 1920, during a retreat he was preaching there. One of his last letters of 23 January 1923 was written to her in view of her solemn profession on January 25. Dame Mary-Fidelis returned to Hayward's Heath shortly before the Second World War. She worked as a librarian there for the rest of her life.[260]

1 May, 30 December: Letters to the Poor Clares in Cork.[261]

22 June: Letter to Dame Bénédicte Bayart.[262]

11 July: Letter to an unknown Religious.[263]

29 July: Letter to a Poor Clare.[264]

5 and 21 August; 21 October; 1 November: Letters to Dame Raphaël Vauvrecy.[265]

23 August: Letter to Mother Xavier Gavin, Prioress of the Carmel of Delgany. Blessed Columba visited the Carmel two times: on 30 April 1919 and 3 May 1919.[266]

---

257 *Ibid.*, "Index: Hamelin, Emmanuelle," p. 1293.
258 *Ibid.*, "Index: Smeets, Marie-Cécile," p. 1310.
259 *Ibid.*, "Chronologie des Lettres et de la vie du Bienheureux Columba Marmion," p. 1358.
260 *Ibid.*, "Index: Tidmarsh, Mary-Fidelis," p. 1312.
261 *Ibid.*, "Chronologie des Lettres et de la vie du Bienheureux Columba Marmion," pp. 1359, 1361.
262 *Ibid.*, p. 1359.
263 *Ibid.*
264 *Ibid.*
265 *Ibid.*, pp. 1359–1360.
266 *Ibid.*, "Index: Gavin, Xavier," p. 1291.

Appendix

(Undated) October: Letter to Mother Mary-Berchmans Durrant.[267]

3–10 November: Retreat preached to the Benedictines "de la Rue Monsieur a Paris".[268]

20 November: Letter to an unknown Religious.[269]

1 December: Letter to Mother Dorothy Wharton (1894–1976). She was born in at Port of Spain at Trinidad on 21 December 1894. She entered the Benedictines at Rue Monsieur on 7 December 1918 and there made profession on 5 April 1920. In 1923, she transferred her stability to the Abbey of Notre-Dame at Jouarre (France), where she died on 7 April 1976. She was a spiritual daughter of Dom Mayeul de Caigny and of Blessed Columba, whom she met at Rue Monsieur in 1922 during a retreat.[270]

5, 21, and 23 December: Letters to Mother Marguerite-Marie de Richoufftz.[271]

17 December: Last conference to the nuns of Maredret.[272]

1923 *8 January:* Letter to Mother Marie-Joseph van Aerden.[273]

16 January: Letter to Sister Hedwige Netter (1896–1961). She was a French Jewess who converted to Catholicism. Her father, Nathan Netter, was a rabbi in Metz (France). He never approved of her conversion. After her conversion, her father never spoken to her or saw her again. He symbolically buried her in his synagogue. She was baptized in 1920. Blessed Columba met her at the Benedictine nuns' retreat at Rue Monsieur in November 1922. She entered Rue Monsieur on 20 June 1921, made profession on 3 January 1923, and died on 6 January 1961.[274]

21 and 23 January: Letters to Mother Marguerite-Marie de Richoufftz.[275]

23 January: Letter to Dame Mary Fidelis Tidmarsh.[276]

---

267   Ibid., "*Chronologie des Lettres et de la vie du Bienheureux Columba Marmion,*" p. 1360.
268   Ibid.
269   Ibid.
270   Ibid., "Index: Wharton, Dorothy," p. 1317.
271   Ibid., "*Chronologie des Lettres et de la vie du Bienheureux Columba Marmion,*" p. 1360.
272   Ibid. See Thibaut, *Abbot Columba Marmion: A Master of the Spiritual Life: 1858–1923,* p. 178.
273   Marmion, *Correspondance 1881–1923,* "*Chronologie des Lettres et de la vie du Bienheureux Columba Marmion,*" p. 1361.
274   Ibid., "Index: Netter, Hedwige," p. 1303.
275   Ibid., "*Chronologie des Lettres et de la vie du Bienheureux Columba Marmion,*"p. 1361.
276   Ibid.

FVRTHER READING

WORKS BY BLESSED COLUMBA MARMION:

Christ in His Mysteries
(The Cenacle Press, 2022)

Christ, The Ideal of the Monk
(The Cenacle Press 2022)

Christ, The Life of the Soul
(Angelico Press, 2012)

Christ, The Ideal of the Priest
(Ignatius Press, 2005)

Sponsa Verbi
(Johannes Press, 2022)

Words of Life on the Margin of the Missal
(The Cenacle Press, 2023)

Union with God
(Angelico Press, 2022)

WORKS ABOUT BLESSED COLUMBA MARMION:

*The Grace of Nothingness: Navigating the Spiritual
Life with Blessed Columba Marmion*
(Angelico Press, 2021)

Abbot Columba Marmion: A Master of the Spiritual Life
(The Cenacle Press, forthcoming 2023)

www.ingramcontent.com/pod-product-compliance
Lightning Source LLC
Chambersburg PA
CBHW030051100526
44591CB00008B/97